Da Capo

BEST MUS

WRITING

2006

Da Capo
BEST MUSIC
WRITING
2006

The Year's Finest Writing on Rock,
Hip-Hop, Jazz, Pop, Country, and More

Mary Gaitskill
GUEST EDITOR

Daphne Carr
SERIES EDITOR

DA CAPO PRESS
A Member of the Perseus Books Group

List of credits/permissions for all pieces can be found on page 327.

Copyright © 2006 by Da Capo Press
Introduction copyright © 2006 by Mary Gaitskill

Set in 10-point Janson Text by the Perseus Books Group

Cataloging-in-Publication data for this book is available from the Library of Congress.

First Da Capo Press edition 2006
ISBN-13: 978-0-306-81499-0
ISBN-10: 0-306-81499-4

Published by Da Capo Press
A Member of the Perseus Books Group
www.dacapopress.com

Da Capo Press books are available at special discounts for bulk purchases in the U.S. by corporations, institutions, and other organizations. For more information, please contact the Special Markets Department at the Perseus Books Group, 11 Cambridge Center, Cambridge, MA 02142, or call (800) 255-1514 or (617) 252-5298, or e-mail special.markets@perseusbooks.com.

1 2 3 4 5 6 7 8 9

*For Maxiel Muñoz, who introduced me to reggaetón,
and who loves music more than anyone I know*

Contents

about J. Robert Oppenheimer, the inventor of the atomic
bomb over, Jon Caramanica writes about tragicomic rap-
y Bastard—putting in proximity two strange, poetic and
a, one who destroyed two cities, one who destroyed him-
eth Méndez Berry covers the war between men and
the power of honesty and directness. Charles Michener
the same thing differently in his review of operatic love
descriptions of violent emotion so piercing and refined
almost a kind of psychic violence, cutting elegant shapes
flesh of love. Geoffrey O'Brien's Brill Building essay
story about Bob Dylan, and Geoff Boucher's piece on ex-
Densmore starts with one. To which Dave Tompkins's
piece says, "What the fuck?" and starts something new.
Relic asks Bushwick Bill whether he's a gangster or a
ill answers as a gangster, then acts like a prankster—he's
David Thorpe pranking on R. Kelly, who gets blasted off
Raquel Cepeda's "Riddims by the Reggaetón." Mike
ps in and out, his short reviews like imp faces peeping
the headlines.

t, in a beautiful introduction to his 2004 anthology, said:
can be strong and relentless and there is no mercy for
timid." I agree; this is true of any art form. But while
strong in this book, I also wanted to make a place for
wanted to do this because the weak love music too, and
ey can avoid being crushed, their voices can be moving.
re exquisitely attuned to the large forces around them;
de by circumstance to confront and live with emotions
l can forcibly repress or avoid altogether. Sensitivity,
ceptivity, and vulnerability are weak in some contexts,
ualities are necessary for the strongest artist: Notice the
vity of Timbaland's ear, or how Kevin Whitehead hears
"bending" and "swerving" notes inside Monk's "ham-
ano technique. Only a playful and delicate mind could

Introduction

This book is titled *Best Music Writin*
that way, not in the set-in-stone typ
gether like a mix tape of sounds a per
in the morning, put on an old T. Rex
Digger" coming out of somebody's ca
out of somebody else's. A guy walks t
an aria from Bizet's *Carmen*; somethi
of a passing boy's iPod. Go into a sto
the sound system singing some artifi
songs fly past; some get lost in traffi
nation and take strange dream-shape
and feelings and make them differen
M.I.A. says, "We *do* hear everything
hard to *feel* everything at once, to *g*
that limitation when putting this col
says I picked are not the only great
was choosing I hated to think of th
that for some reason flew past witho

Like songs on a tape, I put these p
or bang them together, to create a c
with invisible linguistic links—som
Kevin Whitehead sees (on page 148)
and "anti-virtuoso" Thelonious M

Ross wr
bomb;
per Ol'
creative
self. Eli
women
talks ab
wars, art
that they
in the c
ends wit
Door Jo
Timbala
When P
prankste
followed
the page
McGuirk
from beh

Mickey
"The mu
the weak
honoring
weakness
because i
The weak
they are
the powe
delicacy,
but these
fine recep
the suppl
fingered"

hear yodeling the way John Biguenet hears it, as "an expression of inbetweenness"; only an imaginative and delicate hand (Frank Kogan's) could open a lyrical door in Shannon Brown's "Corn Fed" and find a whole "insane" community living inside. It took adolescent sensitivity (not used negatively here) for David Marchese to connect the power of High On Fire's "punishing" hell metal to the strength he once saw in the eyes of a crushed and dying little animal. When Caramanica describes Ol' Dirty going from wretched comedy to pain to hope while singing "Good Morning Heartache," he is describing fearless vulnerability.

It is a great thing, a luxurious thing, that our music is so fine and fierce, that it is able to go so many places and speak of so many things, and that there are people with the nimble intelligence to appreciate it in so many forums. But Marchese's High On Fire story is finally about someone trapped in a soft life that's gone dead inside, and too much luxury has a way of turning into an artificial heaven sitting atop a real hell. Pay attention to Moustafa Bayoumi's report on the ways pop, rock, and hip-hop are being used as instruments of torture in the "war on terror": It is a grim and necessary account of how hell can thrive on the desire to protect an artificial heaven. Peter Relic quotes Geto Boy Willie D. rapping—"Mess with my money, I'ma kick you in the asshole"—and it's possible that he's doing just that on an epic scale, that his music has been turned into a giant foot to be used against people he has nothing against by a government he probably despises. Maybe I shouldn't say that because I don't know what Willie D. feels about it. But, after reading Bayoumi, I do know what Metallica's James Hetfield feels. In an interview on the NPR radio show *Fresh Air*, he apparently said about the use of his music as torture that he is "proud" if his music offends Iraqis, and that ". . . if they're not used to freedom, I'm glad to be part of the exposure."

Strangely, after reading that, I thought of an actual song someone put on an actual mix tape he made for me. It is the sort of joke song that people put on mix tapes, a live recording of Elvis in his twilight years doing a horribly shit-faced version of "Are You Lonesome Tonight?" He is completely screwing it up, and not caring, singing dumb joke lyrics and lapsing into fits of mirthless cackling. Less strangely, I thought of Metallica's 1991 hit "Enter Sandman," a grinding, efficient sludge of dark sounds and flickering images, a story of primitive dream evil triumphantly emerging to bear away a sleeping child, despite his earnest prayers. The songs don't normally go together in my mind, but right then they did. Elvis's performance is the sound of something wonderful turning into something horrible, with the audience clapping at the end as if it's all the same to them. It's also the sound of someone teetering between playfulness and ruin. "Enter Sandman" gloats over its clownish horror, makes you enjoy it and fear it a little, like a kid shining a flashlight under his face in a dark room can sometimes suddenly reveal something truly eerie in that kid. A pop culture that can casually entertain such ambivalent trifles is highly developed. It is also decadent, its passion spent on violent fantasies, its sensitivity spent on trivia dressed up to look urgent. James Hetfield may have turned out to be a soft and foolishly cruel man, blithely wishing pain he has no concept of on people he knows nothing about. But in "Enter Sandman" he described something powerful: Timeless destruction that takes form in the unconscious of a praying child, offers the boy its hand and takes him away to Never Never Land. *Boom*. Giant guitars fill the sky. *Boom*. And we're there.

MARY GAITSKILL
May 24, 2006
New York, NY

Stories of a Bad Song

I'm going to talk about how meaning is generated in cultural work, over time; I'm going to talk about how it is that bad art, a bad song, can make its way through time so persistently that questions of good and bad become absolutely moot. I'm going to talk about a very old song by Bob Dylan.

Last year Mojo magazine ranked Bob Dylan's "Masters of War," his 1963 song about arms merchants, number one on a chart of "The 100 Greatest Protest Songs." It was followed by Pete Seeger's "We Shall Overcome," the anthem of the 1960s Civil Rights Movement, by James Brown's "Say It Loud—I'm Black and I'm Proud" from 1968, an anthem of the Black Power movement, the Sex Pistols' "God Save the Queen" from 1977, an attack on Queen Elizabeth's Silver Jubilee, and Billie Holiday's "Strange Fruit" from 1939, a song about the lynching of southern black men by southern whites. Not to mention Lesley Gore's 1963 "You Don't Own Me" and Eddie Cochran's 1958 "Summertime Blues"—a record about a teenager with a mean boss, mean parents, and a congressman who won't help because the kid's too young to vote.

But for "Masters of War" the lack of subtlety was perhaps the point. "Come you masters of war, you that build the big guns," Dylan begins slowly: "You build the death planes / You that build the big bombs." He goes on, stepping on a somehow mysterious, inviting melody. "Not even Jesus would forgive what you do," the twenty-two-year-old Bob Dylan sings. And then he does something that, even for a protest song, was shocking in 1963 and is shocking now: he calls for the death of the people he's singing about. "I hope that you die," he says flatly.

> *And your death will come soon*
> *I'll follow your casket*
> *In the pale afternoon*
> *And I'll watch while you're lowered*
> *Down to your deathbed*
> *And I'll stand over your grave till I'm sure*
> *that you're dead*

Now, no matter what Bob Dylan has done in the last forty-two years or what he will do for the rest of his life, his obituary has already been written: "Bob Dylan, best known as a protest singer from the 1960s, died yesterday . . ." The media loves a simple idea. No matter how famous you are, when you die you get one idea, and one only.

In 1963, in the small world of folk music, protest songs were the currency. They said that the world should be changed, even implied that songs could change it, and no one wrote better protest songs—or as many—as Bob Dylan. It was a way of getting on the train of his own career, he'd say years later—but to the tens of thousands of high school and college students who had begun to listen to Bob Dylan because, they said, he could draw on their own unshaped anger and rage, terror and fear, and make it all real, even make it poetry, that was not how the songs felt.

They felt like warnings the world couldn't turn away from, crimes that had to be paid, promises that had to be kept. Bob Dylan wrote songs about the nuclear war that in 1963 almost everyone was sure would take place sometime, somewhere—and in 1962, with the Cuban Missile Crisis, almost had: the war that, as Robert McNamara,

Secretary of Defense in 1962, said in the recent film *The Fog of War*, came closer than even the most paranoid protest singer dared imagine. Dylan wrote and sang long, detailed songs about racial injustice, he wrote funny protest songs like "Talking World War III Blues," visionary protest songs like "A Hard Rain's A-Gonna Fall"—but mostly he wrote and sang songs that told stories about the wrong inside a nation that believed it was always right: "With God on Our Side," "The Times They Are A-Changin'," "Blowin' in the Wind." These were the songs that brought Bob Dylan into the common imagination of the nation, and those were the songs that fixed him there.

But even in the heyday of the protest song, "Masters of War" seemed like too much. Too sententious, too self-righteous—stilted, as if it was less a matter of someone writing a protest song than the protest song as such spontaneously generating its own copy, or its own cartoon. "You hide in your mansion / While young people's blood / flows out of their bodies / And into the mud," Dylan sang in "Masters of War." Still, that was almost poetry compared to "You Been Hiding Too Long," another Bob Dylan protest song from the same moment. "Come all you phony super-patriotic"—OK, stop right there, we don't need to hear any more, but there is more, a lot more, no melody, no rhythm, no heart, no conviction, but press a button and the protest song comes out: "You like and mislead / You—for your aims and your selfish greed . . . Don't think that I'll ever stand on your side . . ." and on, and on. It's so awful it's been erased from Dylan's song collections; he probably never recorded it. He may have only performed it once, at a concert in New York in 1963, when he also sang "Masters of War"—but this horrible song is inside "Masters of War," and for one night at least it got out.

"Masters of War" does have a melody—the melody of "Nottamun Town," an ancient British folk song. It's often described as a nonsense song; that's the last thing it is. Today it communicates as twentieth-century surrealism in sixteenth-century clothes: "Not a soul would look up, not a soul would look down . . . Come a stark-naked drummer a-beating the drum . . . Ten thousand stood round

me, yet I was alone . . . Ten thousand got drowned that never was
born." This is the first protest song, and the last; this is the end of
the world. Traditional versions found in Kentucky or North Carolina were in a major key, which put a sardonic smile in the music,
but around "the green pastures of Harvard University," as Dylan
once put it, he heard a version in a minor key by the Cambridge folk
singer Jackie Washington. That put a chill on the melody, gave him
an opening into the bad dream he was after: shadowed, doomstruck,
the sound of funeral procession, or a line of flagellants in the plague
years.

Dylan had stopped singing "Masters of War" by 1964. Songs like
that were "lies that life is black and white," he sang that year. He
brought it back into his repertoire in the 1980s; he was playing
more than a hundred shows a year, and to fill the nights he brought
back everything. It was a crowd-pleaser, the number one protest
song. But nothing in the song hinted at what it would turn into on
February 21, 1991, at the Grammy Awards telecast, where Dylan
was to receive a Lifetime Achievement Award.

The show came square in the middle of the first Iraqi-American
War—a break from round-the-clock footage of the bombing of
Baghdad. "Uncle Bobby," Jack Nicholson said, introducing Dylan,
as Dylan and his four-piece band came onstage to play one song. In
dark suits, with fedoras pulled down over their faces, the musicians
looked like small-time hipster gangsters who'd spent the previous
ten years in the same bar waiting for the right deal to break and finally said the hell with it; Dylan held himself with authority, like the
bartender.

It was an instantly infamous performance, and one of the greatest
of Dylan's career. He sang the song in disguise; at first, you couldn't
tell what it was. He slurred the words as if their narrative was irrelevant and the performance had to communicate as a symbol or not at
all. He broke the words down and smashed them up until they
worked as pure excitement, until the appearance of a single, whole
signifier—"Jesus," "Guns," "Die"—lit up the night like tracer bul-

lets. The performance was faster, the beat snapping back on itself, then fragmenting as guitar lines shot out of the music as if without human agency—and it might have been a minute, it might have been two, it might have been as long as the performance lasted for the melody to creep out of the noise and the song to reveal itself for what it was.

Dylan was asked why, on this night of all nights, he chose to sing "Masters of War."

"The war going on," he said.

Why did he slur the words, he was asked.

"I had a cold," he said.

With that night, the song began its second life. In the fall of 2002, when George W. Bush made plain his intent to launch a second Iraq war—on November 11, just after the midterm elections that Bush had used the specter of war to win—Dylan appeared at Madison Square Garden and again offered "Masters of War" as an answer record to real life. He gathered three musicians in a circle, with himself at the center: playing acoustic guitars and a bass fiddle, seated on chairs, they looked like a coven, and the song sounded like a curse dug out of the ground.

The song began to travel. In May of 2003, with the war under way, Scott Amendola and Carla Bozulich of Berkeley put a nine-minute version on the Internet. They made a storm; they took the song's rage into the realm of abstraction, until the end, when there was nothing left but drum taps, silence, and a single voice, letting you imagine that this was all that was left, after the war.

More than a year later, in October 2004, with Bush and John Kerry battling for the presidency and Minnesota up for grabs, a Minneapolis record-store owner named Mark Treehouse put out a version of the song as a pure rant—with, on the cover, Bush, Dick Cheney, Donald Rumsfeld, and John Ashcroft in red, white, and blue. A month after that, on election night, November 2, in Oshkosh, Wisconsin, with the votes cast but the outcome still unknown, Dylan offered the song once more, again in the middle of a war—a middle, that night, without an end. At first his delivery was clipped, the words rushed and stuttered. As certain lines seemed to draw more from Dylan, the song seemed to rewrite itself. "You put a gun to my head." An electric guitar came down hard, and the music turned fierce. "I'll stand over your grave till I'm sure that you're dead"—as the words came out of Dylan's mouth his voice was shaking. And none of this matched what happened at Boulder High School, in Boulder, Colorado, the very next day.

On November 3, students staged a sit-in in the school library: "Bush will directly affect our generation's future," one Boulder freshman said, "and we were upset we didn't have a voice in that." The principal refused to have the students removed; Congressman Mark Udall came to the school to speak; so did Senator-elect Ken Salazar. TV crews arrived. And then the stakes were raised.

The annual school talent show was scheduled for November 12; a teacher named Jim Kavanagh helped bring a group of students together as a band. "Your basic juvenile delinquent types," he said in plain English, then dropping into teacher's language: "at risk." Fooling around on guitar, someone began playing in D minor. "That sounds like 'Masters of War,'" one student said. That wasn't what the guitar player thought he was doing, but in a moment it was what the group was doing.

The students came up with a name for their group: the Taliband. A singer came forward, a student named Allyse Wojtanek: "Not a singer," Kavanagh says, "a very brave kid." The group went to the audition, which was filled with Britney Spears imitations. "Nobody did anything close to what we did," Kavanagh said—at the start, he and another teacher were in the group—"and we really sucked. I never heard such a horrible sound. We found out the next day that not only did we make the show, we were the last act. And at this point, one of the kids who was doing karaoke stuff went home, and said to her mother, 'I didn't make the show, but this other band that wants to kill Bush did.'" Instead of "I hope that you die," the student had heard "Die, Bush, die." The mother got on the phone to the local Clear Channel AM stations—and once again news trucks hit the school. Talk show hosts called for the Taliband to be kicked out of the talent show. The Secret Police arrived—they took the lyrics to "Masters of War" and left—and the story went over the AP wire.

The band changed its name—to Coalition of the Willing. They negotiated with the school administration over video footage to be projected onto the musicians as they played: first, footage of Bush and Iraq. Does it have to be Bush, the principal asked. "Why not lots of masters of war," a student suggested: Bush, Hitler, and Stalin. Why do there have to be any faces, the administration begged. They settled for generic war footage and the American flag.

As the talent show began, three gangly boys came on to MC the show, miming to ZZ Top's "Sharp-Dressed Man." They didn't miss a step all night.

A twelve-student assemblage did the Eurythmics' "Sweet Dreams (Are Made of This)." A student played a Debussy piano piece. Another danced. The crowd gave everyone wild applause.

As one of the MCs began a routine, an off-stage electric guitar drowned him out. "I can't work under these conditions!" he shouted. "I'm going to protest this next act!" "Oh my God," said a second MC. "You're protesting it? Can you do that? This is national-newsworthy!" Dressed now in a black suit, the third MC pulled out a video camera and began filming the other two. The three accused each other of planning to burn down the school—not a casual joke, thirty-five miles from Columbine. "This next act," said one MC, "is the controversial act you've been waiting for—the Russian Jugglers!"

Aside from Coalition of the Willing, brother and sister Olga and Vova Galdrenko were the highlight of the show. There were ten more acts—and then the seven-student Coalition came out, with Allyse Wojtanek in a black halter. The sound was big and atonal, with guitar and saxophone on the top and Wojtanek screaming. When she got to "I hope that you die," she talked the line, making each word stand alone. When she hit "SURE THAT YOU'RE DEAD," she all but tore her throat out.

There were video battlefield images of Korea, Vietnam, Iraq then, Iraq now. For the moment, for the students, the war was theirs, perhaps waiting for them six months or a year down the line, and the song was theirs, waiting for them for more than forty years.

It became clear that, beyond new wars, what has kept the song alive is its melody, and its vehemence: that final "I hope that you die." It's the elegance of the melody and the extremism of the words that attract people—the way the song does go too far, to the limits of free speech. It's a scary line to sing; you need courage to do it. You can't come to the song as if it's a joke; you can't come away from it pretending you didn't mean what you've just said. That's what people want: a chance to go that far. Because "Masters of War" gives people permission to go that far, the song continues to make meaning, to find new bodies to inhabit, new voices to ride.

About a year ago, at the Berkeley Farmers' Market, there was a black man in his sixties or seventies singing versions of folk ballads like "Stagger Lee"; there was a black man in his fifties singing deep versions of soul hits like "He Will Break Your Heart"; and there was a toothless white singer who never sings anything but Bob Dylan songs. So ruined he could be anything from thirty to sixty, he's been there for years, butchering one tune after another—but this day he was singing "Masters of War," which I'd never heard him sing before, and it changed him. The melody erased the cracks in his voice. And it was so queer: when he got to the lines, "But there's one thing I know / Though I'm younger than you / Even Jesus would never forgive what you do," you realized that he was probably at least as old as the arms merchants who, today, are doing the work he was singing about. As old as some, and probably older than most.

ALEX ROSS

Doctor Atomic "Countdown"

At the northern end of the White Sands Missile Range, in the semi-arid desert of central New Mexico, a road stretches toward the charcoal-colored rockface of the Oscura Mountains, which rise to nearly nine thousand feet. At the end of the road is a neat circular shape, about a half mile in diameter. This is the site of the first atomic explosion, which took place on July 16, 1945. When the bomb went off, it obliterated the creosote bushes that had been growing here, along with every other living thing inside the circle. When plant life returned to the spot, grass and yucca plants took the place of the creosote. The change in vegetation explains why the site is visible from miles away, and probably from space.

White Sands is a mesmerizing place—an outdoor museum of mankind's highest ambitions and deepest fears. The missile range is still an active facility. Lately, the Defense Threat Reduction Agency has been using an area nearby to study the effects of explosives on underground bunkers. One corner of White Sands is occupied by LINEAR, the Lincoln Near Earth Asteroid Research project, which scans the skies for errant asteroids, particularly those big enough to cause mass extinctions. At the same time, the range functions as an unofficial wildlife refuge, the secrecy of the place serving to protect various species. It is home to herds of oryx, an African antelope.

They are noble animals with horns like medieval spikes, and they can go for extended periods without water.

J. Robert Oppenheimer, the man who oversaw the building of the first atomic bombs, called the test site Trinity, in honor of John Donne's sonnet "Batter my heart, three-person'd God." The poem contains the words "break, blow, burn, and make me new." Oppenheimer was made new by the explosion, or, at least, was not the same afterward. The terrain beneath the bomb—Ground Zero, it was called—also underwent a transformation, which scientists are still trying to understand. When Trinity personnel came back to inspect the site, they found a green, glassy substance covering the ground. The latest hypothesis is that this artificial mineral, which was named trinitite, formed when soil, water, and organic matter were lifted off the ground and fused in the heat of the blast. Over the years, tourists have carried away much of the trinitite in their pockets—the site is open to visitors twice a year—and most of the rest was buried beneath the soil. Looking down at the ground, you would never know that anything out of the ordinary had happened here.

What happened at Trinity is the subject of "Doctor Atomic," a new opera, with music by John Adams and a libretto by Peter Sellars. The opening scenes take place at Los Alamos, the headquarters of the Manhattan Project, two weeks before the test. The rest takes place on the night of July 15th–16th, in the hours leading up to the detonation. It will have its première at the San Francisco Opera on October 1st.

"Some people claim that it's the world's first countdown," Sellars said to me, in a hotel lobby in Santa Fe, New Mexico, a few days before the rehearsals for "Doctor Atomic" began. "Every second is charged, because it is a new thing in the history of time—this massive pressure behind every minute and every second in a way that never counted before. At the end of the opera, you can feel the passage of time in the most real way, as with the Doomsday Clock of the Bulletin of the Atomic Scientists, showing how many minutes remain until midnight. You get the hands of that clock, and inside every minute is a universe. A twenty-minute countdown takes forty minutes. From zero minus one minute up to the explosion takes four minutes. The music actually connects with the most formative experiences in your life, which you want to never live again yet you're living over and over—those moments when you were more alive than you ever were alive before or since. This is 'Götterdämmerung' for our generation, with our speed, with our tension points, with our nervous energy, but with nothing being a metaphor and everything being a reality."

Sellars—director of opera and theatre, activist, professor of "art as moral action" at U.C.L.A.—actually does talk like this. He speaks better than most writers write, moving through thickets of erudition toward exact epiphanies. His orations and incantations well up without warning, and break off with a giggle, or a profanity, or a burst of California slang. He has a compact, almost elfin body; his shoulders slope down sharply from his neck, and his feet pad the floor in short, quick steps. His hair shoots straight up, giving him the air of being perpetually electrified. He has a boyish quality, and dresses in boyish clothes. A typical ensemble may consist of cargo pants, an oversized flannel shirt, and a track jacket. Yet, when he is in the grip of one of his rhetorical tours de force, he takes on the look of an elderly sage: his head turns toward the heavens, his arms stretch upward in supplicant gestures, his face twists into an attitude of ecstatic pain. The blend of mental power and depth of feeling in one man is almost fearsome. But the most distinctive thing about him is his warmth: his customary way of greeting a stranger is to wrap him in a hug.

It was the peak of the atomic season—midway between the sixtieth anniversary of Trinity, on July 16th, and the sixtieth anniversary of Hiroshima, on August 6th. Books about Oppenheimer and the bomb were being published, seemingly, at the rate of one a week.

Sellars, who was in town to direct a production of Osvaldo Golijov's "Ainadamar," at the Santa Fe Opera, pointed out that there were traces of atomic history all around: we were sitting a few hundred feet from 109 East Palace Avenue, the studiously inconspicuous front office for Los Alamos, where Dorothy McKibbin, Oppenheimer's gatekeeper, took in bewildered émigré physicists and sent them on the road to the laboratories, twenty-five miles to the northwest.

Sellars has long been in the habit of dragging opera into danger-ous places. When he was an undergraduate theatre prodigy at Har-vard, in the late nineteen-seventies, he staged an abridged version of Wagner's "Ring," with lip-synching puppets. In the eighties, in a se-ries of productions both notorious and revered, he placed "Don Giovanni" in Spanish Harlem, "The Marriage of Figaro" in Trump Tower, Handel's "Julius Caesar" in Beirut. His first collaboration with John Adams was "Nixon in China," in 1987; the title more or less explains the plot of the opera, though not its dreamlike atmo-sphere. His second Adams collaboration, "The Death of Klinghof-fer," ventured into the even riskier territory of Israeli-Palestinian relations and international terrorism. The librettist for both of those projects was Alice Goodman, who also was to have written the text of "Doctor Atomic." When Goodman backed out, Sellars de-cided to write the libretto himself. Or, rather, he decided to assem-ble a libretto from extant material, because he realized that the subject resisted a conventional treatment.

"My mother lived in Kobe, Japan, for five years, one hour away from Hiroshima," Sellars told me. "I went there several times, and there's a whole museum filled with bad Holocaust art. The great material is Kenzaburo Oe's 'A Personal Matter,' where the word 'Hiroshima' appears once. How to make a Hiroshima piece or a Holocaust piece—that's a really serious question. Art can't get above itself. It has also to recognize its own limits." He went on, "The nightmare of all art, as well as of all politics, is generalities. You can-not generalize. You've got to keep things as specific to the minute, as down to the wire, as possible."

The classic book on the Manhattan Project is Richard Rhodes's "The Making of the Atomic Bomb." Rhodes wrote it only after he had tried and failed to produce a fictional work on the same theme. Rhodes recently appeared at a panel discussion in San Francisco with Sellars and Adams—an event sponsored by the Exploratorium, which was founded by Robert Oppenheimer's brother Frank— where he reflected on the dangers of treating the bomb melodramatically. "This whole story is slowly moving into a mythological compressed state," Rhodes said. "You have one person, Oppenheimer, and his scientists, and one place, Los Alamos, and one city, Hiroshima. Poor Nagasaki—we always forget Nagasaki every August. But, in fact, this was a huge project of a hundred thirty thousand people, on a physical plant on the scale of the American automobile industry by 1945."

Rhodes was impressed to hear of Sellars's prolonged immersion in the Los Alamos story. The libretto is an ingenious collage, stitching together declassified documents, transcripts of meetings, interviews with participants, and standard histories. Events are sometimes condensed, but almost every line can be checked against a source. The cast of characters includes Oppenheimer, in all his brilliant, arrogant, magnetic, cryptic glory; his wife, Kitty, seething against the confines of Los Alamos and losing herself in drink; Robert Wilson, an idealistic young scientist, who opposes the use of atomic bombs on Japan; General Leslie R. Groves, the oversized bulldog in charge of the entire operation; and Jack Hubbard, the Trinity meteorologist, whose predictions of thunderstorms drive Groves into an impotent rage. Lurking to the side is the Hungarian-born physicist Edward Teller, who is beginning to feel the resentment that will lead him, at the height of the Communist hysteria of the nineteen-fifties, to denounce Oppenheimer as a security risk.

Oppenheimer reveals his inner life by reciting poetic texts that had special meaning for him. In addition to Donne's "Batter my heart," the libretto features Baudelaire—a volume of whose poetry was in Oppenheimer's pocket at Trinity—and the Bhagavad Gita, which the physicist had read in the original Sanskrit. (He later claimed to have thought of a line from the Bhagavad Gita—"I am become Death, the destroyer of worlds"—after the bomb went off. Jack Hubbard's diary has Oppenheimer saying, "My faith in the human mind is somewhat restored.") There is little record of what Kitty Oppenheimer was doing or saying in this period; Sellars fleshes her out by giving her lines from the mid-century poet Muriel Rukeyser, whose life overlapped with that of the Oppenheimers in fascinating ways (wealthy New York background; hard-left politics; visionary tendencies). And there is one semi-fictional character, a Tewa Pueblo maid named Pasqualita, who baby-sits for the Oppenheimer children. Many Native Americans were employed at Los Alamos, including, Sellars says, a maid with this name. It is not implausible that, during a summer storm, a servant would have comforted a baby with a Tewa song: "In the north the cloudflower blossoms / And now the lightning flashes, / And now the thunder clashes, / And now the rain comes down!"

In Sellars's "Doctor Atomic" libretto, as in Oe's "A Personal Matter," the word "Hiroshima" appears once. In the first scene of the opera, which depicts a staff meeting at Los Alamos, Oppenheimer goes through a list of potential Japanese targets with Teller and Wilson. (Some of the dialogue is taken from a Washington, D.C., meeting that occurred a few weeks earlier.) When the physicist gets to Hiroshima, the strings and brass play a soft groan of a chord, containing multiple, clashing major triads, and then the dialogue moves on. That same chord returns, in modified form, at the end of the opera. Here the advantage of opera as a dramatic medium becomes clear. The characters do not know what is coming. The orchestra, brooding from the start, knows everything.

The first person to theorize nuclear weapons was the Hungarian physicist Leo Szilard, who, as Richard Rhodes relates, pictured an explosive chain reaction while crossing a London street in 1933. The first person to theorize "Doctor Atomic" was Pamela Rosenberg, who was appointed the general director of the San Francisco Opera in 1999. An administrator of sharp intellect, Rosenberg arrived with the conviction that opera should be more than an opulent entertainment. She decided that a new work by John Adams should be central to her tenure. Rosenberg has sometimes been a controversial figure in San Francisco, but her productions have had a strong impact, and few have faulted her for launching "Doctor Atomic," which will travel to at least four opera houses over the next few years, including the Met. Rosenberg leaves next year to become the general manager of the Berlin Philharmonic. She will, as she says, go out with a bang.

"I was doing this Faust series here, and wanted to commission an American Faust," Rosenberg told me one day, at a picnic table in the Presidio. She presented the idea to the opera's board of trustees; afterward, Michael Harrison, a professor emeritus at the University of California, at Berkeley, approached her. Rosenberg recalled him saying, "You know, all your subjects are sitting over there, and they can't sleep at night because of the genie they let out of the bottle." She told him, "The man I have been thinking of is Oppenheimer." Rosenberg zeroed in on Adams because she considers him "the greatest composer alive."

Adams's ability to attract lofty epithets has aroused envy among his colleagues, but he has won his eminence fair and square: he has aimed high, he has addressed life as it is lived now, and he has found a language that makes sense to a wide audience. As a music student at Harvard, in the late nineteen-sixties, he received the gospel according to Arnold Schoenberg, who held that composers of integrity should flee the profaned temples of mass culture and cry out in a wilderness of dissonance. Adams bought into all that when he was young, and even wrote a letter to Leonard Bernstein chiding him for the tonal simplicities of "Chichester Psalms." He then began to find his way outside academic language, investigating the chance methods of John Cage and embracing New York minimalism. Most important, perhaps, he moved to Northern California, settling eventually in a house in the hills of Berkeley.

Adams and Sellars met in 1983, in the composer's home state of New Hampshire, where they talked over the idea that became "Nixon in China." That opera and the later Sellars-Adams collaborations ("Klinghoffer," "I Was Looking at the Ceiling and Then I Saw the Sky," and "El Niño") delved into what Adams calls "psychic complexes of American consciousness—Communism, the market economy, Presidential politics, terrorism, racism." Adams matches these sprawling themes with sprawling musical vistas, in which multiple forces are in motion. He can react to a huge variety of dramatic stimuli, and is as comfortable creating the peculiar Chinese-accented big-band jazz of "Nixon" as he is writing the hieratic Bachian chorales of the Exiled Jews and Palestinians in "Klinghoffer." His method is often to link a character or a situation to a favorite musical gesture or texture in his memory bank; he then extrapolates from that kernel to fashion his narrative.

Adams took a long break from large-scale opera after he finished "Klinghoffer." The protracted controversy over that work, in the course of which he was called both an anti-Semite and a terrorist sympathizer, left him discouraged; he began to think that the genre was not worth the trouble. When I interviewed him five years ago, he said that he didn't think he had another opera in him. But the Oppenheimer story proved irresistible. It offered him the psychic complex to end all psychic complexes.

At the "Doctor Atomic" panel at the Exploratorium, Adams said, "I knew almost within the hour of first talking to Pamela that this was what I wanted to do." He went on, "The atomic bomb was the ultimate archetype, the ultimate looming presence. And I do remember, as a kid—I don't know how old I was, maybe seven or eight years old—living in the most secure, Steven Spielbergesque, idyllic village in New Hampshire . . . getting into bed one night, and my mother gave me a kiss and turned out the light. I heard a jet plane way, way high up in the sky, and I went into a panic, because I wondered if that was the Russians coming to bomb us." He said that the bomb represented a "dividing line in human history, when the hu-

man species was no longer riding along with the rest of God's creation . . . but suddenly was in a position to destroy the nest, to literally destroy the planet. That seemed to be a theme that was worthy
of my time."

When Adams sat down with Sellars and looked through the
sources, his eyes soon landed on some sentences in Henry DeWolf
Smyth's pamphlet "Atomic Energy for Military Purposes," which
was published just after Hiroshima: "The end of June 1945 finds us
expecting from day to day to hear of the explosion of the first
atomic bomb devised by man. All the problems are believed to have
been solved at least well enough to make a bomb practicable." A
fast, relentless eighth-note figure—what Sellars would later call "the
Stravinsky emergency music"—darted through the composer's
head. A less promising verbal cue could hardly be imagined—had
the word "practicable" ever been set to music?—but Adams had
found his groove.

The working relationship of Adams and Sellars is intimate and
complex. Each has his fiefdom, and negotiations between the two
regimes are unending. Adams's control of musical matters is absolute. He entertains suggestions from Sellars, which are sometimes
very detailed—"Give me something like the Adagio of the Bruckner
Fourth," Sellars said of one passage in "Doctor Atomic"—but when
Adams sits down to write, his inner voice often takes him elsewhere.
The passage that was supposed to sound like Bruckner—Jack Hubbard's final weather report, shortly before the detonation—came out
sounding like, well, John Adams. When the score was finished,
Sellars was puzzled that certain choice lines had been unceremoni-
ously dropped. But he was too thrilled by the over-all result to fret.
Adams, for his part, retires from the battlefield once rehearsals begin. As he watches Sellars at work, he comments on the musical exe-
cution rather than on the stage action. He may have reservations
about the sheer amount of activity that Sellars sometimes unleashes
onstage, but if he were to say anything Sellars would likely become
all the more convinced that his instincts were right—the director is

sunny and steely in equal measure. Adams is usually won over, and his gratitude is immense.

The strength of the partnership lies as much in its opposing traits as in its similarities. Sellars is pure charisma, enthusiasm, happy intensity. Adams is wry, folksy, detached. Sellars is outspoken in his politics, Adams more reserved. Sellars talks about the atomic story in terms of a battle between light and darkness, although he is too intelligent to confine his characters to one side or the other. In Adams's telling, the bomb bears down like Fate incarnate, inevitable and irrevocable. Sellars sees unexpected grace and hope blossoming around the explosion; his motto for this opera is Muriel Rukeyser's line "Love must imagine the world." Adams, too, supplies moments of dizzying beauty, but in the end he has written a three-hour symphony of dread.

It would be a stretch to compare the staging of "Doctor Atomic" to the Manhattan Project, but the undertaking is gigantic all the same. Under the troika of Adams, Sellars, and Rosenberg, a miniature city has been working to bring the opera to life. Some five hundred people are contributing to one or another aspect of the production. Only in the final week do all the components—singers, chorus, orchestra, costumes, scenery, lighting, and the rest—come together onstage; before that, most components are prepared separately. This being a Sellars show, there are extra complications. Lucinda Childs has been devising fluid, geometric choreography for a squad of dancers. At the core of the production team are three people who have worked with Sellars since the nineteen-eighties: Adrianne Lobel, the set designer; Dunya Ramicova, the costume designer; and James F. Ingalls, the lighting designer. They have devised an overarching color scheme for the show. Graphite represents the will to kill; "true blues" represent whatever remains of the human impulse; gray and ochre tones represent the muddled middle. The colors were inspired in part by a photograph of the mountains and sky at Trinity on the eve of the test.

The San Francisco Opera costume shop is in a cavernous three-story building on Ninth Street. Twenty-eight stitchers, drapers, and tailors are running up period garb for the singers, chorus, supernumeraries, and dancers. The supervisor for "Atomic" is Jai Alltizer, a soft-spoken art punk with a red-and-purple Mohawk and a long goatee. He has spent the past year trying to reconstruct the way people at Los Alamos dressed, and to master such arcana as the project's system of I.D. buttons, which were coded white, blue, or red to identify levels of clearance, and of temporary passes—"to let you come to the after-party," Alltizer joked. He showed me Teller's suits (graphite), Kitty Oppenheimer's dress (a watery-blue silk number, made from leftover Valentino fabric), and Oppenheimer's hat— a rakish porkpie, which was famous enough in its day to be pictured on the cover of *Physics Today* with no caption. It is being stretched and distressed to simulate the effect of conditions on the mesa.

The scene shop is in the Potrero Hill neighborhood, in an old steelyard warehouse. Last November, Jay Kotcher, the head scenic artist, and Jack Kostelnik, the foreman of the construction crew, worked with eight carpenters, four scenic artists, and a sculptor, building the scenery for the show: the huts and fences of Los Alamos; the tower at Trinity, on which the bomb was placed; an enormous protective container called Jumbo, which was never used; and the hundred-and-two-foot-wide sloping floor on which the action takes place. And, of course, Kotcher and Kostelnik built the bomb itself. For the frame, they used wood; for the shell, Styrofoam; for the skin, fibreglass. Lobel asked them to paint it a dull silver color, to give it a suitably ominous sheen.

Sitting in a cramped, dusty office next to the carpentry shop, Kotcher told me, "The fun part was coming up with all these doodads, these mysterious electrical things that come out of the shell. Lori Harrison, our master of properties, did some shopping and came in with a carful of miscellaneous weird stuff. A colleague of hers had gone to a restaurant-supply place down the street, where she found some liquor pourers—those spigots you see sticking out of liquor bottles at a bar. We just glued them in the wooden box and stuck wires on them."

Kostelnik called up a spreadsheet on his computer to check how much the entire thing had cost. The original Gadget, as it was called, consumed hundreds of millions of dollars. The Kotcher-Kostelnik Gadget came in at $30,164, including parts and labor. It had been moved to the backstage area of the opera house, where it sat under a transparent plastic tarp, glowering at passersby.

In a rehearsal space one block from the opera house, Sellars was working with a group of singers in a piano rehearsal. Adelle Eslinger, one of the music coaches, was at the keyboard, trying to summon up the sound of a hundred-piece Adamsian orchestra. Donato Cabrera, the assistant conductor, gave the singers their cues and sang the part of the chorus or vocalized a significant instrumental solo. Props were scattered around the room, to give the singers inspiration. There was a blackboard with a daunting equation written on it: $2 + 2 = x$ squared $+ 2$ to the x $(3\pi CO) / 10$ cubed. Sellars and the singers amused themselves by scrawling new equations each day.

The session focussed on Act I, Scene 1, in which Oppenheimer, Teller, and Wilson debate the wisdom of deploying the bomb in Japan. The dialogue begins with a line adapted from Teller's memoirs: "First of all, let me say that I have no hope of clearing my conscience. The things we are working on are so terrible that no amount of protesting or fiddling with politics will save our souls." In Adams's setting of the words, the melody moves along in shadowy, groping fashion, the notes drawn generally from the whole-tone scale.

The man singing Oppenheimer is Gerald Finley, a forty-five-year-old Canadian with a firm jaw and a hypnotically expressive baritone voice. In the past few years, he has scored international triumphs in such mainstream roles as Don Giovanni and Figaro. He has also worked steadily in the less glamorous realm of contemporary opera, and seems happiest when taking on thorny, elusive characters. In the "Atomic" rehearsals, he was tireless in his pursuit of nuances, and often could be seen in the corner, puffing on a fake cigarette—Oppenheimer's chain-smoking is a leitmotif of the opera—and trying out different readings of a line. Like almost everyone involved in the production, he had become an enthusiast of the atomic literature, and, naturally, he had thought harder than most about the central character.

"He wanted to believe in the beauty of natural forces," Finley told me at lunch one day. In the opera, Oppenheimer speaks of the "brilliant luminescence" of the explosion. "When there was an imperfection, it would drive him crazy," Finley said. "Faust is the obvious connection—the craving for knowledge and the cruelty of having that knowledge, if you like, and the punishment of having that knowledge."

Teller was being sung by Joshua Bloom, a young Australian baritone. He was one of a group of cover singers who were attending all the rehearsals, studying the principals' every move in the slender hope that they might be called to do the same onstage. Today, Bloom was happy to be standing in for Richard Paul Fink, who had been assigned the role at the last minute and was not yet in town. Bloom sang his opening line elegantly, with perfect accuracy of pitch. Sellars stopped him, seeking more.

"This whole night is about the atomic bomb," Sellars said, "and I want actually to begin with the most important words—that, at the end of the day, yes, it's wrong, and everyone knows it. Yes, it's wrong. When you say 'terrible,' terrible is"—Sellars paused—"terrible. Look at it in the eye."

"Terrible"? "Wrong"? As a New Yorker who thinks regularly about the possibility of a stray nuclear bomb wiping out not only my life but everything I love, I didn't doubt him for a moment. But I wondered whether the director was politically stacking the deck. He was, however, merely setting up one pole of the debate. Oppenheimer answers Teller by archly quoting Baudelaire: "The soul is a thing so impalpable, so often useless, and sometimes so embarrassing that at this loss I felt only a little more emotion than if, during a walk, I had lost my visiting card." Sellars gave Finley an indication of what this allusion might mean: "It's like, 'Oh, really, Edward, you're worried about losing your soul? Well, I lost my bus ticket yesterday. I was upset. That transfer is an extra quarter!' The most soulful character in the history of science is acting like a soul is a trivial thing. Get a little pyrotechnic with it. With your butterfly mind, just feel that you can literally go rings around him."

Finley ran through the Baudelaire lines in a lighter, airier tone. The words "visiting card" fluttered in the air, and the singer accentuated them by wiggling his fingers.

"Great great great great great great great great great great great cool cool cool cool," Sellars said, in about the time that most people would say, "Great, cool."

Later in the scene, Robert Wilson registers his objections to using the bomb in combat. The part is played by Tom Randle, who is the sort of singer that Sellars loves—alert to psychological detail, physically agile, extremely well prepared. (He often mouthed the words to other singers' parts.) Sellars urged him to invest his words with humanitarian passion and patriotic fervor. "What I always hate are right-wingers who say that progressives can't be patriotic," he said. Wilson's argument, in brief, is that the Japanese should be given more time to surrender, and if the bomb is to be used it should be dropped on an uninhabited area, as a demonstration.

Again, Oppenheimer engages in a masterly manipulation. Sellars said to his lead singer, "When Wilson starts speaking, would you start very slowly coming the entire distance—smoking, listening—and then say something that is going to be very unpopular with all these young people: 'What do we know about Japanese psychology? How can we scientists judge the way to end the war?' Be prickly. You're saying, Look, you've come this far in the countdown. Five minutes before, two billion dollars later, twenty thousand people working for two and a half years, and now you say, 'Uh, O.K., go home, thanks'? Physics in the last twenty years has become the most powerful thing in the world, the single greatest power in the history of the human race. As a scientist, you want to know if it works."

Randle nodded. "There's something sympathetic about this," he said, on behalf of his character. "I understand that, his curiosity."

Finley sang the words with his usual nobility. Sellars instructed, "Gerry, come straight down, like a piranha. You have to be the bad guy, and what that means for you to have to be the bad guy is what I want to feel. You're somebody who's into the nuances of Baudelaire and you're talking about 'Japanese psychology'? It's offensive, what you're saying. You're saying this just to provoke them." Sellars also said, "As you know, Oppenheimer is being grilled around the clock by these government security people about every damn thing about your past. They've missed Klaus Fuchs, who is actually reporting on the bomb to Stalin, and meanwhile you're being harassed on a weekly basis about"—Sellars snarled—"minuscule shit. These people will not rest until you are dead."

Sellars wrote his undergraduate thesis on Vsevolod Meyerhold and his avant-garde theatre of abstraction and defamiliarization. At the same time, Sellars studied Konstantin Stanislavsky's art of psychological naturalism. You could say that his lifelong project has been to try to reconcile the two giants of early-twentieth-century Russian theatre. He devises challenging, disorienting frames for drama, and then fills those frames with lavish knowledge of the characters' inner lives. If he sometimes seeks the unattainable—at one point, he asked one of the singers to "get Martin Luther King's entire 'I have a dream' speech in that melisma"—he never fails to provide the wealth of context and backstory that actors crave. Above all, he won't hang cards around characters' necks saying "good" or "evil"; that is why some people rejected "Klinghoffer," and why others may reject "Doctor Atomic." In the end, the main objection that can be levelled against some of Sellars's work is not that it presents a limited point of view but, rather, that it presents too many points of view. His productions, Andrew Porter wrote in the *New Yorker* two decades ago, are "meant for nimble minds."

The following day, Sellars rehearsed this same Act I scene on the main stage of the house. He was in his element, hollering instructions and channeling history as the dancers swirled around him, supernumeraries carried boxes of explosives, the women of the chorus sang an ode to the plutonium core, and the male principals ran through their chamber play of protest and intellectual seduction. The composer was there, too, though you had to go to the back of the hall to find him.

Adams began "Doctor Atomic" in November, 2003, and finished it on May 24th of this year. He worked at a steady pace, hitting relatively few major obstacles as he went along. He composed directly onto thirty-six-staff orchestral music paper, without making an initial piano sketch. It's a bit like painting directly onto canvas without first pencilling in a drawing underneath. Although Adams solved some musical problems on the computer, using various forms of compositional software, he wrote out the score the old-fashioned way, by hand. The manuscript is a mammoth thing, taking up five hundred and forty-eight pages. It sits now in his studio in Berkeley, divided into manila envelopes.

For Adams, the tensest day of the process was the first orchestral rehearsal. It took place in a long, low-ceilinged hall on the grounds of the Presidio; Adams noted the appropriateness of first hearing the orchestral music of "Doctor Atomic" on a decommissioned military base. The composer walked in, saw an array of twenty gongs, and said, "My God, what have I done?" He greeted various players, some of whom he had known since the seventies, when he was a hippie-ish instructor at the San Francisco Conservatory. He went over to a table at the front of the orchestra and sat down next to Sellars, who was studying the music.

Donald Runnicles, who will conduct the première, walked in with the two big volumes of the score under his arm. He is an amiable, shaggy-haired, unprepossessing maestro, a native of Scotland, who has been living in California long enough that his burr has softened. He has been the chief conductor of the San Francisco Opera since 1992. This week he was preparing not only "Doctor Atomic" but also "L'Italiana in Algeri," which would play at the opera's opening-night gala. When I talked with him at his favorite pub, a place called

Liverpool Lil's, he joked about the absurdity of going back and forth between Rossini's frothy comedy and Adams's dire nuclear drama. He then drew a fascinating comparison between Oppenheimer and the figure of Captain Vere, in "Billy Budd." Vere's decision to send Billy to his death, he said, was not unlike Oppenheimer's decision to support the dropping of the bomb on Hiroshima: each man wills himself to uphold the official line, at enormous inner cost. "He conforms to the pressure of the state," Runnicles said. "But he's forever haunted by his decision."

Several times during the first rehearsals, Runnicles invited Adams and Sellars to talk to the musicians. This was an unusual move. Orchestral players like to concentrate on the technical nuts and bolts—Should it be soft or loud? When does the crescendo start?—and they tend to snicker at airy generalities about what the music means. So it was a bit brave of Sellars to stand up and chant Baudelaire. He then unleashed one of his verbal reveries, giving the players the same sort of Stanislavskian motivation that he had offered to the singers.

"In Act I, you're basically providing a lot of bad weather," Sellars said, standing on the tips of his toes so he could see the brass players and the percussionists in the back. "But when you make this thunder and do these sudden explosions it's not purely descriptive. You are indicating moral heights and depth of knowing. Those strange wind solos, for example—the oboe solos that play when they are talking about radiation poisoning—they show how cancer works in the body, how radiation functions. Or these weird, dark wind chords: the physicists are saying one thing, but you in the orchestra are telling us there's a whole lot more. The Stravinsky emergency music keeps hammering, because people did not always have the luxury of making decisions in a calm, quiet place." He added, "It's a real honor to do this piece at this time in the history of our country. The arts are not just entertainment, sideshow, and distraction."

Whether these instructions made any difference was not immediately apparent, but, during the break, several players came up to

Sellars to thank him. Then it was back to business as usual: adjusting balances, establishing crisp entrances, making sure that a fast figure was relayed cleanly from one section to another. The orchestra was mastering Adams's tricky textures, but, as the afternoon went on, their energy waned. By the time they arrived at the climax of Act I, Oppenheimer's recitation of "Batter my heart," they were tired out. Adams, who, a little earlier, had been rocking delightedly in his seat, was now bent over his score with a tight expression, scribbling notes on a yellow pad. He decided, at one point, that it was too much to ask the double basses to play some high, spidery figures in unison, so he gave the passage to a single bass player.

"Donald should just send them home," he muttered. "They're beat."

Sellars, though, was transported. "John Adams," he said, "you have written an unfucking-believable opera."

"Doctor Atomic" begins not with music but with noise: a two-minute electronic collage of industrial groans and screeches, into which is mixed the roar of airplanes, military voices, and a snippet of Jo Stafford singing "The Things We Did Last Summer." It suggests the buzzing of the innards of the bomb as it bleeds through radio static. All this will rain down on the audience from speakers that the sound designer, Mark Grey, has installed all over the War Memorial Opera House.

Jo Stafford's voice breaks up, cuts off, and gives way to a brutally dissonant passage for full orchestra, which feels like a detonation in progress. Adams had in mind not so much the explosion itself as the mental conflict of the Los Alamos physicists, who were mortally afraid of what would happen if their bomb did not work and no less afraid of what might happen if it did. Adams says that he was inspired in part by Edgard Varèse, who composed some of the most earsplitting music of the early modernist period. A recording of Varèse's work "Ionisation" apparently entertained some physicists in the Manhattan Project. But the real model is one of Adams's classic early works, his hyper-Romantic symphonic poem "Harmonie-lehre." The trombone and tuba have an identical floor-rattling fig-ure (a rising minor ninth) in both works. What had been darkly exuberant is now exuberantly dark.

The chorus barges in with its report on the progress of atomic research. The manic, scurrying pattern underneath—the Stravinsky emergency music—indeed takes off from Stravinsky's Symphony in Three Movements, which was itself inspired by the images and sounds of the Second World War: newsreels of goose-stepping Ger-man soldiers, of "scorched earth" tactics in China, of Allied forces on the march. The great Russian exile began writing it in the spring of 1942, around the time Oppenheimer was organizing a team of Berkeley physicists to work on the bomb, and finished it on August 7, 1945. Listening to Adams's music, I pictured Stravinsky in a hut at Los Alamos, working away on an intricate problem of seemingly tangential yet ultimately crucial significance.

A little later, a kind of explosive fusion occurs: the two main elements of the opening section, the dissonant chords and the driving lines, are rammed together. Throughout the scene, there are premonitions of the detonation to come. The word "Hi-roshima" is uttered, with its accompanying low-brass moan. When Oppenheimer rhapsodically describes the "brilliant luminescence" of the explosion, the winds swirl like particles in rapid motion and the strings play shivery tremolo chords. Many of these sounds are familiar from the forbidding archives of modern music past, not to mention a hundred sci-fi movies. There's a sense in "Doctor Atomic" that Adams is mobilizing the entire ghoulish army of twentieth-century styles.

In the second scene comes another shock, this one of beauty. We are in the Oppenheimers' bedroom, in the middle of the night. The physicist is sitting up in bed. Kitty wakes up and sings a setting of Rukeyser's "Three Sides of a Coin": "Am I in your light? No, go on reading." The poem is used to conjure up Kitty's sardonic, plaintive, and finally angry attempts to command the attention of a husband whose mind is buried in the mysteries of the atom. Oppenheimer, after putting aside his work, answers her with the Baudelaire prose poem that begins "Long let me inhale, deeply, the odor of your hair"—the "opium bath," as Adams calls it. They can relate to each other only in these precious terms. Kitty acknowledges as much when she moves on to another Rukeyser poem, beginning "The motive of it all was loneliness": it suggests that the Oppenheimers are together less out of love than out of fear. The interaction is edgy and charged, but Adams allows his music to become ravishingly sensuous. On close inspection, those blaring dissonances turn out to be simple chords nested together. They detach, breathe, sing out. The Baudelaire suggested to Adams a very French sound—surging, shimmering textures out of Debussy. It's a drugged, drunken beauty, not quite real.

In the final scene of Act I, the action moves to Trinity, on the eve of the test. A violent storm breaks over the desert. General Groves, who is played by Eric Owens, bellows, in a Lear-like tantrum, "What the hell is wrong with the weather?" Later on, after much sound and fury surrounding the arrival, raising, and arming of the bomb, Groves drops his bluster and begins to talk about his various attempts to lose weight. The oddly haunting tone of this "diet aria" illustrates what I think of as the Gadget Effect: even the most mundane chatter takes on spooky significance in light of the bomb. The crux of the opera arrives: Oppenheimer, alone at the bottom of the tower, sings "Batter my heart, three person'd God." The most telling lines may be the last: "for I / Except you enthrall me, never shall be free, / Nor ever chaste, except you ravish me." The aria is in the key of D minor, in the manner of a Renaissance lament, with a hint of synagogue chant; Oppenheimer sings a grand, doleful, nobly stammering melody, while the orchestra mimics the sound of viols and lutes.

"That music just sort of fluttered down and landed on my desk one day," Adams told me. "Part of me said, 'No, you can't do that,' and the other half said, 'That's it, go ahead and do it.' Afterward, I realized the reason it was right. Naming the site after a John Donne

sonnet was itself an archaic gesture. Oppenheimer was always referring back to ancient things, summing up his state through very dignified forms."

Act II is one long hallucination. The low brass lean for long
stretches on black Wagnerian chords; the strings emit clattering
noises and siren-like glissando tones. The electronic component in-
trudes more insistently, until it produces an almost continuous rum-
ble. It's as if we were hearing the hum of power lines in the desert,
the glistening of the grid. Weird shapes emerge from the sonic
gloom—sci-fi creatures, perhaps, including an irradiated version of
the dragon of "The Ring." Pulses compete against each other;
clocks tick away, but not in unison. They seem to speed up even as
the countdown slows in real time. The chorus stops singing and begins muttering, or, at one point, shouting. It also erupts into a mon-
umental, timpani-driven setting of verses from the Bhagavad Gita, a
hymn of praise to Vishnu: "At the sight of this, your Shape stupen-
dous, / Full of mouths and eyes, feet, thighs and bellies, / Terrible
with fangs, O mighty master, / All the words are fear-struck, even
just as I am." Robert Wilson reflects that Los Alamos reminds him
of Thomas Mann's "Magic Mountain."

The private world of the opera—the world of poetry and
prayer—seeps into the "official" world of lingo and debate. The action cuts between Trinity, where Oppenheimer and the rest take
bets on the kiloton yield, and Los Alamos, where Kitty is staying up
all night with her maid, Pasqualita. The Rukeyser poems and
Pasqualita's Tewa song become a constant, nagging presence amid
the solemn jibber-jabber of the countdown. Sellars wanted to break
up this mostly male melodrama by having women infiltrate the
scene. Adams, for his part, keeps interrupting the general death
march in the orchestra with passages of aching simplicity. You
would never expect to find so much delicate writing for harp and ce-
lesta, or so many plaintive solos for horn and trumpet, in a work on
this subject. So why do you remain tense as you listen? Because the
other shoe must drop.

It is left to Kitty Oppenheimer, that volatile, alcoholic, widely disliked woman, to announce what Sellars sees as the moral of the opera. Act II opens with a setting of Rukeyser's poem "Easter Eve 1945," which tries to find rays of light in the blackness of war:

> *Whatever world I know shines ritual death,*
> *wide under this moon they stand gathering fire,*
> *fighting with flame, stand fighting in their graves.*
> *All shining with life as the leaf, as the wing shines,*
> *the stone deep in the mountain, the drop in the green wave.*
> *Lit by their energies, secretly, all things shine.*
> *Nothing can black that glow of life.*

Some of Rukeyser's work is dense to the point of impenetrability, and some of it is tendentious, as Communist-inflected literature of the nineteen-thirties and forties often could be. Much of it, however, is breathtaking, and "Easter Eve 1945" is a masterpiece. It takes on an added power in the context of "Doctor Atomic": those images of luminous death play almost like a prophetic vision, as if Kitty, lost in her cups, were seeing the blinding flash to come.

The role of Kitty was to have been sung by Lorraine Hunt Lieberson. When that matchless artist withdrew for medical reasons, early in the summer, Kristine Jepson, an Iowa-born mezzo-soprano of rising reputation, gamely stepped in. Jepson is about as far from Kitty in temperament as can be imagined—ebullient, easy-going, self-effacing. But she soon found the sympathetic side of her character, who is, on the one hand, a neurotic, drunken mess and, on the other, the chief truthteller and moral compass of the opera. "She speaks only in poetry a hundred per cent of the time," Jepson told me, a few hours before her first rehearsal in costume. "She's having a vision of the mountains being on fire, she feels that she's hearing the cries of the children. All of those—if you want to call them—hallucinations are very real to her." And the bomb turns her hallucinations into reality.

Early in the morning on July 16, 1945, Mrs. H. E. Wieselman was driving over the border from Arizona to New Mexico when a huge light filled her field of vision. That day, she told the *El Paso Herald-Post*, "It was just like the sun had come up and suddenly gone down again." Dorothy McKibbin was watching from a hilltop near Albuquerque, and described the experience in terms that resonate with the imagery of Rukeyser's "Easter Eve 1945": "The leaves of the green native trees were kind of shining with the gold. It was different. Everything was different. The world was changed."

How to depict the detonation puzzled Adams from the start. He talked about the problem one day as we drove across the San Francisco Bay Bridge, on the way to a rehearsal. He knew better than to put a mushroom cloud onstage. "I can't compete with George Lucas," he told me. What he decided to do, in the end, was to visualize the explosion from afar—from the perspective not of the scientists in their bunkers but of the women back at Los Alamos. He sent a query to Richard Rhodes, asking whether the blast would have been perceptible from two hundred miles away. Rhodes told him that "people would have noticed a dawn coming from the entirely wrong direction." So Adams wrote a slow crescendo for trilling strings, to which is added a flash of winds and brass—a chord that dazzles and fades, like a false dawn.

If "Doctor Atomic" is considered the saga of Robert Oppenheimer—and it is more than that—then the hero's final line is important. It is "Lord, these affairs are hard on the heart." The music seems like a reprise of "Batter my heart," but it falters after two bars. Oppenheimer begins the opera by saying, "The soul is a thing so impalpable," and returns many times to the soul, the spirit, and the heart. We are confronted, at last, with the question of Oppenheimer's soul. Pamela Rosenberg had asked Adams to write an American Faust, and his title had a Faustian ring, but the composer came to fear the implications of that association. Any sort of demonic narrative would severely oversimplify the situation of Oppenheimer and his staff, who conceived the bomb, after all, in the belief that Hitler was preparing to drop a bomb on them. (Hitler, it turned out, was perplexed by the idea of atomic bombs; he didn't like the idea that they might kill everyone on the planet.)

Once Adams was done, though, he admitted that the Faust metaphor still interested him, as long as it was not taken too literally. It helps to expose the blinkered mentality of the scientists, and particularly of Oppenheimer, who assumed that science had every right to discover whatever lay within its grasp, and that it was someone else's job to figure out the moral consequences. Oppenheimer once had this to say: "It is my judgment in these things that when you see something that is technically sweet, you go ahead and do it and you argue about what to do about it only after you have had your technical success." As he read the literature, Adams seesawed between an intense admiration for Oppenheimer and an equally intense dislike of him. The physicist had a violent streak, and it is unsettling to read of his more bloodthirsty initiatives—for example, his notion, floated briefly during the war, that Germans could be killed en masse by radiation poisoning. Such a program would be worth pursuing, Oppenheimer said, if it could yield the death of five hundred thousand or more people.

Oppenheimer liked to float above the rest of humanity, not just intellectually but geographically. If you go to see the places where he lived, you notice that he made a habit of perching like an eagle on the rim of the world. When he lived in Berkeley, he took a house high in the hills; it had the address No. 1, Eagle Hill. In New Mexico, he had a cabin on Grass Mountain, a surreally lush meadow at nearly ten thousand feet. He was instrumental in placing the Manhattan Project atop the Los Alamos mesa. In his youth, he said that his two great loves were physics and New Mexico, and that he wished he could unite them. And he did, but only at the price of ruining, for his own purposes, the landscapes that he loved. It's said that he felt the mushroom cloud hanging over the Sangre de Cristo Mountains, where his cabin was. One tremendous passage in Adams's opera is an interlude called "Rain Over the Sangre de

Cristo Mountains": it is nothing more than a tremulous chain of chords, one blurring into the next. I think of it as a radioactive cloud bearing down on Oppenheimer's aerie.

A few months before his death, as cancer was spreading from his throat through his body, Oppenheimer went to hear the world pre-mière of Stravinsky's Requiem Canticles. The same work was played at his memorial service, in February, 1967. It is no accident that the "chords of death" that end Stravinsky's valedictory compo-sition—a tolling of spectral bells—are echoed in the chords that end "Doctor Atomic." There are nineteen of them, and the high gongs create strange resonances in the upper frequencies. Previ-ously, during the countdown, time slowed to a surreal crawl, but now it seems to be racing forward, to the moment of Oppen-heimer's death. It is also moving to a nearer destination, to the Ground Zero of August 6, 1945. How Adams succeeds in trans-muting Trinity into Hiroshima is not something that should be re-vealed in advance, for it is the most dramatic turn of the entire opera, albeit one that takes place át low volume. It has happened, and it is about to happen again.

One day in early September, Sellars worked on the final scene of the opera with most of the principals, including Beth Clayton, who sings Pasqualita, and James Maddalena, who is Hubbard, the weath-erman. The scene begins with Oppenheimer once more savoring lines of Baudelaire: "To what benevolent demon do I owe the joy of being thus surrounded with mystery, with silence, with peace and with perfumes?"

Sellars went through the poem with Finley word by word, work-ing out gestures and facial expressions. The singer got to the line "That supreme life which I now know and which I am tasting minute by minute." Sellars, uncharacteristically, made no comment. Finley asked, "Do you want anything special on 'tasting'?" Sellars re-sponded, "Oh, God, yes." The passage ends, "Time has disappeared;

it is Eternity that reigns now!" Oppenheimer, at this late stage, seems far gone, lost in the desert of his mind.

Maddalena stood all the way upstage. He is a longtime Sellars collaborator, and has given many piercing performances in the title role of "Nixon in China." In that opera, he played the troubled soul; here he plays an ordinary man who tries to keep his bearings. Sellars asked Maddalena to deliver his final weather report in a state of wonder, as if he were describing not the sky above but a paradise beyond it. As Sellars recited and meandered about, Maddalena walked right behind him, matching his gestures like a shadow. To Beth Clayton, Sellars gave the task of purifying and blessing the terrain; by the end, Pasqualita becomes a dream figure, perhaps a representative of the ancient Tewa people who once occupied the Los Alamos mesa.

Sellars's vision for the very end was not yet complete. He talked of having all the performers lie face down, arms behind their heads, as waves of light poured across the stage.

At one point, Sellars stopped to describe for Clayton the scene at Trinity today, even though he had never been there. "There is incredible regeneration in this world," he said. "The good thing is that this bomb is going to go off and fifty years from this night there will be wildflowers growing among the trinitite at this test site. All our private storms, which seem like the end of the world, blow over, and there is a new day. That's the deepest thing in life. The person who seems most hopeless turns out to be the very person who is the hope. There is some part of life that will never be extinguished and will always stay evergreen. I feel that some weird, strange hope exists in the created universe."

MIKE McGUIRK

Rush, *Hemispheres*

Apart from the 20-minute odyssey that opens this overlooked album, Rush also delivered "The Trees," one of the greatest songs there is about trouble in the forest. You don't have to be a druid to get it either, although Neil Peart had to be a total druid to write it. As always, every member of the band plays their instruments like they're more evolved than the rest of us.

London Calling—For Congo, Colombo, Sri Lanka . . .

In 1976, Cory Daye recorded a song called "Sunshower" with Dr. Buzzard's Original Savannah Band. She was 24. The band were well outside a recording deadline from RCA; when the album was eventually released, the label failed to notify the band.

"Sunshower" has been sampled for almost 20 years now; there's a snatch of its warped Hawaiian guitars and splintered percussion towards the end of A Tribe Called Quest's "Can I Kick It?" but, like attempts by De La Soul and Doug E. Fresh, it's just dressing. The appropriations always seem piecemeal and placeless: Busta Rhymes' "Take It Off" is slick, but not convincing. Ghostface Killah's "Ghost Showers" attempts to wholly inhabit the song; it swallows him whole. There's simply too much in the original: swooping Hawaiian guitars, child-like chants, ambient noise, guitar barely recognizable in a flood of in reverb. The percussion is so richly syncopated, so densely layered, that it leaves Daye's vocal somehow isolated, exposed, as if shimmering in a cloud of dust. The melody itself sounds free and ungrounded, and takes on an almost atonal quality. The groove is wood-like, organic, pulmonary. Nobody has done anything as remotely convincing, assured, or unique with the same materials. Until M.I.A.'s "Sunshowers."

The difference between the original and M.I.A.'s second single, produced last year by Steve Mackey and Ross Orton, is more than one of genre or period; it is a difference in aesthetics, a difference in the place given to popular culture. The original material itself is gutted. The slightly adrenaline bliss of Davy's chorus sounds highly phased, over-exposed, washed-out at the edges. A percussive bass glissandi, which in the original gracefully eases the song into a final elaboration of the chorus, is ripped out and looped throughout the piece. The groove is a relentless throb that hammers its way throughout the entire song, rattling and lurching between violence and grace. "Sunshowers" erases the spirit of the original as it goes along.

Where Dr. Buzzard's Original Savannah Band brought a wispy lyricism to disco, a feeling of dreamy nostalgia wrapped in their elaborate big band arrangements, M.I.A.'s use of the song is—like the rest of her material—a blend of hard unsentimentality and pop-like glee. It's a striking contrast: strident political stances sit along-side made-for-ringtone hooks. There's no middle ground on *Arular*, her debut album. Even the wordplay is taken to a level of abstraction, with playground chants in place of intimacy and wit. There is very little that deals with the minutiae of personal relationships; even "URAQT," a song about betrayal, revolves more around the exchange of postures than of emotions. Relationships are almost transactions. There is no trust in this music.

It's a stance that echoes the details of her life: M.I.A. witnessed at first hand the violence of Sri Lanka's civil war, followed by an abrupt relocation to a neglected council estate on the outskirts of London.

London shapes much of her music. The touch of gleeful—almost naive—joy in her sound recalls early British experiments with hip-hop. It is the sound of the Wild Bunch, of Fresh Four's "Wishing on a Star," of Carlton's forgotten *The Call Is Strong*, where the sing-song lilt of Lovers Rock met the swallowed aggression of dub, where the structure and confidence of American hip-hop met the residual brashness of punk and ska. Though those influences have been replaced in the contemporary sound of London by dancehall, crunk, grime, and American R&B, the aesthetic is the same—and one unique to London. "The thing that I'm a part of," M.I.A. agrees, "is that I listen to everything. And so do the grime kids. There are grime tunes where Lethal B could rap over a Kylie Minogue backing, because he knows it—he hears it: he's on a bus, he's in a cab, he's in a Chinese takeaway."

The vocal cadence that is a part of her singing voice—the rise in intonation at the end of almost every line—is now near-ubiquitous among Londoners of a certain age. It is not, curiously, part of her speaking voice, which is a fairly cool and unremarkable London accent. "Everybody has access to all kinds of genres of music every day when you wake up. So why not reflect that? It's way more realistic than me saying 'I only hear dancehall when I walk down the street. I only hear dancehall for eight years of my life walking around in this city.' That's wrong. Because that's not the case. Every day I wake up in this city, the cosmopolitan Westernized fast first-world amazing foreign land that's got amazing technology, amazing information access, speedway, highway—let's not kid ourselves: we *do* hear everything at once, so whether it's through television, on the radio, on people's CDs, people's cars going past you—so why not reflect that in what you do?"

While race relations over the last two decades in London have hardly been exemplary—something M.I.A. knows about at first hand—the capital's density and diversity have made possible a mixture of cultures that sets it apart from most other Western cities. Even so, M.I.A. sees this process as increasingly under threat. "I knew someone like me could never come out of America, and I knew that I couldn't come out of Sri Lanka either. It was really important to be in Britain to come out the way I did. But at the same time, I just think it's really, really sad that I'm the only person here, when there could be a damn lot more. There could be more people making a crossbreed sound and referencing each other's communities. But there isn't. The Asians do stick to the Asians. The Somalians stick to the Somalians. The Palestinians stick to the Palestinians. The Moroccans stick to the Moroccans. The white kids stick to the white kids. The black kids stick to the black kids. And that's only a new thing that's happening."

Since the late '90s, concerns have been voiced that "economic migrants" are using the UK's asylum system as a backdoor. This argument has increasingly come to drive British political debate (not to mention newspaper sales), intensifying around election cycles despite a fall in the number of people seeking asylum. Since 2001, the debate has taken on an additional overtone of paranoia and "racial profiling" amid fears about international terrorism. Local community workers admit to noticing a correlation between incidents of racial harassment and the intensity of the national debate. Steve Griffin, Deputy Director of Groundwork Merton, a local regeneration agency covering the area in which M.I.A. grew up, notes, "You get Islamophobia going. There's been more attacks on Asians and more problems for Asians since 9/11 in this country."

M.I.A. is outraged by this situation—and the smothering effect it is having on cultural interaction in London. "I've followed British culture, the underground culture, and musically I feel like I've been a part of different movements that have happened. But for the first time, everything is kinda just quiet, you know? Back when I was sort of walking around there seemed to be more of an identity amongst young people, and there was just stuff happening, and it was real sort of energetic and colorful. And then, it seems like everybody's bogged down by all this immigration stuff, and newspapers are like 'Immigrants go back home!' and for the first time they can say it on the front page without it being politically incorrect. And then with all this terrorism stuff where they're like 'Muslim kids are bad.' There's some weird atmosphere going on. Girls have started wearing yashmacs, and there's divides amongst communities and stuff. And that's when I decided to go, 'Look: the only thing that Britain always ever goes on about, and is proud of going on about, is that it's a cosmopolitan city, and it's multicultural.' So unless everybody starts waking up in England and starts shouting about it, and saying that's a really great thing, you're not even doing what you said you're good at doing in the first place."

Maya Arulpragasam was born in London in 1976. Her father moved to London in 1971 after graduating in Moscow with a master's degree in engineering. His name is sometimes rendered A.R. Arudpragasam, sometimes Arul Pragasam; his *nom de guerre* is Arular. In January 1975, he was instrumental in founding the Eelam Revolutionary Organization of Students (EROS) in Wandsworth. In June of that year, EROS staged demonstrations at the inaugural cricket World Cup, prompting clashes between Sri Lanka's Tamil and Sinhalese supporters, and bringing the conflict in Sri Lanka to international attention for the first time. In March 1976 he was one of three EROS members selected to train for six months in Lebanon with Palestinian militants associated with the Fatah wing of the PLO. He left after three months of training, returning to Sri Lanka with his family. Maya was six months old.

By 1976, Sri Lanka was well on its way to the internecine ethnic violence that would erupt in full a few years later. Following the withdrawal of the British in 1948, and the electoral triumph of Sinhalese Buddhist nationalism in 1956, the island's Tamil minority was gradually coerced into a position of second-class status; economic discrimination went hand-in-hand with a gradual displacement of Tamils from the education and administrative institutions. A handful of bloody incidents—on both sides—eventually tipped the balance in favor of militancy: land grabs, armed attacks, mob violence, and the destruction of symbolic and cultural treasures, sometimes with official connivance. By the early 1980s, more than thirty Tamil militant groups had emerged, of which EROS was one.

In Sri Lanka, Maya and her siblings rarely saw their father. He was introduced to them as an uncle. They temporarily relocated to the outskirts of Chennai (then Madras), where they lived in a derelict house. Her sister contracted typhoid. They returned to Sri Lanka and remained constantly on the move. She remembers a childhood "inundated with violence": the convent at which she attended school was destroyed during one of the government's aerial bombing campaigns. She watched as some of her friends died. Family members were incarcerated.

In 1986, they fled. Her father remained in Sri Lanka; the rest of the family made it to London. Maya was 11.

They were allocated an apartment in Phipps Bridge Housing Estate, a development in the borough of Merton, which sits in the middle of the vast band of conurban sprawl that constitutes outer London. At the time Phipps Bridge consisted of five high-rise tower blocks and ten low-rise buildings. Of the 4,000 residents, about 65 percent were on income support. It was built in 1976, when institutional inertia and hamstrung development budgets continued to license the building of high-rise estates, despite mounting evidence that they anchored social deprivation and institutional neglect.

By the mid-1980s, life on Phipps Bridge was an experience in misery. Sue Johns, a local resident, wrote in a poem of "the piss-filled lift" and "the shells of wrecked cars," of "Fifties design faults holding on / By the skin of their teeth in the eighties." She pictured residents waiting for a long-promised redevelopment "behind Chubb locks and net curtains." Television cop shows used the estate to film scenes depicting the most run-down, graffiti-stained dead-end estates in the country. It was hardly the perfect environment for a refugee family; Donna Neblett, a longtime resident and now a manager in the community center, remembers: "Police would not come onto the estate; they'd never come by themselves. They'd always be in cars, they'd never get out and walk. It was a very notorious estate. Everything: drug dealers, needles on the floor. Worse things than you can imagine was Phipps Bridge twenty years ago." Maya was placed in special needs education to improve her English. Her mother worked from home as a seamstress. Maya remembers watching as their home was burgled. When her radio was stolen by crack-addicted neighbors, Maya listened to hip-hop from the teenage boy who lived next door.

Maya's family was one of only two Asian families on Phipps Bridge in 1986. The mid-1980s were hardly a golden period in British race relations. Steve Shanley, until recently a housing officer for the estate, insists that despite Phipps Bridge's reputation as "a fairly tough estate," there were not "any racial tensions or any great problems." The local council records a relatively low number of reported racist incidents. By contrast, Donna Neblett remembers an estate rife with racist sentiment: "There were people [living on the estate] that were the leaders of the National Front, so this is where they had their offices and their meetings, in the houses on the estate." The statistics may reflect the tiny proportion of black and ethnic minority residents at the time. "People knew not to come on Phipps if you were from the [black and ethnic minority] community."

Racial tensions—conditions in general—have eased considerably on Phipps Bridge over the last few years. But the obvious question is how an Asian family might have been placed—in near isolation—in such an environment in the first place. Local authorities are adamant that they are not in the business of social engineering. According to Steve Shanley, individual requests for location tend to be accommodated, but "one thing that councils make sure of is that they don't proactively put people together. It wouldn't be seen as 'equal opportunities' to find out people's nationalities and think, 'Right, well we'll put them there.'"

One resident guardedly confided a suspicion: "I think basically what they tend to do—in my experience—is that's where they'll put [black and ethnic minority residents] anyway. It's normally run-down, notorious, them sort of estates. That's how it used to be. I'm not going to say it's like that now, but I know back then it was. And that's when you . . . That's all I'm going to say on that."

Maya used the aesthetic template of hip-hop to pull together her range of influences and interests—at first in the field of visual art. She graduated from Central St. Martins College of Art and Design, and a book of her graffiti-influenced artwork was published by independent label Pocko. It caught the eye of Nick Hackworth, who in

2002 established the Alternative Turner Prize to critique the narrow criteria of Britain's leading art prize. Maya was among the six artists shortlisted. Hackworth—Arts Editor of *Dazed and Confused*—was immediately impressed by "the combination of the political content from her Sri Lankan background through the Tamil Tigers, with the kind of street aesthetic." He remembers a boldness of vision that fused well with the improvisational nature of her technique: "She was just spray painting on bits of board, so it was pretty DIY kind of stuff with the actual media, tying in with the spraycan-type aesthetic. So it's kind of rough, ready, and graphically quite powerful, because she doesn't use too many elements; she repeats some of the elements; she keeps it visually quite clean, she doesn't overload the images . . . It's about graphic boldness. That was the best thing about it." The work attracted the attention of Justine Frischmann of Elastica, who commissioned an album cover and a tour documentary. It was on tour that she met electro-revivalist Peaches, who first showed her around a Roland 505.

Her visual style is on display on the video for "Galang," her first single. The video was directed by Ruben Fleischer, who notes that "using her artwork as a way to define her and inform people is very important. I mean how many other beautiful singers are performing in front of tanks, burning palm trees, bombs, Molotov cocktails, and helicopters? All of the stencils we made were completely based on her aesthetic, and were meant to be an extension of her. Many of them she either helped us make or made herself."

The video's imagery—alongside the lyrical content of "Sunshowers"—has attracted some criticism of her political stance. There are the brightly colored burning trees, bombs, tanks, Molotov cocktails, London housing estates, and cell phones—and the video is punctuated by images of a racing tiger, a motif that recurs in her concert visuals and designs. A portrait of a Tamil militant leader appears at one moment.

For some critics, this is simply *revolutionary chic:* an attempt to commercialize the color and exoticism of distant struggles while

safely draining it of any real-world political context. Nick Hackworth is aware of that tendency. "I think it was that unusual combination which I hadn't really seen before in too much stuff. And
also—I suppose it sounds potentially pejorative—it was slightly exotic, seeing something that dealt with non-English or non-European
political problems in that kind of way, visually." There are longstanding European traditions of seeing the "orient" as repository of
color, creativity, and vibrancy—as a nest of cultures alien enough
not to have to be inspected for political markers. Other critics are
more troubled, arguing from her father's biography and a handful of
details (for instance, for a brief period after the December 26
tsunami, her website carried links to an aid organization closely
associated with Tamil militants) that she is a closet supporter of
terrorism—in particular, of the Tamil Tigers.

From the early 1980s, the Liberation Tigers of Tamil Eelam
(LTTE) quickly became the dominant body in Tamil militancy, and
Tamil nationalism in general, not least because of the viciousness
with which they dispatched rival groups. In April 1986, for example, hundreds of members of rivals TELO (the Tamil Eelam Liberation Organisation) were killed in a sequence of attacks, despite
their being armed, trained, and supported by the Indian government. From 1987, the "Black Tigers" developed suicide bombing
as a tactic, their victims including former Indian prime minister
Rajiv Gandhi. UNICEF and Amnesty International have censured
them for the forced conscription of child soldiers, including 40
since the December 26 tsunami. They have been accused of mur-
dering civilians in border areas to induce population displacement.
The Sri Lankan government, meanwhile, has continued a series of
depredations, including extensive—and sometimes apparently indiscriminate—aerial bombing campaigns. Over 65,000 people have
died; at one point, up to 30 percent of the Tamil population was estimated to have fled the island, with over a million people—from
all ethnic groups—temporarily or permanently displaced. A 1991
report estimated that perhaps ten percent of the population had

been displaced. Sri Lanka is one of the most heavily landmined countries in the world.

This is a far cry from the revolutionary panache suggested by M.I.A.'s work. Some of the associative imagery of "Galang" and "Sunshowers" implies a connection to the Palestinian Intifada, the Zapatistas, the Black Panthers, and the anti-Apartheid movement. Some see these as valid comparisons; Dr. Dagmar Hellmann-Rajanayagam notes, "The LTTE also fights against linguistic, ethnic and class/caste discrimination and oppression. The methods might be open to question, the aim is certainly not." M. R. Narayan Swamy, author of *Inside an Elusive Mind*, the first biography of LTTE leader Velupillai Prabhakaran, disagrees, citing the LTTE's murderous reputation. "This does not mean that LTTE has no support; on the contrary it does. It controls vast areas in Sri Lanka's north and rules a de facto Tamil Eelam. But it will be very difficult to say how much of the support it enjoys comes out of genuine respect or genuine fear. The support is real, and so is the fear."

M.I.A.'s stance, inevitably, is more complicated—and conflicted—than critics suggest, not least because of family involvement. Her father's group, EROS, reached a working arrangement with the LTTE as the other groups were being eliminated. When Arular returned to Sri Lanka in 1976, he was apparently in close contact with Prabhakaran; according to some sources, EROS established a training camp at a farm in Kannady which was used by the LTTE. Arular and Prabhakaran are reported to have shared bomb-making knowledge, equipment, and chemicals. According to M. R. Narayan Swamy, "Arular was never in LTTE. Yes, he was with EROS in the early stages, but he left it but kept in touch with most of the actors in the militancy scene." Arular's official biography—which is to say, the one that appears on the jackets of his books—insists that he now writes history, and has mediated between the Sri Lankan government and the LTTE. In any event, relations between M.I.A. and her father, whom she has referred to as "insane," are not close. She has not seen him since 1995. *Arular* is titled in an apparent attempt to bait him, citing her mother's complaint that "the only thing he ever gave you was your name." She has doggedly refused his request to change it.

What's more, if tiger imagery does predominate M.I.A.'s vision of the world, it's not necessarily advocacy. The overdominant LTTE imagery—if indeed it is that—does accurately reflect the totalitarian hegemony that the LTTE and Prabhakaran exercise over the northern part of the island, and Tamil nationalism as a whole. The tiger, as a symbol, has been associated with Tamil nationalism for centuries; her use of it does not necessarily signal support for LTTE, though the gesture may be somewhat naive.

But it's an issue that goes to the heart of her identity as an artist. She sees herself not as an individual, but a spokesperson. "In the beginning they told me [in England] that being an artist was about being an individual and reflecting society. And in Sri Lanka I was brought up with a different value system, which was that you talk for other people, and it's always 'we.' It's never 'me.' You never think selfishly. Nobody cares, nobody wants to hear what your particular opinion is. It's the opinions of thousands that count." Hence the urgency: "It's too soon for me to get censored before people know what I'm talking about. There's so much confusion about what I stand for and what I'm saying that that's the whole point: there *have* to be discussions; there *has* to be people talking, and there has to be young people talking about politics if they want. They have to have a chance to hear different opinions. And that's really what it's about."

There's a personal edge to this, of course: Maya *was* personally caught up in Sri Lanka's violence, and she's aware of the impetus that experience gave her. But the instinct is deeply intertwined with an instinct to represent others. "I feel the reason why I'm really like outspoken and stuff is because all of these things were inflicted upon me, and I never went and caused any trouble, you know? I just feel like I was kind of skipping along in some country and somebody decides to drop a bomb and shake up my life and then it's all been survival from then on. And that's the reality for thousands—and millions—of people today. Why should I get censored for talking about a life that half the time I didn't choose to live?"

Given the extent to which her viewpoint is grounded in personal experience, what is impressive about the maturity of her songwriting is her ability to write convincingly in the third person. "Sunshowers," for instance, outlines—with some economy—the fate of a victim of racial profiling who is not a clear stand-in for either herself or her father.

There's a sense, too, that Western critics (such as they are) are simply missing the point when they object to the sense of indiscriminate violence in her music. Violence is not often represented in Western popular music; where it is it tends to be—as in gangsta rap, say, or death metal—ritualized at source and translated into a marketable commodity. Violence in the Western popular imagination is abstract, organized, refined. In much of the developing world, Sri Lanka in particular, the experience of the last few decades has been one of arbitrary, unannounced, and spectacular slaughter. M.I.A.'s music and politics might sound like an assault without coherence or strategy; that doesn't necessarily mean they lack realism.

Ruben Fleischer, who directed "Galang," thinks "the principal idea behind M.I.A.'s artwork is to have pretty heavy/political ideas, but to present them in a poppy candy-coated wrapper. So someone might buy her painting because it is pretty to the eye, and not necessarily consider that it is a rebellious image that she is presenting. However, after they've had it for a while, they might start to think— why do I have a pink tank on my wall? . . . I think that ['Galang'] is a very successful video in that we have true images of revolution playing on MTV. However, because there's lots of pretty colors and a pretty girl dancing, no one blinks an eye. Hopefully we have succeeded in subconsciously starting the revolution."

The superficiality of M.I.A.'s chosen media—graffiti stencil art and popular music—makes politics a risky business. Her approach is the opposite of that of radical artists like Fernando Solanas and Octavio Gettino, who followed Franz Fanon in calling for an art that documented resistance while breaking down the barriers between spectator and artist. They called for artistic processes—and exhibition—that involved the audience directly, making them reexamine their role and forge a new, collective, identity. M.I.A.'s art and music, by contrast, are *all* spectacle. The two-dimensional stencils and the catchy hooks can only subvert the audience's role after their immediate appeal has worn off, and they lack the breadth to contain a full alternative program. What's more, the distance that comes from rendering real-world political conflicts in such a stylized, vibrant medium feels very much like the distance afforded by nostalgia, hero-worship, and romanticism. Graffiti—like hip-hop—is a superficial, ephemeral medium, with its own set of artistic risks.

But the realm of the image is what M.I.A. is most determined to contest: the media role models, the conformity of mainstream popular culture. "When [XL] first signed me, they sat me down and they were like, 'You know we only sign artists that are like "fuck you."'' I was like, 'Hmm. What part of "fuck you" don't you get about me? Me being on MTV is way more "fuck you" than me not being on MTV.' Because of where I come from. I haven't seen anyone like me on there before. And that's what would be really fun to do."

The narrow range of images presented by "the commercial media" appalls her. "There's only so much controlled generic brainwashing you can do. And the thing is it would be fine if the audience weren't reduced to being so dumb. I feel like they constantly think that we're just stupid and that all we can handle is more songs about champagne and Bentleys . . . We don't all have access to millions of pounds and Bentleys and £50,000 diamond necklaces. Where do those people go to be content with how they live, if constantly we're being fed images of 'this is what you need to aspire to be; this is what you need to aspire to be'?"

There's a common thread that runs from her concern with racism to the assumptions made about audiences. It's prejudice, the ugly side of London's cosmopolitan mosaic, and the DNA of Sri Lanka's remorseless conflict. "What I want to say is, just be careful how you judge people, because you never know. And I'm a living proof of that. Every step of the way, people thought I was shittier than I actually was, or people thought I was worse than I was, or people thought I exist as something bad on the planet. Politics shaped that in the beginning for me. But right now it's just a messy situation. All I want to do is exist as a voice for the other people that you don't get to hear from. That's all."

Ghetto Gospel

Considering how colorful the man was, Ol' Dirty Bastard's funeral was a quiet, reserved affair. Held at a preposterously huge church in the Canarsie section of Brooklyn, it wasn't somber so much as *measured*. Everything about the space—the high ceiling, the elevated stage, the slick minister—seemed to dwarf the possibility of authentic emotional intimacy. Some well-wishers huddled near the front of the auditorium, while others were sprinkled throughout the room, and up in the balcony. As mourners took their seats, the church band played a dismal lite-rock instrumental version of Mariah Carey's "One Sweet Day."

After family members shared their memories of the dearly departed, the band's keyboardist gingerly kicked into the signature opening phrase from "Shimmy Shimmy Ya." It's a nervous, angsty passage, though in such a huge space it felt somewhat cold. That is, until one young man realized this was no proper send-off for the man born Russell Tyrone Jones, alternately known as Ason Unique, ODB, Dirt McGirt, Dirt Dog, Big Baby Jesus and Osirus. Jumping up from his seat, the animated mourner began enthusiastically rapping along: "Oooooh baby, I like it raw! Yeah baby, I like it raaaawwwwww!"

For the two minutes that the band indulged him, he flailed his arms and exhorted others to join him—only one person did—causing a very localized storm in an otherwise tranquil room. No one seemed to mind, though. They realized that right there was the spirit of Ol' Dirty calling, a reminder that it wouldn't be denied.

Sometimes it seemed like that was the role Dirty played, not only in his group the Wu-Tang Clan, but in hip-hop itself. Within the Clan, with its byzantine iconography and ideology, he was clearly the loose cannon, the Flavor Flav of the set. But as crew leader RZA's cousin, Dirty was doubtless forgiven all his eccentricities and destructive tendencies, including the drug habit that would end up costing him his life this past November, when he collapsed and died from the combined effects of cocaine and the prescription painkiller Tramadol.

Hip-hop has been quick to ossify a limited set of acceptable images—hustler, gangster, player, thug—and, almost to a man, big-name MCs can be neatly slotted into one of these categories, whether they want to admit it or not. Moreover, rappers guard their image with almost perverse fanaticism. Heaven forbid they might change in light of commentary or criticism. Stagnation is preferable to concession.

Over the course of his career, Ol' Dirty fell victim to that sort of shortsightedness, but the root cause was different. He was one of the genre's few true characters. While his peers were busy micro-managing their personas, he seemed genuinely impervious to judg-ment—he's almost certainly the only rapper who'd let a protégé take the name Shorty Shit Stain. His life became fodder for a starv-ing media. Whether he was taking MTV cameras in a limousine to pick up food stamps, storming the stage at the Grammys to protest "Wu-Tang is for the children!" or getting arrested in the parking lot of a Philadelphia McDonald's after stopping to give autographs to kids, his exploits made him a regular feature on TV news "you're-not-going-to-believe-this" reports and in newspapers' "strange-but-true" sections.

Dirty the man, then, posed a perpetual threat to Dirty the artist. Not only did his continuous intoxication and frequent incarceration make it difficult for him to maintain a regular recording schedule, his fraught life story obscured his professional achievements in the minds of the public. People loved Dirty, but mostly they loved his oddity—the circus sideshow rather than the rapper. Which is a shame, because during his too-short career, Ol' Dirty Bastard made worthy contributions to hip-hop as an artist. A potent cross between surrealism and outsider art, his records are an indelible part of the rap canon—difficult to parse at times, but that became a statement in and of itself, a sort of stylistic onomatopoeia. His best songs sound deliciously and deliriously unmediated.

Even from the beginning he was an outlier, and on 1993's *Enter the Wu-Tang (36 Chambers)*, RZA knew better than to try to rein him in. Dirty's more of an idea than a presence on the album, appearing on less than half the tracks and not at all on crucial numbers like "Can It Be All So Simple," "Wu-Tang Clan Ain't Nuthing ta F' Wit'" and "C.R.E.A.M." *36 Chambers* is an album about tragedy, and Dirty's style—closer to the tragicomic and the absurd—wasn't always the easiest fit.

"First thing's first, man, you're fuckin' with the worst / I'll be sticking pins in your head like a fuckin' nurse" is how he introduced himself on the Clan's first volley "Protect Ya Neck." "Bite my style, I'll bite your muthafuckin' ass!" he shouted, but that wasn't something he really had to worry about. Even among his ever-dynamic Clanmates, no one came close to fiddling so with emphasis, tenor, vocal tone and pitch. On "Shame on a Nigga," the only song that really relies on Dirty for its personality and character, he's explosive: "Hut one, hut two, hut three, hut! / Ol' Dirty Bastard, live and un-cut!" And then he's off, going soft to loud and dropping back again as if suddenly succumbing to the effects of gravity: "To the young youth, you wanna get a gun? / Shoot! / BLAAAAOOOW! / How you like me now?"

The answer to that question became evident two years later, when Dirty became the second Clan member to release a solo album, following only the intensely charismatic Method Man. Considering how small a lyrical presence he was on *36 Chambers*, it was clearly his personality that got his album fast-tracked. *Return to the 36 Chambers: The Dirty Version* is by far the loosest of all the Clan solo projects, a fitting representation of its author. "You taping this?" he asks at the beginning of "Brooklyn Zoo II (Tiger Cane)"; the rest of the album seems almost as oblivious. At times, it sounds as if Dirty, even though songs like "The Stomp" and "Hippa to da Hoppa" exploit his vocal quirks, is so used to sharing the spotlight that he's just trying to fill up space. "Shimmy Shimmy Ya," perhaps his best-known song, repeats the same verse twice. Some songs don't have any discernible verse-chorus structure at all. The closest he comes to studied form is at the beginning of "Cuttin' Headz," when he and RZA trade lines back and forth in a style that suggests years of practice. On "Goin' Down," Dirty takes cues from the original old school, back before rapping became, you know, complicated—"I'm the U-N-I, the Q-U-E, the G to the O-D / I said I go by the unforgettable name of the man called Unique G"—and he's at his best with straightforward boasts, like these on "Damage": "One verse, then you're out for the count / Bring the ammonia / Make sure he sniffs the right amount."

But *Return* also showed that a hip-hop album could have atypical strengths. Like Biz Markie and TJ Swann before him, Ol' Dirty Bastard loved to sing. He does it on the album intro, changing a tender Roberta Flack classic into "The first time / Ever you sucked my dick." "Drunk Game (Sweet Sugar Pie)" is almost entirely sung (slurred, actually, but who's counting). On "Don't U Know," he breaks out a surprisingly deep vibrato for four bars of "Over the Rainbow."

When he settles into a groove, though, Dirty's raps hold the beat tightly. The opening bars of "Brooklyn Zoo," for example, are among the most unforgettable lines in the wider Clan catalog: "I'm the one-man army, Ason / I never been tooken out / I keep MCs lookin' out / I drop science like girls be dropping babies / Enough to make a nigga go craaaazy / Energy building, taking all types of

medicines / Your ass thought you were better than / Ason? / I keep
planets in orbit / While I be coming with deeper and more shit."

Deeper? Perhaps. More? Not really. On the Clan's highly anticipated second album *Wu-Tang Forever,* Dirty's barely present, log-
ging fewer bars even than U-God. The verses he does get—on
"Reunited" and "Dog Shit" in particular—are almost completely
without anchor.

He does, however, kick off the comeback single "Triumph" with
verve, asking the question, "What? Y'all thought y'all wasn't gonna
see me?" One suspects that, by this time, no one knew his erratic
behavior better than he, qualifying this as a rare moment of self-
awareness. RZA, knowing the strength of Dirty's allure, lets him bat
first but doesn't give him a real verse, instead letting Inspectah Deck
take over ("I bomb atomically . . . ").

At this point, in 1997, it was beginning to feel like every moment with Dirty was borrowed time. Nevertheless, he remained
very much a force in hip-hop, largely because his peculiar musical
stamp was getting put to use helping other artists who needed the
particular shot of adrenaline only he could provide. Simply put,
having an Ol' Dirty Bastard cameo on your remix was enough to
make it hot. New-Jill Swingers SWV learned it in 1994 on "Anything (Old Skool Radio Remix)": "Ooohhhlll Dirty Bas' / Style
cuts like glass . . ." But no one benefited from Dirty's quirks more
than Mariah Carey. Her song "Fantasy" was just another trifle before Dirty showed up to deliver a uniquely leaky performance. On
the hit '95 remix the two proved to be an irresistible odd couple;
when Dirty intoned, "Me and Mariah / Go back like babies and
pacifiers," it seemed like the two opposing flavors had always
meant to be together. (The union proved to be a lasting one: years
later, in 2003, after Dirty was released from jail, Mariah appeared
at the press conference where he announced his signing to Roc-A-
Fella.) Mariah's been flirting with hip-hop ever since, but her appreciation never seemed more puzzling, or sincere, than it did on
this first go-round.

By the time he came to assist Busta Rhymes on the remix for "Woo Hah!! Go You All in Check" and injected the unbearable Pras/Mya collabo "Ghetto Supastar" with a bit of woozy charm (and loose-limbed political understanding), it seemed like Dirty might never use his talents for his own gain, or that of his crew, again. (In fact, of the 21 Clan member solo albums, he appeared on only four: two by his cousin GZA and two by cousin RZA.) His talent needed focus, a channel to operate in, and on his second solo album, 1999's *Nigga Please*, he found collaborators—namely the Neptunes and Irv Gotti—who saw more in him than a mere foil for other artists.

Of course, judging by the sound of *Nigga Please*, there's no way it could have been anything other than a producers' album. Unlike *Return*, which was given to rambling numbers—rhymes stretching 16, 32, 48 bars at a time—the songs here are concise and taut. It's not that Dirty corralled himself so much as his outbursts were filed and sanded into more immediately recognizable and compelling shapes. "Recognize," featuring ad-libs from Chris Rock, opens the album in sprightly fashion; Dirty's howls sound fierce and present. "I Can't Wait" sounds like proto-crunk, both in beat and in rhyme. His patented nonsequitur style is in full effect—"It ain't lambskin / You can't use the word napkin"—and he emerges from his haze for two bars of precious lucidity: "Nigga, I'm from the ghetto / How many celebrities from the ghetto?" At the end of the song, Dirty sends shout-outs to Eskimos, submarines, schoolteachers and "umm, umm, myself." The title track, featuring sloppy horns courtesy of RZA, sports some of Dirty's best shambolic rhymes: "I fuck in my vest, drive an armored tank y'all / I dead niggas like a dog bury a bone / You could never set me up / I raise the pain volume." But perhaps nothing beats Dirty's twisted proclamations on "You Don't Want to Fuck with Me": "I got the government lost on *Gilligan's Island* / By December, CIA getting paid taxes back / From the candy cane / Santa came, back in the big hurricane." Try though you may, you can't smooth out all the man's rough edges, it turns out. Or, as he croons at the end of "Got Your Money": "Recognize I'm a fool and you looovvve me!"

Nigga Please could have been the starting point for a renaissance, both popular and critical. Instead, it became something like an exclamation point, followed by a paragraph break. Dirty was in jail for most of the three years following the album's release. In that time, the Clan released two albums, *The W* and *Iron Flag*, which collectively featured him on only one track, the sinuous Snoop Dogg collaboration "Conditioner." Furthermore, 2002 saw the release of *The Trials and Tribulations of Russell Jones*, a cobbled-together set of what sound like reworked outtakes—featuring Insane Clown Posse, E-40, C-Murder and Too $hort, among others—that Dirty didn't know about until it hit stores. (Additional odds and ends are available on two strong mixtapes: J-Love's *Ol' Dirty Bastard—Uncut Raw Throwback Vol. 3*, and *R.I.P Dirt McGirt* by Vin Tha Chin and Scram Jones.) Since his jail release and signing to Roc-A-Fella, Dirty had been recording steadily for an upcoming comeback album, leaked tracks from which indicate a tightly controlled direction like that of *Nigga Please*. Until the disposition of that album is determined, fans can track down the scattered collection *Osirus: The Official Mixtape* (out in January), which features production from DJ Premier, Mark Ronson and Chops.

As his personal struggles took center stage in the years since *Nigga Please*, it's become even easier to dismiss the style and content of Dirty's raps. But careful listening reveals keenly felt hurt in between the base libertinism and untempered free association. On *Return to the 36 Chambers*' "Raw Hide," he turns a typical rap rant into a stark promise: "Who the fuck wanna be an MC / If you can't get paid to be a fuckin' MC? / I came out my mama pussy, I'm on welfare / 26 years old, still on welfare / So I gotta get paid fully / Whether it's truthfully or untruthfully."

Dirty's finest moment, though, came on *Nigga Please*'s version of the crooner standard "Good Morning Heartache." Originally performed by Billie Holiday, and since covered by everyone from Sam

Cooke to Rosemary Clooney to Diana Ross, it's one of the great laments in all of pop music. Rather than defiling the song's proud legacy, Dirty's rendition—a duet with Lil' Mo—rewrites it. He sounds like the last guy sitting at the bar at closing time, and at the outset Mo's sweet vocals are the optimistic counterpart to his depressed mumble. But then, for a few glorious bars, against all logic and hope, they begin to harmonize. It's a remarkably beautiful moment and a window into the sort of emotional honesty pop music often obscures. Dirty hurt, for sure, but sometimes that pain could be elegant. These were the sing-rap blues, and no one in the game was ever better equipped for the job.

ELIZABETH MÉNDEZ BERRY

Love Hurts

Before going to sleep, many little girls pray for a new Barbie, an Xbox game, or a trip to Disney World. At age 7, Vanessa Rios asked only that "Papi would stop hitting Mami."

It was May 1999, and Vanessa was staying with her aunt, Penelope Rios Santiago, in Miami. After Santiago overheard her niece's bedtime prayer, she confronted her brother, Christopher Rios. His reaction? It wasn't true, he said.

Though he had much in common with other abusers, Christopher Rios was also different: He was Big Pun, a famous rap star. He first hit his wife, Liza, when she was 16, and over the course of their 10-year relationship, she claims he sent her to the hospital three times and prevented her from seeking needed medical attention on many other occasions. "One time he told me to change the batteries in his beeper," says Liza Rios, now 31. "I totally forgot about it, and he took this lead pipe and started swinging on me. I had my daughter in my arms, and I told Cuban [Link, who was there] to take the baby. After he finished beating me, my elbow was twisted out of place. I was limping for two months."

Each time Rios got up the courage to leave, Pun tracked her down and convinced her to come back to him. "After we got married and he had that paper, it was like he had bought me," she says. Still, though she was financially reliant on him, Rios began to loathe

58

his extravagant displays. "I didn't even enjoy the jewelry, because it was, like, I got the extra bracelet because you punched me extra hard," she says.

Rios did leave Pun twice, but returned both times, and she was with him when he died of a heart attack in 2000. Backed by footage of Pun pistol-whipping her, she and other witnesses described his beatings in the 2002 documentary *Big Pun: Still Not a Player*, which she coproduced. Many criticized her for going public, among them Fat Joe, who argued that if there was abuse, Pun must've been justified. Others wondered why Rios waited until he died to tell her story.

For some women, speaking out while their abuser is alive is not an option. Murder at the hands of a romantic partner is a leading cause of death among African-American women between the ages of 15 and 24, according to the National Center for Health Statistics. The Centers for Disease Control and Prevention reports that intimate-partner violence in the United States leads to two million injuries annually and nearly 1,300 murders. "I tried to use my life as a testimony. I hope that somebody can learn from this story," Rios says during a phone interview.

Another factor motivated Rios: Chris's assaults have had a huge and lasting impact on their children. "My son was smacking my girls up for any little thing," says Rios. "Even though they love Chris, my kids have a lot of anger, too. They still have nightmares, but my son has calmed down a lot. He hasn't hit his sisters in a long time."

Rios's revelation struck a nerve in the community that turned the phrase "smack my bitch up" into a catchy chorus (on the Ultramagnetic MC's 1988 song "Give the Drummer Some," later sampled by the UK rave act Prodigy). Many argue that mainstream rap's verbal violence against women is just entertainment, but there's evidence to the contrary. For example: Dr. Dre, in a 1991 *Rolling Stone* article, admitted to attacking TV host Dee Barnes in a nightclub, and in 2002, radio personality Steph Lova charged DJ Funkmaster Flex

with hitting and choking her over a perceived slight. Barnes and Dr.
Dre settled their suit in 1993; Lova and Flex settled in 2003. If
prominent industry figures feel comfortable attacking women pub-
licly, what are they doing in private? When you get paid big money
to call every woman a ho, at what point do you start believing you're
a pimp?

In fact, a number of high-profile personalities have been accused
of violence against women; most can't be named in print because
the victims are unwilling to go on the record with their stories. But
legal records and interviews corroborate a tragic pattern of brutality
and denial. Ten years ago, Mystikal condemned the violent murder
of his sister. In January 2004, Mystikal himself pleaded guilty to sexual battery after sexually assaulting a woman, an incident that was
captured on videotape.

He's far from the only hip hop figure to have faced serious allegations. Hip hop mogul Damon Dash is the object of a $15 million
civil lawsuit in New York, filed by a woman who says he raped her
after a party in Brazil in 2003, a claim he heatedly denies. Dash has
been accused of violence against women on several occasions. The
Washington Post recently reported that when Dash was 16, a 14-year-
old girl at his upstate New York summer camp accused him of raping her. Dash says he was never accused of rape, just "sexual
misconduct," and that he was vindicated when a lawsuit and a related arrest warrant in the case never went anywhere.

Between 1990 and 1996, cops were called on multiple occasions
to quell "domestic disturbances" at the Long Island home Dash
shared with Linda Williams, the mother of his eldest child, Damon
II. Dash was arrested multiple times, at least one order of protection
was granted, and police records indicate that Williams reported that
she was injured; a caseworker who interviewed their then 6-year-old
son noted that the boy said "he had seen his father hit his mother in
the stomach," and that "he was afraid his father was going to kill his
mother." Dash also refutes these charges, noting that he was

awarded custody of the child after a bitter fight. Still, to many there seems to be a disturbing pattern to these accusations.

Like Dash, Busta Rhymes has also had to fend off accusations. In January 2004, a woman claiming to be the mother of his children appeared on *The Wendy Williams Experience* on WBLS radio in New York, saying Rhymes was chronically abusive and had thrown her down the stairs while she was pregnant. Also, court records show that a woman who had children by him was granted a restraining order against him in 1999. Rhymes declined to comment for this story, and attempts to reach the woman were unsuccessful. But according to Williams, after that interview, Rhymes saw to it that the woman did not speak out again. "He threw her a few dollars, and a few threats," says Williams. "She's no longer doing interviews. She buckled."

Several women who have had relationships with well-known abusers declined to speak on the record for this piece and said they feared reprisal. The ex-girlfriend of a famed MC mentions a chart-topping rapper who attacked his wife (and mother of his children) with a champagne bottle; a multiplatinum producer tells VIBE matter-of-factly that he has seen many physical fights between artists and their romantic partners over the years. Neither witness cares to elaborate. Says Nzingha Gumbs, a prominent makeup artist, "People are unwilling to come forward and talk about what's going on. They're scared that they'll lose their jobs."

Rapper Charli Baltimore experienced similar complacency when there was much less money involved: As a teenager, she says she endured four brutal years with the father of her eldest daughter. Her boyfriend was a big guy—6 feet 3 inches, and she was a skinny 5 feet 7 inches. She says he attacked her regularly from the age of 14, even while she was pregnant with their daughter. "I remember one time he had the door shut, and I was supposed to knock but I didn't. I walked in and he and three guys were playing a dice game," she recalls. "I walked out with a black eye. His friends didn't say anything. They were probably laughing."

At 17, Baltimore finally escaped her abuser, but many young women today are trapped in the same situation. And attitudes among young men may be hardening. According to the market research firm Motivational Educational Entertainment (MEE) Productions, which surveyed thousands of low-income African-American youths for a 2003 study, acceptance of abuse is on the rise. Many felt there were plenty of situations in which violence against a woman is justified.

The Notorious B.I.G. set that mentality to music. On the track "Me & My Bitch," he raps to his beloved, "You talk slick, I beat you right." Apparently, he was keeping it real: Since Big's death, his widow, Faith Evans, has taken a public stand against domestic violence. She sang the chorus on Eve's indictment of abusers, "Love Is Blind" (remix), and appeared in Eve Ensler's V Day event in Harlem, opposing violence against women. Evans declined to comment for this article, but according to two people who worked closely with her, her face was bruised throughout her marriage to Biggie and didn't stop being black-and-blue until after he died.

"Biggie treated women like a pimp with his hos," says a childhood buddy, who also noticed Evans's bruises. "He would talk about hitting them. He'd say things like, 'She was out of pocket, so I had to put that bitch back in line.'" Baltimore, who dated Big for two years, acknowledges that he was physically violent with her during their relationship, and in the VH1 episode of *Driven* that focused on Lil' Kim, numerous friends of hers allege that he was vicious. Apparently, she wore the giant Jackie O. sunglasses to shield black eyes.

Rappers like Biggie figure prominently in young lives. The participants in the MEE survey listened to the radio and watched TV for an average of three hours each per day—76 percent called BET their favorite station. Like Big Pun, who grew up in an abusive household, these youths are learning by example. According to the

MEE surveys, both young men and women used almost exclusively negative words to describe the females they knew—they were either hos, sluts, or bitches—and many young males boasted about "running trains," groups of men having sex with and sometimes raping one woman.

Violence against women crosses class and racial lines, but it affects certain groups disproportionately, including police officers, among whom domestic violence is two to four times more common than the U.S. average, according to the National Center for Women & Policing. Another academic study indicates that partner abuse against Latino women is 50 percent higher than among white women. Minorities are less likely to talk about it, however. "Communities find it easier to focus on oppression that comes from outside than on what we do to ourselves," says Dr. Oliver Williams, executive director of the University of Minnesota's Institute on Domestic Violence in the African American Community.

The complex legacy of racism has given gender dynamics a particular twist in communities of color, according to Marcus Flowers, 28, a community educator and trainer at Atlanta's Men Stopping Violence. "Because of socioeconomic factors, African-American men have a harder time fulfilling the protector and provider roles, so they overcompensate in other areas," says Flowers. "They focus on wielding power where they can—in their own communities and in their intimate relationships." Author and activist Kevin Powell has called this "bootleg masculinity"—and hip hop's studio pimps and gangstas are its poster children. "Of course, hip hop didn't create violence against women, but it can endorse and accelerate it," says Powell, who admits that he has himself been violent toward women in the past. "If you listened to mainstream hip hop over the last 10 years, you would think that we men of color hate women."

Flowers uses the strip club–themed video "P-Poppin'," by Ludacris, to make a point when he's talking with teenagers. "The way that the women are paraded in front of fully clothed customers, their bodies for sale, reminds me of how half-naked slaves were exhibited to white buyers at auctions, as if they were animals," he says. "Now it's not the whip—it's the dollar bill. We black men have become slave masters in our own community."

And it's not just men who buy into this tough-guy myth. "Some young women define jealousy, controlling behavior, and abuse as expressions of interest, caring, and love," says Dr. Williams. "When there's emotional abuse, some women start believing that they deserve the violence," adds Tara Borelli, a staff attorney with Break the Cycle, a nonprofit that provides free legal services. "For men, partly, it's the importance of looking tough," says Dr. Williams. "Partly, it's a lack of problem-solving skills. Young people see violence as the primary approach to conflict."

Laci Peterson's case may have made it to Court TV, but thousands of women have suffered similar fates out of the limelight. After two neighborhood girls were killed in Brooklyn, a community youth organization called Sista II Sista turned its energies to addressing the dilemma. "Young women deal with violence daily, from drama at home with family to getting harassed walking down the street," says Adjoa Jones de Almeida, 31, a Sista II Sista staff member. "Just the other day, we saw this girl getting dragged down the street by her hair by her boyfriend. It's everywhere, but we are taught to see it as normal, until somebody dies."

In interviews for this article, many men preferred to discuss male victims, though they represent just one in nine cases. Both men and women used euphemistic language like "the situation" to describe assaults—a common trap people fall into when discussing domestic violence. Many blamed a woman for what she said or did, instead of holding the man accountable for his decision to react violently. Several men also tended to minimize their attacks; one said "it wasn't no black eyes," another, "I never sent her to the hospital." Few recognized that most relationships that end in murder start with something much more minor. According to Liza Rios, the first time Pun slapped her, when they were in high school, he apologized and said it would never happen again.

As a teenager, Juelz Santana, 21, was arrested after attacking his longtime girlfriend, and subsequently wrote a song called "My Problem (Jealousy)." The assault occurred after he heard gossip that she was unfaithful. "I was 19 at the time, my career was popping off," says Santana. "I was like, I'm the dude, I can't be hearing this about my girl! People gonna be looking at me bad." They had an argument, and it escalated. "She hit me in the back of the head," he says, "and I hit her on the arms, grabbed her up, controlled her. She was crying."

That incident led the couple to re-evaluate their relationship, and since then, he says, he hasn't hit her. "I found other ways to resolve things," he says. "Fighting proves nothing. I had to realize that in order to love her, I had to trust her."

Though Santana's candor and self-awareness—both in conversation and on record—are impressive, hip hop attitudes in general may be even less supportive of women today than they were when many rushed to Dee Barnes's side after Dre attacked her in 1991. In 2002, few in the community spoke out on Steph Lova's behalf. Although a settlement was reached quietly, it didn't seem to scare away any of Funkmaster Flex's endorsements. When Liza Rios's story emerged, she got little support or coverage. One person told VIBE that a major rap publication pulled a story about her for fear of offending Pun's camp. It wasn't just the media that turned a blind eye. Plenty of people repeated rumors that she had been unfaithful, and, therefore, deserved to be beaten.

Called hos or called housewives, too many women in relationships with men in the hip hop community find that they get treated like prostitutes—wham, bam, and bam some more. Those who don't stick to the script—or take the hush money—face isolation.

Liza Rios attempted to do a tribute tour in Pun's honor to raise funds for a foundation for battered women and children that she had created. But after the DVD came out, people stopped returning her calls.

"The industry closed a lot of doors to me, I guess it made them uncomfortable," says Rios. "Maybe it's too close to home."

CHARLES MICHENER

Going Bonkers at the Opera

Glimmerglass Flirts with Chaos

Opera, it might be said, is a kind of madhouse: Musically, it pushes vocal capacities to the breaking point; dramatically, its protagonists are often in the grip of something so grievous that suicide may be the only way out. In Cooperstown, N.Y., where Glimmerglass Opera is celebrating its 30th season, operatic derangement is in full swing. In Poulenc's *La Voix Humaine* ("The Human Voice"), a woman falls to pieces during a desperate phone conversation with her faithless lover. In Donizetti's *Lucie de Lammermoor* (the French version of the more familiar *Lucia di Lammermoor*), the heroine indulges in opera's most famous "mad scene" before taking her life. In Britten's *Death in Venice*, a celebrated, austere writer becomes so obsessed with a beautiful youth that he allows himself to die in an outbreak of cholera. In Mozart's *Cosi Fan Tutte*, a cynical hoax unleashes passions that scramble the engagement vows of four young lovers (I have yet to see the Glimmerglass production). To paraphrase the Sondheim lyric, the theme this summer seems to be "losing control while falling apart."

La Voix Humaine is the second half of a French double bill that begins with a trifle: Massenet's *Le Portrait de Manon*, a pallid sequel to the intoxicating, full-length Manon, in which an embittered

Chevalier des Grieux finds peace long after the death of his way-
ward courtesan. Perhaps a staging more perfumed with fin-de-siècle
wistfulness would have masked the scent of mothballs, but I doubt
it. Poulenc's one-act monodrama, on the other hand, has lost none
of the insidious glamour that I remember from the classic 1959
recording with Denise Duval, the soprano for whom it was written.
In few operas are music and text so well joined. With microscopic
voyeurism, Jean Cocteau's play examined a young and elegant
Parisian woman clinging to the disembodied voice of her "cheri,"
who has abandoned her.

This was caviar to Poulenc, whose personality combined a
bourgeois homosexual's refinement with a Roman Catholic's pen-
chant for self-punishment. Poulenc's limpid melodies aspire to an
elevation they never quite reach, and he was perfectly suited to
bringing out the not-so-latent sadomasochism in both the
Cocteau text and a heroine who luxuriates in her own pain.
Wisely, the Glimmerglass production didn't try to update the action to the age of the cell phone. David Newell's glossy, unclut-
tered set, Miranda Hoffman's pert organdy couture and Robert
Wierzel's melodramatic lighting kept the piece firmly rooted in
the 1950's, when a woman changed dresses and matching shoes according to her mood. Denise Duval, who was the composer's close
friend, has long been regarded as the unsurpassable Elle, the
opera's only audible voice. But at Glimmerglass, Amy Burton—
supported by the sensitive conducting of Stewart Robertson—
seemed to me just about ideal in this extraordinarily taxing role,
arresting in her desperate solitude, like a cat miserably in heat, and
expressive in her easy handling of the torrential French text. Ms.
Burton's Elle was the most compelling performance I've seen by
this City Opera stalwart, whom I have previously admired more
for intelligence than allure. Here, she has it all.

I was less convinced by the decision of the director, Sam Helf-
rich, to mute the presence of the other key character onstage: the
telephone, which sits throughout on a table, its receiver off the

hook. Instead of listening to the call itself, we eavesdrop on the woman as she replays (or perhaps merely imagines) the conversation. This Proustian approach adds to the sense of internal breakdown and allows for greater freedom of stage movement, as Ms. Burton prowled the apartment from bedroom to refrigerator. But Cocteau's libretto specifies that the telephone be used both to chart the woman's turmoil and to sharpen the opera's fundamental irony—which is that the most useful of modern conveniences can be worse than useless in the most human of predicaments. In the stage directions, the telephone raises the woman's hopes when it rings after she's inexplicably been cut off. It provides cold comfort when she takes it to bed. And it signals that it may even become a means of suicide when at one point she winds the cord around her neck. In this otherwise masterly production, *La Voix Humaine* still packs a wallop—at least one feminist friend confessed to being "devastated" by it. But I suspect that it would have been even more devastating if it hadn't gone cordless.

Donizetti's French version of *Lucia di Lammermoor* had its premiere in Paris in 1839, and it hasn't, as far as I know, been performed in this country for nearly 100 years. The composer's relentlessly tuneful style, which is like a faucet you can't turn off, is Italian to the core and somewhat incongruous with French speech (which, in any event, seemed largely absent from the Glimmerglass performance). Even so, the French *Lucie* is, in several respects, an improvement over the original—more dramatically compressed; more generous about Henri, the weak, overbearing brother (who now has a brutish lieutenant, Gilbert); and more focused on the isolation of the hapless heroine, who now lacks her female companion, Alisa. Lillian Groag's production, which was vigorously conducted by Beatrice Jona Affron, distilled the Gothic gloom of the Sir Walter Scott novel into a claustrophobic hothouse of tilted mirrors. (The designer was John Conklin.) This had the effect of concentrating one's attention on the title character, in the person of a young American soprano, Sarah Coburn.

When Ms. Coburn fetchingly sang the title role in Gilbert and Sullivan's *Patience* last summer, she gave no indication that she was up to one of the most demanding coloratura assignments in opera. But she turns out to have qualities that have made legends out of so many of her predecessors, from Adelina Patti to Maria Callas: stage charisma, a thrilling upper register and, crucially, a fearlessness about abandoning herself to opera's most abandoned heroine. On a blistering Sunday afternoon, this was not a completely satisfying performance. Ms. Coburn's mad scene was stagy, with lots of finger pointing at the hallucinatory "bird" of the accompanying flute. I heard nothing in her brilliant top notes that resembled a melting pianissimo. In the lower registers, she indulged in some mannered crooning reminiscent of today's most vocally willful diva, Renee Fleming. But this is a palpably exciting voice, and if the rest of the cast seemed a little dazed by her (the best of them was the steadily impassioned Edgard of Raul Hernandez), that's as it should be. Ms. Coburn is a budding prima donna of exceptional promise.

When the Met staged Britten's *Death in Venice* in 1974, the work seemed small in the huge red auditorium, despite a superb musical performance, led by the composer's longtime partner and vocal muse, Sir Peter Pears. In the intimacy of Glimmerglass' 900-seat theater, Britten's most enigmatic work for the stage fills the house gloriously. In librettist Myfanwy Piper's adaptation of Thomas Mann's novella, the cast of characters includes tourists, a strawberry seller, strolling players, a travel agent, gondoliers, the god Apollo and a half-dozen Mephistophelean characters, ranging from an elderly fop to the Voice of Dionysus, who function as agents of doom (all six are sung by one baritone). The "action," however, takes place entirely inside the head of the doomed protagonist, the novelist Gustav von Aschenbach. With a running time of two hours and 45 minutes, this must be the longest—and richest—operatic monologue ever written. It begins (there's no overture) with the blocked writer thinking aloud: He sings, "My mind beats on," and those four words take us into an internal universe of clandestine desire that comes to signify as much as the public universe ushered in by the opening four notes of Beethoven's Fifth Symphony.

Mann's story (in Michael Henry Heim's recent brilliant translation) situates Aschenbach in a state of "torpid discontent"—a condition that no composer was better equipped than Britten to explore. His music ratchets up the Olympian detachment of Mann's prose to a tense turbulence that is expressive on enough levels for a dozen operas: the city's mysterious, watery foundations; the disease-ridden sirocco; echoes of the Platonic dialogue about whether beauty is a path to wisdom or chaos; Aschenbach's attempts to get an intellectual grip on the "perilous sweetness" of his obsession, which are set to an eerie piano accompaniment that rebukes him while indulging his imagination. And much more.

Most of Britten's operas represent an ongoing dialogue with himself and with the public—art made to explain himself as a passionate dissenter from a world devoted to war and as a flawed individual, conflicted by his search for grace and the pederastic desires of his homosexuality (desires he managed to suppress). By the time Britten composed *Death in Venice*, four years before his death in 1976, he had distilled his unmistakable musical language—spidery, translucent, fraught with treacherous sensuality—into an expressionism comparable in its brazen immediacy to Titian's last painting, Apollo's *Slaying of Marsyas*. As the god did with the satyr, Britten's opera flays. If the Glimmerglass staging doesn't quite fulfill the work's strange power, it makes an awfully good stab at it. Tazewell Thompson's production (with sets by Donald Eastman) shrewdly situates the fluid events in a single setting—the lobby of a decaying grand hotel whose back panels open to reveal the stupefying Venetian light. Led by Stewart Robertson, the young Glimmerglass orchestra overcame an initial tentativeness to bring real fire to this rigorously demanding score. William Burden sang the marathon role of Aschenbach with unfailing sensitivity—though the youthful attractiveness of his tenor (so different from the hollowed-out eloquence of Pears) worked against our belief in a man in his twilight years. As the six agents of doom, David Pittsinger proved a nimbly sinister chameleon. I found Scott Chiba as Tadzio, the object of Aschenbach's fatal attraction, problematic. Given that his appearances are accompanied by exotic orchestral colors that reflect Britten's longstanding interest in Balinese gamelan music, the casting of an Asian actor as the Polish boy made some sense—and would have made more sense if Asian performers had also been cast as his mother and sisters. Mr. Chiba is unquestionably eye-catching, but he projected the air of an experienced stage creature who's used to being looked at. He struck me as altogether too knowing to convey what is most disturbing about *Death in Venice*. In this, Britten's last and most overtly autobiographical opera, the composer looked more deeply into the concern that had informed his best earlier work, from *Peter Grimes* to *The Turn of the Screw*—the corruption of innocence. Here, the corruption resides in innocence itself.

MIKE McGUIRK

Charlie Rich,
Behind Closed Doors

When Charlie Rich sings about being in love, the gentleness of his voice, the inexplicable sadness of his piano playing and the slight echo on everything can make even the most stable among us want to slit our wrists and write "I loved you" on the wall in blood. *Behind Closed Doors* is the best record ever that will make you wish you were dead and gone.

Crazy Is as Crazy Does

Sometime in the course of your unpredictable life, you've probably loved a crazy person. There are just so many of them out there. How could anyone avoid it? And before you get started on me, yes, I know I'm using a politically incorrect term here. I should say "bipolar," or "coping with OCD" or "just really very moody." But I'll stick to the old-fashioned word, because it's short and sharp and etymologically linked to the infinitive "to shatter," which pretty well describes what happens when a crazy person, whether it's your boyfriend or sister or some sad new version of yourself, takes over your life. That's what craziness does. It draws us in, especially those of us who love the magnified realities of art. The energy of craziness can be sexy and wondrous—before its relentlessness shuts everything down.

In rock circles, mental instability is fetishized in familiar ways—as a sign of intensity and, even more so, purity. The inability to function within ordinary society shelters such artists from the temptations of "selling out"; the Syd Barretts and Roky Ericksons of the world couldn't make a wishy-washy commercial record if they wanted to. The filter-free directness of many mentally troubled people can also produce an air of honesty, both within lyrics so artless that they seem innocent and through music so inept it seems spontaneous.

Indie rock, with its lo-fi aesthetic and anti-commercial ethic, particularly favors eccentrics. Some function perfectly well in society while making incredible music; David Thomas of Pere Ubu and Victoria Williams spring to mind. Others have a harder time. The most troubling case is that of Daniel Johnston, whose simple songs, initially self-released on cassettes that were in themselves a form of folk art, warrant acclaim—but perhaps not at the level they've received. Johnston's mania has obviously fed his myth; his insistence that his talent rivals the Beatles is charming. But this is a truly screwed-up man, violent at times. And, now 44, he's pretty much in the same place artistically as he was two decades ago. He's not a failure, but he's no inspiration, either, at least not to me.

What I've noticed about "crazy" rock musicians is that the ones whose music offers the most insight into the turmoil of emotion tend to be women, and that these crazies tend to receive less hero worship than their male counterparts. Not to minimize the pain Johnston or Syd Barrett endured when institutionalized, or the suicides of Drake or Elliott Smith—but these guys walked out on that edge, willfully or not, and (with the exception of Drake, a flop when alive) their reputations grew.

Not so for Mary Margaret O'Hara, who made one ecstatic album in the late '80s and virtually disappeared, or for Barbara Manning, who's getting her undergraduate degree after two decades of struggling at the margins of indie. Or for Kristin Hersh, who lost custody of her son Dylan because a court ruled that her medicated bipolar disorder and her dedication to playing rock were a lethal combination for a child. (Dylan's now college-age and reunited with his mother.) Or Lisa Germano, currently "fighting with her muse," according to one missive floating around the Internet, after ten years of not fitting into anyone's cultural categories. Or for Courtney . . . but I'm not opening that can of Medusa-snakes right now.

One reason for the complexity and power of these women artists' work is that their inner demons are in constant dialogue with a world that already demonizes anything less than neat that emanates from the feminine realm. A male artist getting crazy can come off as threatening, but he's also often greeted as a prophet or, conversely, an endearing holy fool. A woman artist getting crazy is a different kind of mess—one that raises the general discomfort level by raising the specter of uncontrolled sexuality, irresponsible motherhood, violence done to or by the sacred "gentler sex"—all elements of our common consciousness that have haunted us since Medea's time and have never been resolved.

Hersh touches on these scary subjects in her stark folk albums, like The Grotto and her collection of irresistibly creepy American ballads, Murder, Misery and then Goodnight. In the music Hersh makes with Throwing Muses, a band she's reincarnated numerous times over her 20-year career, the disquiet lives in whorling beats and jagged guitars, a veritable house tornado of melodic noise. Rocking even harder at almost 40 than she did as a 16-year-old Meat Puppets fan, Hersh has found a way to employ music's catharsis as a kind of driver constantly carrying her into deeper regions of self-understanding. Early on, before she mastered her psychic imbalances, the music drove Hersh, and that was exciting to listen to. But it's more exciting to keep journeying with her as she's harnessed her power.

If Hersh has gone inward only to barrel through the darkness and come out free and clean, Lisa Germano has stayed inside, in beautiful darkness. This multi-instrumentalist first gained unlikely fame as a member of John Mellencamp's band—that's her playing fiddle on The Lonesome Jubilee and Big Daddy—but her own compositions are as knotty and internal as her old boss's are anthemic. In her early masterpiece, 1994's Geek the Girl, she builds a Sistine Chapel of self-doubt and ambivalence. These song-miniatures, constructed with the careful grace of a Joseph Cornell box from found sound, quiet effects and Germano's own delicate playing and deceptively offhand vocals, come from a disturbed consciousness, for sure, but Germano is as freaked out by real external threats like rape and stalking as she is by the vicissitudes of her own psyche. In "A Psychopath," she uses bits of old recordings and a very creepy tape of a 911 call to capture the awful feeling every woman knows: of being alone in a dark house with a threat—imagined? real?—at the door. Other songs, like the title track, perfectly nail that sense of self-sabotage smart women often feel as they try to figure out the relationship between misogyny and self-doubt. Though Germano focuses on a particularly female brand of torment on this album and others, like the funnier if slightly less pointed Happiness or the luxurious Excerpts from a Love Circus, she has enough empathy to realize all people struggle with confusion like hers. As she sings in Geek's hymn-like "of love and colors":

> People. All us fucked-up people,
> What are we gonna do
> With ourselves
> And our addictions
> And our desire to kill each other?
> And special things, your own dreams?

As for today's landscape of rock crazies, it seems to be getting better for the girls. Outsider artists like Joanna Newsom and Tywanna Jo Baskette are garnering acclaim, and Chan Marshall, who records her stark dreamscapes under the name Cat Power, is a certified indie star. I'll happily benefit from these artists' observations as I wait for Lisa Germano to make up with her muse and take me on another trip into her rich underworld.

Ted Nugent, *Cat Scratch Fever*

Album No. 3 from the Motor City Madman cemented his place in history with the smash hit single "Cat Scratch Fever," one of the all-time great juvenile vocabulary lessons. Throughout the album, Nugent's totally burnin' guitar is matched by the cock-rockin' vocals of Derek St. Holmes. Don't forget to play "Homebound" anytime you are returning from the hunt.

Kevin Blechdom

I don't much like being called mad. I'm funny like that. I don't like being accused of being a psycho bitch from hell; being compared by a boy I hardly know to a nutter who flung pots at his head. I don't much like asking what seems to be a pretty innocuous question and getting The Look instead: a Look I might expect if I had, I don't know, ripped open the buttons of my summer frock, hoiked my tits out of their ribbon-trimmed aqua balconette brassiere, and started rubbing handfuls of raw meat into my exposed areolae while wailing, "Are you fucking with me? OR ARE YOU FUCKING WITH ME?" at the top of my lungs. I guess I'm just unusual. I particularly don't like someone comparing arguing with me to the experience of listening to Kevin Blechdom's new album, *Eat My Heart Out*. I mean, *have you heard it?*

Kevin Blechdom doesn't mind being called mad, because, for the purposes of that album, she was. I mean, not mental asylum straight-jackets thinking everybody's taping you through radios in your fillings kind of mad—the other kind. The whimpering sobbing caught-on-a-loop not-eating shattering lying-on-pavements utterly broken kind of crazy you only get after the Big Relationship Break-Up. Everyone gets that at least once. Even boys.

Eat My Heart Out is an electronic masterpiece which mixes homegrown laptop ditties with country songs, pirate shanties, electro-skronk anthems, max/msp synthesis exercises and heartfelt achy-breaky ballads: yeah, mad alright, and that's just the *music:* we haven't even got to the lyrics yet. It's brilliant-mad; funny, cute, ironic, menacing: danceable-mad. It speeds up. It slows down. It loops a single voice into an army of voices all attempting to outdo each other to meet the high notes; and every song's got at least three different interrelated sections, if not more. There are songs written and recorded on nitrous oxide, songs where the artist didn't even know what she'd said till she played the recording back, where you can hear her gasping and whimpering as she sucks the laughing gas out of the balloon and into her lungs. ROCK. And . . . mad.

As for the album's subject matter, *Eat My Heart Out* is a twisted kind of one-woman off-off-Broadway music hall show about the break-up of a long-distance relationship. We're talking raw emotional states, clinical depression, near-hysteria: you know: *feelings.* Ugh. Feelings and all that they entail, from the over-saturated metaphors ("Youuuu are my torrrrtttuuuure / and IIIIII am your chhaaaaammmmber / get OUT of me" she squeals, operatically) and hideous moments of clarity ("I don't wanna get over you / but I'm so scared that I might have to / in order for me to get on with me / I can't wait around indefinitely"), to the nauseatingly repetitive loops of the futile crush ("I want out of this situation I can't stop thinking about . . . are you fucking with me? Or are you fucking with me?" etc. ad infinitum). Phew! And yet, even though it's dealing with serious, horrible shit, the album's also funny—piss-takey and irreverent, sticky with irony and self-mockery and awareness of cliché, like the mortifying moment you realise you've been reading your sister's copy of "He's Just Not That Into You" and actually *underlining things.*

But, you know, the creative female has been accused of being mad so fucking often—a hysterical harpy: disturbed, hormonal, her own muse before she is an artist—think Sylvia Plath, think Tracy Emin, think Anne Sexton—that it's tempting to want to reconfigure this album's outpouring in a postmodern, death-of-the-author kind of way. No, of course Kevin Blechdom's not mad, dear—she's just *playing* with the notion of the female confessional mode, transforming her emotion into art through her *quite considerable* technical mastery. Why, it's a *mediated and deliberate self-reconstruction:* not mere emotional exhibitionism, but a *counter-aesthetic designed to reclaim female subjectivity*—right, Kevin?

Er, nope. "Oh, I definitely was going crazy while I was making the record," says Kevin (real name Kristin Erikson, a matter we shall go into in more detail later), in a breezy, matter-of-fact manner. "I was pretty depressed most of the time. But I wasn't hiding the depression. I was like, I'm gonna use it, because I'm feeling that way, so fuck it."

OK. So you're cool with the notion of entering the pantheon of disfunctional female artists like Tracy Emin or Sylvia Plath? Are you down with "Kevin Blechdom" being a name that can be used to critique female behaviour?

"What do you mean?"

Well, when I was in Berlin I had a fight with this boy I was seeing, and he said that arguing with me felt like listening to your album.

(KEVY B LAUGHS REALLY HARD FOR ABOUT HALF AN HOUR)

"Well . . . I don't like the crazy woman stereotype so much, or a comparison to me being used as an insult, but awkward situations *can* drive women crazy, so what you gonna do? I used to be even more crazy, because I didn't know what to do with the energy, whereas this time I put it into the record. This is cheesy, but I had a dream where a witch came to me. I was so emotionally confused at the time that I didn't know what was happening. I was travelling a lot, and felt really disjointed and fucked up. And the witch in the dream said to me, 'If you want to know what's going on, write a song every day, and then you'll figure it out.' And I did!"

OK. Witch. One of three classic archetypes of woman—virgin, mother, crone. The village wise woman, she lives alone, slightly outside of the society. She is the bearer of knowledge and medicine, knows which herbs will induce a miscarriage, and is therefore friend to the female—and the enemy of man. What the *fuck?* Dreams, female archetypes, the confessional mode—is this shit for *real?* I mean, since when did digital, computer music—the traditional domain of the navy-blue hoody wearing boy, the traditional speccy IDM geek—ever—EVER—involve talk of such things?

Don't stop reading, losers. Kevin Blechdom is not some kind of hippy. Kevin Blechdom is cooler than you'll ever be. Born in 1978, she attended the prestigious Mills music college in San Francisco, where she learned all about computer music, generating tracks with software she programmed in Max / MSP. She met ex-collaborator Bevin Kelley while both were playing at a Halloween party in 1998: they recorded their first record that weekend and started making music together as "Blectum from Blechdom," which they released on the prestigious Tigerbeat 6 label. After five years and several releases on Tigerbeat 6 the duo split and Kevin decamped to Berlin, where her first full-length album, *Bitches without Britches*, came out on Chicks on Speed records in 2003.

And Blechdom wasn't always such a heart-in-hand, female-confessional-mode kind of lady. When Blectum from Blechdom first started out, the duo avoided involvement with gender issues by simply pretending to be men.

"Back then, I wanted people to listen to the music without thinking about gender at all. At the time, when I was a bit younger, I thought the best compliment I could receive as a female artist was for someone to listen to my electronic music and think that a man made it. If I read a review containing the phrase 'Blectum from Blechdom are two guys from San Francisco,' I would be like, 'Thank you!!!!' It's kind of sad really. But it was a reality."

Right now Kevy B couldn't be outing herself as female much more if she tried. The aforementioned cover, for example, features Kevin clutching a handful of animal guts to her exposed and freckly tits. It's both a homage to and a piss-take of '60s and '70s feminist performance art, such as the work of Carolee Schneemann, who organised a show in 1964 called 'Meat Joy,' in which the artist and a host of nude participants frenziedly smeared each other with dead fish, chicken parts and raw sausages.

"I love playing with those clichés of feminist art from the past! Like, OK, I'm a performance artist now! And I'm gonna take my shirt off and rub myself with guts! It's like the stupidest thing a female artist could possibly do. But on some levels I'm also serious, like: 'OK, let's bring it on, all this sex shit. All these rap musicians are showing their tits and asses and that and I say I'm not gonna do that and then I'm like . . . wait!!! I can do that!!! I don't even give a shit! I don't have the same physical beauty standard but I'm going to fucking do it anyway!' You'd hear all these rumours about why one record sold better than another—'oh she showed her tits, oh she showed her ass'—and I'm like, OK fine if that's how it works I'm gonna play the same game! It's like—hey, media! You want tits? You GOT THEM!"

Only, not. The cover artwork, showing a topless Kevin clutching some raw meat, directly subverts the conventions of the female nude (passively accepting the gaze, coyly displaying her parts, yada yada ad infinitum), to such an extent that the record company decided to conceal the image beneath a more innocuous cartoon cover in order to avoid censorship in Japan, the UK and the US.

"It's ridiculous. You give them tits but then they get mad when they're not plastic tits! Then it's suddenly *illegal!* I mean, I'm just standing there casually. I'm not sticking my tits out. My shoulders aren't back. They're just like another part of my body, like my elbow or something. And that's seen as more offensive than someone who's thrusting their tits forward in this really sexual way! It's like, what is going ON with this world????"

Speaking at a conference at the University of Virginia back in 2000, Gloria Steinem pointed out that women tend to be more conservative in their early years, and become "radicalized" once they

enter the workplace and encounter discrimination, or when they become mothers and find themselves working two jobs with little help.
Feminists are made, not born. Blechdom's shift in perspective—
from literally pretending to be male to appearing on her album
sleeve with her floppy, freckly tits out and yelling about love, heart-
break and disappointment, would seem to bear this out.

"It would be great to feel that you didn't have to talk about feminism, and a lot of people I know say that you should only talk about
the music, and not about gender politics. But I'm like, fuck that!
Gender politics is FUCKED UP! Music is like a boys' club—look at
how many female artists are released on Warp. Across their whole
roster maybe 5 percent of their artists are girls. It's like the most sex-
ist fucking boys club ever and I'm just really tired of it. It's just boring. I want to see some girls rock the mic. Let them talk their minds
about their side of the relationship! BRING IT ON, MOTHER-
FUCKERS!"

You know what? I don't think I mind being compared to Kevin
Blechdom any more. This woman's just made the most ferocious,
impassioned, visceral electronic album the decade's seen so far, exploring stereotypes of what it means to be fucked-up, heart-broken,
artistic—then wrapping it all up in a layer of piss-take, cleverness
and irony and genius glitched-up beats (just so we don't get too
fucking serious, like). She's putting a human—no—a *female* face on
the esoteric landscape of digital music—and it's laughing right at us.
Arguing with me's like listening to a Blechdom album? I'll take that
shit as a compliment.

KIMBERLY CHUN

Touched by a Woman

*Dolly Parton Sings 'bout Peace,
Love & Understanding*

It was as if an unlikely angel had alit amid San Francisco's hairy fairies and graying hippies, jam-band twirlers and drag kings. Proto-yuppies and mountain bikers bumped helmets with heavily tattooed gearheads. Vegan bike messengers rubbed shoulders with straight-laced Financial District trench workers in one of the most diverse crowds in a city that prides itself on its freak parade.

Still, you can imagine, imagine all the people and their ardent jostling when Dolly Parton finally took the second stage in Golden Gate Park at the city's free annual Hardly Strictly Bluegrass Festival. The Summer of Love may be long gone, but as the late afternoon sun set on the epicenter of the countercultural revolution—sunlight ricocheting off the blue-green sparkles on the 59-year-old Parton's minidress—it was clear that the love was still there for this once-poor girl from the Smoky Mountains. The smell of weed was blowin' in the wind as Parton remarked, "I don't know what y'all are smoking, but it sure smells *good*!"

The sun was in the singer's eyes, but her demeanor was typically jovial: "I'm in God's spotlight. Hi, God!" Like God, Dolly is bigger than nature, bigger than law, bigger than biology—and there's

enough of her to go around. On Thursday, Dec. 15, Dolly's bubbling joviality will be projected all through Bobcats Arena when the
country legend brings her current "Vintage Tour" to the stage at
8:00 p.m.

She's an unlikely unifier: a bombastic, blonde, über-femme St.
Peter who embodied crossover country-pop superstardom decades
before Shania or Faith. Unlike those divas, Parton has also been
blessed with musical chops and credibility to go with her frankly
faux beauty and radically over-the-top fashion sense. Since her
childhood, when she composed songs before she could read or
write, Parton has stooped to conquer all media: the country and pop
music charts; TV (with early collaborator Porter Wagoner and then
on her own); movies (from breakthrough 1980 feminist comedy *9 to
5* to 1989's archetype-defining *Steel Magnolias*) and entertainment
palaces Dollywood, in Tennessee, and Dixie Stampede, in Branson,
Mizzou. (All she needs now is a podcast.) Yet despite the popularity
of her *Touched by an Angel*–like role in the 1996 Hallmark holiday
fave *Unlikely Angel*, I suspect Parton's bad, bawdy 1982 musical *The
Best Little Whorehouse in Texas* remains closest to her heart.

In *9 to 5*, Parton unveiled the earthy realism and likeable warmth
beneath those humongous wigs—looking like a platinum 'fro-ed
White Panther in the gender wars, and playing the misunderstood,
sexually harassed secretary Doralee. But you can't imagine another
lead in *Whorehouse*, resonating with feeling and jiggling like life force
in a corset. She's effortlessly charismatic and comfortable in her own
formidable skin, while showing off that utterly startling chest, making *Whorehouse* a must-rent for Russ Meyer fetishists. Miss Dolly not
only delivers a memorable rendition of the Broadway hit's center-
piece, "A Lil' Ole Bitty Pissant Country Place," with her ever-
present effervescence, but she also serves up her own songs: the
characteristically knowing "Sneakin' Around" as well as her biggest
hit (in the hands of Whitney Houston), "I Will Always Love You."

Dolly sings that song—eyes and face wide open and adorned with
big, fake, butterfly lashes—to a stricken Burt Reynolds like it's a

weapon to be used only as the last resort. Here, the bombshell sets off a gentle nuclear explosion: She dares Reynolds to turn aside and throw that tremulous, generous love away. How can you walk away from the open doors and welcoming smiles at Parton's palace of excess? As Pamela Wilson writes in her essay "Mountains of Contradictions: Gender, Class, and Region in the Star Image of Dolly Parton": "The Dolly persona *embodies* (there being no other word for it) excessive womanliness, in any interpretation. Parton displays this excess through her construction of a surface identity (her body and appearance) and through her representation of interiority, or a deeper identity (her emotions, desires, and 'dreams')." The caricature finds her power by revealing her roots, her guts, her vulnerability, and her grits.

Like the singer who drags Sly Stallone up to her level in the 1984 stinker *Rhinestones*, Parton brings more than mammaries to the table. Her writing—especially early on and sung in that crystal-clear, watery soprano—displays that feisty Parton mix of sweetness and grit, urban modernity and backwoods tradition. And it's hard to imagine anyone else doing justice to key songs like "Coat of Many Colors," "Touch Your Woman," "My Tennessee Mountain Home," "Jolene," "Love Is Like a Butterfly" and "The Bargain Store."

So when Parton went in to record her latest album, *Those Were the Days* (Sugar Hill); ***), she understood the challenge in dusting off such 60s and 70s protest standards as "Blowin' in the Wind," "Imagine" and "Where Have All the Flowers Gone." She trots these tunes out into the new grass, along with her own, on her current "Vintage Tour." Ever the bridge-builder on this album, Parton enlisted some of the original songs' writers and/or related interpreters to help her out. Yusef Islam (Cat Stevens) plays guitar on "Where Do the Children Play," and Kris Kristofferson tag-teams on "Me and Bobby McGee." The Dylans and Lennons didn't show up for "Blowin'" or "Imagine," but Nickel Creek appears on the former. A few other young artists participated, too, including Norah Jones (on "Flower") and Keith Urban (on a rousing "Twelfth of Never").

So why hasn't Parton suffered the hostility and backlash directed at the Dixie Chicks for articulating similar anti-war sentiments? One reason could be that, two years ago, Parton released the flag-waving *For God and Country*, a collection of right-leaning patriotic tunes such as "God Bless the USA" and "Ballad of the Green Beret."

"I am not protesting anything," Parton has said. "I am not political. But I am a patriot and peace-loving." Perhaps the safe remove of nostalgia—symbolized in Parton's "vintage" hippie-chick chic on the CD cover—protects her. Or maybe Dolly's sunny and grounded charm delivers her from harm, allowing her to express pacifism in song, just as she once manifested feminine strength and workplace empowerment in low-cut frocks. Then again, it could be that the mood in the country has simply shifted, falling in line with Parton's peace 'n' love music-making.

Obviously, Parton still understands what's blowin' in the wind, and like *Whorehouse*'s Mona, she's good-naturedly willing to satisfy, although I'm waiting for her to go further than simply reflecting the current zeitgeist with super-straight hair. I'm wondering when she'll pull a Loretta Lynn and collaborate with a strong, historically minded producer who loves her voice, guitar-playing, and classic songwriting—someone like Jack White, Nigel Godrich or Devendra Banhart. Parton's upcoming Broadway revival of *9 to 5* fits one glittery side of her glam persona, so record-collecting nerds keep dreaming of imagined collaborations with Lambchop, Calexico or Neko Case and the New Pomographers. We are the geeks, freaks and counselors at Camp Dolly, who will always love her while surreptitiously wishing for the return of the big blonde's down-home bandanas and many-hued rainbow stew of aspirational countrypolitan and hillbilly love songs.

MIKE McGUIRK

Kylie Minogue,
I Believe in You

International disco diva Kylie teams up with ultra-hip fruitcakes the Scissor Sisters to deliver a decidedly space-y club single that goes best with soft, solid-color lighting, shooting stars, and slow motion pirouettes—lots of them. Fittingly retro and futuristic at the same time.

FRANK KOGAN

Frank Kogan's Country Music Critics' Ballot 2005 (excerpt)

It's a cliché but accurate to say that country & western is split emotionally between a desire for home and family on the one hand and the urge to range wild and free on the other. This can either be a profound paradox or a lazy inconsistency depending on the artistry involved. Shannon Brown's "Corn Fed" is very catchy but appalling in its stupidity: on the one hand she says that in her happy heartland they leave doors unlocked so as not to keep anybody out, on the other she brags that there ain't nothin' but country on the radio. The average eight-year-old can see the hypocrisy in that one, and for an adult to write such a song and not notice its bullshit requires a deliberate deadening of the intellect. (Gawd, if there were an actual community that said this about itself, how would its teenagers avoid growing up insane? By listening to Young Jeezy records, perhaps, and dreaming of being gangstas.)

But it's the emotional split asserting itself, the gap between one ideal (wild and free, everybody welcome) and another (everybody united in values). Jamie O'Neal's got the split too, which she avoids confronting directly. Her mom-is-a-hero-in-the-home lecture is in one song, her girls'-night blowout is in another. In "Devil On the Left," a song about a stripper—where the two ideals co-exist—the words sidestep just what is supposed to count as the angel's dominion and what the devil's: you assume that the strip show belongs to the devil, but does this mean dancing and pleasure belong to the devil as well? There's a hint in the song that the preacher who prays for her is the one who eventually marries her and takes her to the corn-fed picket-fence land of the happy ending. But in marrying her he gets the carnal dance she'd previously sold to everyone. (The most touching of the many touching moments on Deana Carter's album is where she in effect asks the angels for permission to have a love affair.)

In general I like music that overspills its container, though for this to work well there has to be a good container in the first place. So that's my version of the split (Nietzsche's melding of Dionysius and Apollo, I suppose, though I haven't read *Birth of Tragedy* in thirty years, so don't really know). Anyway, alt-country—alt anything, actually, including the *Nashville Scene* and *New Times* and the *Village Voice*—has its own version of this paradox/inconsistency: it claims to ride free—to be alternative, to overspill its container—and at the same time it turns "we overspill our container" into a container itself, a niche for the likeminded, and without a lot of motion in the niche. Really, Jamie O'Neal's music has way more splish and splash than Mary Gauthier's does, even if the latter claims to be an emotional cascade.

The DeZurik Sisters

Two Farm Girls Who Yodeled
Their Way to the Grand Ole Opry

In his droll travelogue, *A Tramp Abroad*, Mark Twain neatly summarizes the jaundiced response of many music lovers to yodeling: "[D]uring the remainder of the day [we] hired the rest of the jodelers, at a franc apiece, not to jodel any more."

Twain's attitude seems to have prevailed today, but during the first half of the twentieth century, a mania for yodeling seized America, catapulting its greatest practitioners to national celebrity. Though yodelers once numbered among America's best-known vocalists, with the exception of Jimmie Rodgers and a few movie cowboys, their names have faded from public memory.

Arkansas native Elton Britt, for example, who was unofficially known as "The World Champion Yodeler" after triumphing in a yodeling competition in New York organized by horse-opera film star Tom Mix, became the first country singer to earn a gold record for his million-selling 1942 patriotic hit "There's a Star-Spangled Banner Waving Somewhere." Though Britt was billed as "The World's Highest Yodeler" when he performed at the White House for President Franklin Roosevelt (and when he later ran for the presidency himself in 1960), little of his recorded music is available today.

Britt may have reached the highest notes as a yodeler, but neither he nor any other vocalist of the period approached the range of sounds coaxed from the human voice by two girls from a farm just outside Royalton, Minnesota. Among the first female country singers to appear on stage without husbands or fathers, the DeZurik Sisters always appeared as a duet, amazing audiences with their rapid, high-pitched yodels that often spiraled into animal sounds. In fact, so convincing were their chicken yodels that the act was renamed the Cackle Sisters when they joined the Ralston Purina Company's *Checkerboard Time* radio program as regulars from 1937–1941.

Though presented as a novelty (on one transcription, a *Checkerboard Time* announcer introduces the sisters, who only cackle in response to his questions, as "that fine feathered pair of songsters with their trick vocal stunts"), the DeZuriks's animal imitations actually sprang from the very nature of the yodel and its origins in agrarian culture. The period of its popularity in the U.S., however, coincided—perhaps not so surprisingly—with the rapid transformation of an agricultural America into an industrial and urbanized modern state. The yodeling craze may have been, in fact, more nostalgia for a passing way of life than celebration of thriving folkways.

But then, yodeling was the perfect music to serve as threshold between a world that had already begun to disappear and the one that would replace it. For what is a yodel except an expression of betweenness?

Between—isn't that where the yodel warbles as it rapidly alternates from low moan to vertiginous falsetto shriek and back again, emphasizing the transition from one to the other with its distinctive break between those opposing registers? As the dean of yodeling studies, Bart Plantenga, defines it in his fascinating and informative survey of the art, *Yodel-Ay-Ee-Oooo: The Secret History of Yodeling Around the World*, "The yodel, simply put, is most distinguishable from other types of vocalizations by its characteristic emphasis on the noise, that jolt of air, that occurs as the voice passes from bass or low chest voice to high head voice or falsetto—and vice versa. . . . Other vocals may tinker with falsetto, trill, and vibrato, but it's that abrupt, almost rude, leap across the cavern of pitch that makes the yodel *yodel*."

The yodel quavers between word and sound, between voice and instrument, between man and woman, between despair and exultation, between adult and child, between human and animal, between civilization and nature. It reminds one of the cracking voice of a boy on the verge of manhood, of a woman fighting back tears, of a mute struggling for language to express—what? Something melancholy, something quivering between bruised experience and disappointed innocence.

Perhaps that's why the yodel almost always erupts in the midst of a sad story. Caught between desire and rejection, faithfulness and betrayal, love and loss, the balladeer abandons language altogether to express the outraged heart in a "barbaric yawp," as Walt Whitman describes the articulation of that which is "untranslatable" into words.

One cannot prove, of course, that yodeling is older than speaking, but its origins are likely ancient. Plantenga hypothesizes that it is rooted in the domestication of animals, noting similarities in yodels to the lowing and calls of local creatures. Examining types of yodeling among groups all over the world, including the Pygmies of Central Africa, the natives of Papua New Guinea, and the Brazilian Bororo Indians, he documents the first notation of Alpine yodels in 1545 and finds similar yodeling practiced from "northern Sweden to the Caucasus, down into Romania."

Though one might assume nineteenth-century Germanic and Scandinavian immigration to the United States accounts for the introduction of yodeling into American popular culture, another kind of betweenness may have been its source. In *Where Dead Voices Gather*, his revelatory study of the career of Emmett Miller, Nick Tosches traces the rise of yodeling to the tradition of minstrel shows: "That tradition, which dominated American music and show business from the middle of the nineteenth century until after the turn of the twentieth, was—simply, bizarrely, inexplicably—a form of stage entertainment in which men blackened their faces, burlesqued the demeanor and behavior of Southern blacks, and performed what were presented as the songs and music of those blacks."

He establishes that by 1925 yodeling was "a routine aspect of blackface performance," and then goes on to note that the most enduring of all yodelers, Jimmie Rodgers, spent the 1924–1925 season working "blackface in a traveling medicine show." Tosches, however, makes a persuasive case that it was not Rodgers but Emmett Miller, a white Georgian in blackface, who transformed the yodel from novelty to "something plaintive and disarming, something that would become . . . an expressiveness pure and free."

If Tosches is right, the yodeling craze that began in the late '20s depended upon another kind of betweenness, the divide between races, and it was the mad song of a white man with a black face, swooning from the falsetto to the guttural and back again, that had toes tapping across America as the Great Depression approached.

The DeZurik Sisters, although fresh-faced Midwestern farm girls rather than blackface Southerners, brought to their Nashville performances at the Grand Ole Opry something more authentic than the racist parodies of minstrel shows. In their evocation of a natural world in which the human was at home, the two girls hearkened back to the very origins of yodeling with their gift for imitating barnyard animals. The granddaughters of Slovakian immigrants, Mary Jane and younger sister Carolyn grew up to the music of nature. As Carolyn explains, "We listened to the birds and tried to sing with the birds and yodel with them, imitate them. And that is how we got into all the bird stuff and animal sounds, and we would include them in our songs. That was quite a joke to us, too."

How did they sound? An article from the late 1930s in *The Prairie Farmer* provided readers a succinct introduction to the sisters' musical style: "They specialize in trick yodels including Hawaiian yodel, the cackle trill, German, Swiss and triple tongue yodel."

Though usually accompanying themselves on guitar, the DeZuriks often used their wordless vocalizations as instrumental bridges between verses. Their repertoire of yodeled sounds eventually extended to chime bells, trumpets, muted trombones, Hawaiian guitars, mandolins, and even musical saws. But their signature animal yodels, too, were more instrumental sound effects—almost sonic illustrations of animals referenced in their songs—than expressive plaints or *cris de coeur.*

Though their yodeling is astonishing and sometimes exhilarating as they rise to shattering heights together, it is in their beautifully matched voices, where one barely shadows the other, that the extraordinary quality of their music becomes apparent.

The simplicity and authenticity of those voices are still evident in the reminiscences of the duet's surviving sister. In an interview with Christoph Wagner published as liner notes for Trikont's 2003 compilation CD entitled *Flowers in the Wildwood: Women in Early Country Music,* Carolyn recounts how their career began:

> This is 1934. In our town they had a band every Wednesday night. My uncle played in a band and the band leader was everybody's dentist out there. Jane and I were out in the field cutting rye. We saw this truck coming up the road and that was my Uncle Frank. He walked over to us with big grins on his face, and he asked us if we would like to sing at the band concert tonight. We said, "What? We are not good enough yet." But he insisted. He pushed us into it. We knew only three songs well. We were nervous. We almost froze on the spot. So we sang our three songs. We didn't have a microphone. When we finished the first song, they screamed, they howled. It was a big success. After that we started in amateur contests and we won all of them but one.

When a unit from WLS (the call letters of the Sears-Roebuck Agricultural Foundation radio station, standing for the "World's Largest Store") came to the fairgrounds at Little Falls, Minnesota, to stage two days of performances, the DeZurik sisters arrived at the end of the second day and sang two songs to wild audience reaction. Eventually persuaded by a WLS program director to audition, they moved to Chicago—despite their distaste for the city—when they were offered a spot on *National Barn Dance* in 1936.

Their trick yodeling eventually landed them a recording contract with the Vocalion label in 1938. Two years later, Carolyn married Ralph "Rusty" Gill, a WLS staff guitarist from East Texas who would become known for his cowboy songs and mountain ballads; less than a month after her sister's wedding, Mary Jane married WLS staff accordionist Augie Klein. That same year, 1940, the DeZuriks starred in a Republic Pictures movie, *Barnyard Follies*, singing five of their distinctive songs. But the sisters went into temporary retirement the next year (except for radio performances and commercials) in anticipation of the births of their first children.

In 1943, Carolyn joined the Sonja Henie Ice Review. The former Olympic gold medalist skated to Carolyn's yodels for two seasons.

Mary Jane returned from retirement in 1944, and the Cackle/DeZurik Sisters began recording transcriptions for Purina's *Checkerboard Funfest* broadcasts around the country as well as appearing regularly on the *Eddy Arnold Show* and the *Grand Ole Opry*. "But," Carolyn explains, "we had to commute by train from Chicago to Nashville every Friday to be there on Saturday. That was pretty hectic, because that was during the war and the trains were very crowded with soldiers and sailors. The engineers were very good to us because they knew who we were. And they put us on the train before anybody else. Put us in the ladies room and locked the door so nobody else could get in. Then he put a sign on the door: OUT OF ORDER! So we were pretty safe. People got pretty rowdy on those long trips."

Following a serious automobile accident in 1947, Mary Jane retired the next year, but a third sister, Lorraine, took her place, appearing with Carolyn from 1949–1950 on NBC's televised *Midwestern Hayride*. Their partnership ended soon after, and Carolyn became the female vocalist for the Prairie Ramblers, her husband's country band that performed some of the campfire songs Rusty had learned as a horseman in East Texas. Eventually joining the ABC television affiliate in Chicago in 1954, the band was featured on *Chicago Parade*, a popular daily program.

Then, in 1956, the Prairie Ramblers gave up country yodeling for polka tunes. As Wayne W. Daniels writes of their transformation in his liner notes for the American Gramophone & Wireless Co. tape of thirty-eight DeZurik Sister songs, "They swapped their cowboy hats and boots for Bavarian costumes . . . changed their name to the Polka Chips with Carolyn DeZurik, and became one of the polka sensations of Chicago."

Uniting the two styles of music for which she was known, Carolyn ended her career as the yodeling trademark for Busch Bavarian Beer. When she finally retired from show business in 1963, yodeling was already disappearing from the musical scene. The once-famous "World Champion Yodeler" Elton Britt would have one last solo hit, "The Jimmie Rodgers Blues," in 1968, but no revival of the ancient art of yodeling would follow that song.

Perhaps American culture in the following decades simply lost its taste for in-betweenness. Instead of music that celebrated uncertainty, verging, and becoming, we preferred songs that asserted unwavering confidence in something or other, whether it was an emotion or an opinion. Divorced from nature, we were divorced, too, from its bleat and howl and, yes, cackle; the only sounds we recognized were the sounds we made ourselves. And so the yodel became the quaint artifact of a lost world, worthy only of our disdain.

Oh, it is easy enough to point to exceptions. For example, Jewel, the pop singer, yodeled as a child and sometimes performs a rock version of the bluegrass yodeling tune "Chime Bells" in her concerts. And Bart Plantenga catalogues a wide range of occasional yodelers from Bobby McFerrin to Bruce Springsteen to Dave Matthews to k.d. lang. But the general attitude today toward yodeling is perhaps best expressed by filmmaker Tim Burton.

His 1996 film *Mars Attacks!* offers yodeling not as music but as a means of conquering an invading army of Martians. The military is useless, since its bullets bounce off the spaceships from Mars without effect, and the Martians have a little vacuum cleaner that sucks up the nuclear radiation from the missiles fired at them. Burton certainly can't kill them with the common cold or some other virus, because that's how H.G. Wells did it. So what's left? How about Slim Whitman singing "Indian Love Call"? We never quite get an explanation of how it works—maybe it's the resonant frequency of his yodeling—but once the scrappy humans figure out that's all it takes to turn the evil creatures into green goo inside their space helmets, we wipe them out in about thirty seconds.

If it wasn't so funny, it would break your heart—the way the Martians can't take the yodeling at the end of the movie. Of course, is there anything more melancholy than a good yodeler? All that yearning that just can't quite make it out of the throat as words. Maybe that's what killed the Martians: their green hearts bursting with sadness in those scrawny little chests.

KATY ST. CLAIR

A Very Special Concert

*The Enduring Bond Between Huey Lewis
and the Developmentally Disabled*

"Ooooh, man, I can't wait to see Huey!" said my client Sean, busily
brushing his hair. I work with Sean in a day program for people with
developmental disabilities. In addition to some mental retardation,
he has severe obsessive-compulsive disorder. He's a hand-washer
and a germphobe, and he looks exactly like a grown-up version of
Harold from *Harold and the Purple Crayon*. He literally has three
hairs on his head, which he brushes obsessively in between visits to
the beauty college. He goes there for a free cut when things start to
get "shaggy." Part of his disability is that he has to have three of
everything—three water bottles for work, three hats, three nail clip-
pers, three hairs (I guess). So of course he has a big-ass stack of
Huey Lewis CDs and tapes, three of each one.

"Man," he continued, "I'm gonna dance, dance, dance!" When
Sean says he's gonna dance, he means he's gonna dance. I once saw
him at a '50s party, dressed like Kenickie from *Grease* (sans hair,
natch), kicking up dust for over two solid hours. He knows a lot
about music, and I call him the "human jukebox" because he can
name that tune in about three seconds when we have the radio on in
the car. His hands-down favorite performer is Huey Lewis.

Sean has a framed picture of himself and Mr. Lewis locked in an embrace. At first I thought it was cool that he had met the singer and was lucky enough to snap a photo. Then, as I visited other clients' houses, a pattern started to emerge. Rose, Jennifer, Linnea, Donald (whose names, like everyone else's in this story, have been changed to protect their anonymity)—each had a picture of him- or herself posing with Huey Lewis or at a Huey concert. Was Huey Lewis the Pied Piper of the developmentally disabled, only with a harmonica instead of a fife? (How else to explain all those sales of *Sports*?)

Whatever the reason—the catchy tunes, the goofball charisma, or maybe those slapstick videos—developmentally disabled people see something significant and tender in Huey Lewis. He makes them happy.

The band recently celebrated its 25th anniversary by performing at this year's Marin County Fair on a cool summer night a few weeks back. This was Huey Lewis & the News' stomping ground, where they began two decades earlier, playing around San Rafael and Mill Valley. Suffice it to say, the show was something all of my clients were looking forward to.

I was actually only going to escort one person, my friend Bobbi, and meet the rest of our friends there. Sean and Linnea were going, of course. Linnea actually likes the soundtrack to *Dirty Dancing* better than any Huey record, but damn it, she loves "If This Is It" and wouldn't miss it for the world.

Linnea's a young woman with, we think, an as-yet-undiagnosed chromosomal abnormality, a syndrome that has saddled her with a smaller frame than she should have, awkwardly formed bones, and some sort of a delay in neuron transfer. Linnea takes a few beats to respond to you, or to laugh at a joke, or to do things like stock clothing at her work.

We have a lot in common. We both like to eat out at Mexican places with groups of friends and see scary movies. She has what I consider the best quality a person can have: the ability to laugh at herself. I once asked her what exactly her disability was. She responded, after a beat of course, with, "I'm retarded. Duh!"

I often call her "Le Schnoz," because her nose takes up about a third of her face. But the most peculiar thing about Linnea is that she has a curious habit of talking to herself as if she were two people. Listening to her do this is a good window into her soul, really, and earlier in the day I witnessed just how excited she was to go to the concert that night.

Linnea (to herself): "Are you going to the concert tonight?" To which she replied, again to herself, "You got it, baby. You are on, girl. I'm not missing Huey Little."

"Huey Little?" she replied back in her other voice. "Who the heck is Huey Little? You mean Huey Lewis!" Then she laughed at herself, and her other self had to laugh a bit, too.

I have gotten very used to these exchanges, which soothe Linnea and, in turn, have come to soothe me as well. When Linnea isn't talking to herself, she's just not herself.

"Huey LEWIS," she repeated strongly to herself with a chuckle. "Get it right, girl."

There are a lot of stereotypes about retarded people, and most of them are false. Yes, I'm going to refer to people with developmental disabilities as "retarded." After all, what is wrong with the word "retarded"? It means slowed or delayed, and when someone is retarded, that's what's going on (or not going on) somewhere in his brain. Some of my clients are great at math and reading, but cannot tell you what they did the day before, or why a joke was funny. Others cannot speak, see, or say what they want, but they can tell when I'm sad. In each person, something that works in most people's brains is hindered, i.e., is "retarded." If gays can take back "faggot," and blacks can take back "nigger," then surely developmentally disabled folks can take back "retarded." And since they can't do it for themselves, I'm going to do it for them.

So back to the stereotypes about retarded people. When I tell people that I love my work with my retarded clients, they invariably conjure up a picture of a drooling monobrow with one arm curled into his chest and a shit-eating grin on his face. This is a stereotype of a retarded person. Here are some others: All retarded people are happy-go-lucky; all retarded people pull their shorts up as high as they can; all retarded people have bathroom accidents; all retarded people want to hug you. In reality, retarded people are just like you and me: They come in all shapes and sizes. They, too, put their pants on one leg at a time. It's just that sometimes they put theirs on backwards.

Here are some facts about retarded people. First, they are zero-bullshit. If you are a jerk, they will call you on it. If you have a booger hanging out, they'll damn sure let you know. That's all I've ever asked for from a friend.

Retarded people never make fun of someone else, never point and laugh at anybody. In fact, my clients generally see the good in everyone. All of these are generalizations, and of course there are exceptions to the rule, but mostly these are the reasons why I love my work.

There is, however, one stereotype about retarded people that is true, one broad brushstroke that one can make about them all: Good gosh a'mighty, retarded people love them some Huey Lewis. Part of the reason is that Huey is apparently a sweetheart who does a lot of volunteer work with people who have developmental disabilities. But another big part is the music.

My clients have a favorite record, and it's not *Fore!* or *Picture This*. Nope, everyone loves the soundtrack to *Back to the Future*, on which one finds the song "Back in Time." It's a testament to the songwriting prowess of the News, who were asked to write a song for a movie in which the protagonist goes back in time. They put their heads together and came up with the perfect song, a song called "Back in Time." You see, there's no pathos or back story to News songs. They are straightforward ("Stuck With You"), energetic ("The Power of Love"), and easy to relate to ("Hip to Be Square"). These truths are appreciated by a wide variety of music lovers, some of whom just happen to be mentally retarded.

The county fair takes place at the base of the Marin Civic Center, a Disney-ish building designed by Frank Lloyd Wright. Huey would be playing on an island in the middle of a lake.

Bobbi, my date for the evening, is one of my best friends in the program. She is all heart, with an easy laugh, Down syndrome, and a wicked crush on Huey. She first met the songster when she was just 7 years old. She was sure that Huey would remember her.

Bobbi and I arrived a full three hours before the show was set to start, certain we would find decent seating. Bobbi's about 5 feet tall with poor eyesight, and wouldn't be able to see shit if we were stuck in the back. Unfortunately, sitting on my shoulders would be out of the question, because she weighs 200 pounds. When we got there, all of the seats were taken up with retirees in visors and their various beach towels, jackets, and backpacks that they had used to save seats for their brood. I had a hard time not going up to them and saying, "No savesies!" especially after circling the joint for 15 minutes with Bobbi to no avail.

The chivalry of people, or lack thereof, never ceases to amaze me. Bobbi cannot walk very well; she has a sort of circular gait like Billy Barty's. It's easy to see that she has to struggle to get around. Yet no one offered a chair for her to sit in, afraid that he would lose his valuable Huey-viewy. Either that or the two of us were invisible. I've found that it's easy to tune out people with disabilities, and most people do. We ended up standing on the lawn to the right of the stage.

Bobbi had brought her 25th-anniversary DVD that I had given her for her birthday, a couple of Huey tapes, and a Sharpie so the singer could sign them. I went to buy her a Coke and a Polish sausage before we settled in.

"No beans," she reminded me, our inside joke. Whenever we go anywhere—hamburger joint, Chinese restaurant, Mexican place— she always tells the waiter to "hold the beans." Apparently she had a bad reaction a while back, and has been vigilant about legumes in her diet ever since.

"Right," I replied as usual, "extra beans, comin' up."

As I walked to the sausage hut, my attention was immediately drawn to a middle-aged woman in the front row who was crying hysterically. She was clutching a CD, wearing mismatched, age-inappropriate clothes, and rocking back and forth. "They won't let me go up to the stage!" she yelled. "I won't see Huey!" She was telling this to anyone who would listen as if the people around her had known her all her life. She was retarded. Among the several hundred or so gathered for the concert, roughly 10 percent seemed to have some sort of developmental disability. Huey really is a phenomenon; it's not just with my clients.

A bunch of people from a group home had set up camp on the opposite side of the stage, laying out blankets and picnic food. Bobbi recognized some of her friends and waved. "Huuuuueyyyy!" they all yelled back. It was just like people who yell "Bruuuce!" at a Springsteen concert, only more retarded. In fact, Huey Lewis is a retarded version of Bruce Springsteen. Think about it. All of his songs are three-chord chug-a-lugs about working-class schlubs trying to make it through this crazy thing we call life. "Workin' for a Livin'," "Walking on a Thin Line," and "I Want a New Drug" are all slightly less soulful embodiments of the Springsteen ethos. (Communists will note that Huey himself is actually not middle class, but grew up privileged in Marin. He attended private schools and even went to college at Cornell.)

After waiting for a few hours, we finally heard what I knew was coming, the *thump-thump, thump-thump* that signals the intro to "Heart of Rock & Roll." (It's still beating, you see.) "Heart" was the perfect first song for a band celebrating its silver anniversary. Immediately everyone rushed in front of us and packed the front of the stage. Bobbi couldn't see anything, so I had to tell her that Huey looked great. Jesus, he did. He looked and sounded exactly the same. A group of developmentally disabled guys to our right were pumping their fists in the air and clapping out of time. Prim and proper Marin gentry in their folding chairs were tapping their feet.

And, inexplicably, teenage girls with bare midriffs and too much makeup were elbowing their way up front. Once again, no one seemed to pay attention to the short woman with Down syndrome who was trying desperately to see, but then again, the crowd mentality at concerts always turns all Darwin anyway, with the fittest pushing forward to the front while the weaker stay behind.

The island that the News were performing on had long since been sealed off and was packed to the gills with revelers. The band burned through all of its hits, like "Heart and Soul," "Do You Believe in Love," and an a cappella version of "It's Alright." Let's face it, whatever it is that makes a song "catchy," Huey Lewis & the News have it. Even I have to admit a certain affinity for the driving keyboards on "Workin' for a Livin'."

"I tell you, that guy can really play the harmonica," said Sean the next day. We never caught up with any of our friends; there were just too many people. I trusted that they were having just as good a time as the people who surrounded us.

Bobbi was ecstatic at the show, especially when I found a place for her to stand on a chair behind the stage where she could see everything up close. This angered a middle-aged woman with frosted lip gloss. "If you put her up there, no one will be able to see around her," she sneered, referring to Bobbi's ample roundness, doing so as if Bobbi weren't even there to hear it.

"I'll be sure and take that into consideration," I shot back at her with a look that would have melted the polar ice caps.

I helped Bobbi up onto the chair and put my arm around her. We sang along to "Doing It All for My Baby." The bitch-cake lady with the lip gloss had stomped off. Before long, a woman with an *American Idol* baseball hat and a speech impediment joined in on the song we were singing, followed closely by her male friend with something like Asperger syndrome.

Then it happened. Huey noticed us. He acknowledged our presence by strolling toward us and singing into Bobbi's camera lens.

"Huey!" she cried. "It's me!" He seemed to smile in recognition, then did a backward shuffle step to the center of the stage again.

That's when it hit me. My clients all have one thing in common: They want people to "see" them. Huey Lewis sees them. Huey Lewis has gone out of his way to spend time with them. Huey would have given Bobbi a chair if she needed one at a show, or he would have put her on his shoulders so she could see. I just knew it.

Before long Bobbi's knees were really starting to ache from all the standing, so we left during the encore. She never did get her DVD signed, but she didn't seem to care. There would be other opportunities.

"Oh, Huey," sighed Bobbi on the way home, "my Huey."

MIKE McGUIRK

Accept, *Balls to the Wall*

OK, the frontman is an Aryan dwarf who sings like a lurid cross between Bon Scott and Ronnie James Dio, and the song they are most famous for is called "Balls to the Wall," which is about—of all things—having your balls pressed against a wall. And the cover features a guy wearing nothing but a leather jacket and a Speedo. You do the math.

NICK WEIDENFELD

Dying in the Al Gore Suite

David Berman died November 19, 2003. It had been three years since he'd released his fourth album under the moniker Silver Jews. It had been more than four years since he'd published the critically celebrated book *actual air*, which, as contemporary American poetry goes, was incredibly popular. And it had been 16 years since he'd attended the University of Virginia, where he'd met Stephen Malkmus and started playing songs on friends' answering machines. "When I was 23 and he was 24, I got to watch [Malkmus] become famous," Berman remembered of Pavement's success. "There were these really cruel people that I knew, just unlikable people, and he would explain they were likable. I would say you don't know. You can't know! The only way you can judge a person is how they treat someone they have nothing to gain from. And everyone has something to gain from you."

Over the years, Berman grew increasingly dubious of fame—how celebrity and fandom confused fact and fiction, how it disconnected the self from reality. And though Malkmus, Steve West and Bob Nastanovich often played with the Silver Jews, and the Silver Jews were even misnamed "a Pavement side project," the Silver Jew himself did not become famous.

It was not that Berman was without fans. In 1992—the same year Pavement released *Slanted and Enchanted* (a title based on a Berman cartoon)—Kim Gordon included the Silver Jews' first recording *The Dime Map of the Reef* in her year's top 10 for *Rolling Stone*. During the nineties, Berman's fan base grew larger, cultish, and precious of his art. Yet he made few public appearances—mostly small poetry readings or academic lectures. He refused to tour. He rarely played live or spoke to the press. "I live on an island," he said, speaking of his house in suburban Nashville where he moved with his wife, Cassie, and dog, Miles. As he told his mother, "If they told me I couldn't leave the radius of six miles from my house, I really wouldn't care. There's nowhere I really want to go." Especially in the years following the release of his last album *Bright Flight* in 2001, Berman was not seen or heard from. For his fans, a Silver Jews album was not just a milestone in music, it was their only reminder that David Berman existed.

It's not surprising that no one heard what happened that morning, two years ago. How Berman woke up and overdosed. He'd overdosed twice before. This time, however, it was intentional.

He set out to take 300 orange Xanax, ten at a time, between house chores. He brushed his teeth, took ten pills. He made the bed, took ten pills. He showered. He walked Miles. He got the mail. Then he stopped remembering. What must've happened in the next few minutes or hours was that Berman grew incredibly romantic. Like the most honest but self-consciously histrionic moments of his writing, he stumbled to his closet and put on his wedding suit. He tried to scribble some final words. "Cassie I'm sorry. I can't take it anymore. I love you." Then he called his crack dealer. His dealer picked him up and brought him to the place he'd ostensibly been living the past year and a half.

The crack house also doubled as a music venue, and when Berman showed up, a vile Frenchman was performing, the kind of artist who shits on crosses. Against the Xanax, the crack was uplifting. Berman was like a plane just taking off, gaining enough energy to barely walk. Then his wife showed up. Cassie had found the suicide note and her husband gone. She'd called his dealer and was there to take Berman to the hospital. He screamed at her the whole cab ride. He'd never liked being told what to do and he did not want to be saved. Cassie couldn't make the hospital guards take him unwillingly, so she asked him what exactly he wanted to do. He told her to take him to the Loews Vanderbilt; the same hotel Al Gore holed himself up in November of 2000. Three years earlier, the Vice President had traveled to Nashville to make his concession speech, but when questions concerning the Florida ballot arose, Gore waited. And waited. He stayed in his room for two weeks while camera crews from around the world lined West End Avenue, hoping to get a shot of the VP passing his hotel window.

That's what Berman was thinking about when he approached the front desk. "Give me the Al Gore Suite," he demanded. He must've been a sight in the lobby of Nashville's nicest hotel, overdosing on crack and pills. But he was wearing a Brooks Brothers suit, and they gave him the room. Riding the elevator up to the eleventh floor, Berman laughed at the bellboy, "I want to die where the presidency died!" So he stumbled down the hall, opened the doors to the Al Gore suite, and did just that.

It was a year after his suicide attempt, after he'd woken up in the psychiatric ward of Vanderbilt hospital, that Berman decided he was dead. He explains all this, standing in his backyard, holding Miles tightly by his leash. It's raining, and the grass needs mowing. His mom and his wife are inside, tearing down old wallpaper. It feels like a scene stolen from *actual air*. He twists the dog leash around his hand tightly as he explains how disgusting and unethical it was that he'd left such a pathetically short note for Cassie. He tightens the leash even harder when he describes the feeling he had when he woke up in the hospital three days later. He pulled the tubes out of his body. He didn't want to be alive. But he was—at least he thought he was. And he was convinced that he should check in to the Hazelden Foundation, one of the country's oldest rehab centers. Two of his close friends had recently OD'd, and maybe it was sinking in because when he'd checked out of Hazelden 20 days later, he was happy. And he was sober. He bought a house in the suburbs and started going to temple more often. But it was at synagogue, during Yom Kippur service, that Berman realized he was dead and had been for over a year. Yom Kippur, the Day of Atonement, is a lonely, painful day. It is about regret and self-doubt, and for Berman, sitting there, praying and pining over years of sin and remorse, he concluded that all the good that had come to him over the last year couldn't have happened. After overdosing, he'd never woken up in Vanderbilt Psychiatric. He'd never been convinced to go to Hazelden. The last year was a lie. All that good stuff was fake, an illusion. He was dead.

Listening to Berman explain all this as he takes his daily walk down Tanglewood Drive, you ask yourself, How in the world does this happen to someone? How can a man fall this way?

There is a thread, a word, that runs through Berman's confession. He often describes himself as "solipsistic," and it is this quality, a lack of empathy—an inability to relate to the environment—that may explain Berman's predicament.

Suicide, they say, is the most selfish of acts. This may be true, but not in every case. There is a fine line between selfishness and solipsism, the latter more pathological than malicious. And Berman is solipsistic to the bone—someone who cannot comprehend a world outside of the self. This may be the real reason he doesn't tour. "I still believe in putting something out and not asking people to buy the record, then buy a ticket to my show and then buy a T-shirt and then a, like, copy of the show they just saw on CD," he says. "That's undignified to me." But don't his fans *want* to pay to see him perform? Would they mind a live recording? Finding that middle ground requires empathy, and Berman didn't tour. Instead, he retreated even further into himself. For a year and a half he had little contact with the world. Like Conrad's young apostle who's lost at sea—"But the truth was, he died from solitude, the enemy known but to few on this earth, and whom only the simplest of us are fit to withstand"—Berman, shacked up in a Nashville crack house, was losing "all belief in the reality of my action past and to come," as he put it.

A few weeks after that Yom Kippur service, after he concluded he was dead, Berman started seeing his Rabbi and studying the Torah. "I've never been from a certain group," he says of his recent attempt to connect with the world around him. "I've always reserved a space for myself where I'm unattached to any group, but the part of Judaism that I really take away, that means something to me, is the part about community." Identifying with a religious group is one way to battle solitude. Another way may be doing the press he had avoided his whole career.

This is the first extended interview Berman has ever given, and for the last three days straight Berman has talked, rarely pausing. The tone is confessional, as if Berman is finally giving something up, something he'd kept only to himself. But he's not doing press for himself. Without a hint of solipsism in explanation, he explains why he's doing interviews. "It has to do with trying to be a better person and not being such a fucking nightmare for everyone. It's about increasing the general happiness. Making it easier on people at [record label] Drag City. Making it easier on my wife. Making an effort." *Increasing the general happiness . . .*

There is a pad of paper next to Berman's TV that reads the same message. He must remind himself of this constantly, and it seems to be working. "I used to consider myself weak," he admits. "Up until a couple of days ago, I would've had to count myself as a loser by my own yardstick. At night when I have dreams, I lose almost always. I'm being betrayed, or left behind, or somehow losing the game. One of the first things I do when I wake up every day is remember that I'm not really losing."

Tanglewood Numbers, which Drag City will release this summer, is Berman's first album in almost five years. It doesn't sound like a

Silver Jews album. The self-pitying, self-defeating sound is gone. This is a rock album. It's confident and angry. And when you put it on and you hear Berman sing about smoking the gel off a Fentanyl patch and about how things do indeed get really, really bad, know that he's not talking about losing anymore. *Tanglewood Numbers* is not just a reminder to his fans that David Berman isn't dead; it's also a reminder to himself.

TOM EWING

THE BEATLES— "Eleanor Rigby"/ "Yellow Submarine" (Reached No. 1 on 20th August 1966)

Digression

For Christmas I got *Never Had It So Good*, the first part of Dominic Sandbrook's huge new history of Britain in the sixties. Here's what he says about the project:

> This book seeks to rescue "from the enormous condescencion of prosperity" . . . the lives of the kind of people who spent the 1960s in Aberdeen or Welshpool or Wolverhamption, the kind of people for whom mention of the sixties might conjure up memories not of Lady Chatterley, the Pill and the Rolling Stones, but of bingo, Blackpool and Berni Inns.

This leaves me both sympathetic and suspicious. Sympathetic because I agree the point of history writing isn't just to applaud the exciting stuff. Suspicious because the divide is too crude: my Dad, for instance, was an educated middle-class sixties young thing, but until they all closed his regular birthday treat would be a trip to the Berni Inn, and he only owned three pop albums. But then those pop albums included stuff by Dylan and the Doors. The point being that the division Sandbrook makes still gives the canon-sixties too much power, as if taking the Pill or listening to the Stones were magical things that put you beyond the reach of Bernis and bingo. For some people, surely they were; for many, all these things would have existed in jumbled parallel, fitted piecemeal into a life.

The list of sixties number ones works as a fossil record of one part of British pop-culture activity—going to shops, buying singles. It helps make the jumble real, "Green Green Grass of Home" next to "Good Vibrations", Dodd and the Stones in juxtaposition. But taking into account the jumble shouldn't blind you to the obvious—1966 is stuffed with hit records that wouldn't and couldn't have been made five years earlier. "Eleanor Rigby" may be one of them.

Review

One thread running through Ian MacDonald's book about the Beatles is the idea that they were particularly aware of the unique breadth and size of their global audience, and of what they could do with it. Gestures like "All You Need Is Love"—and maybe "Revolution 9"—only make full sense with this kind of scale as a background. Both sides of this single sound to me like a step in creating that audience—a deliberate reaching out to a wider context than the shining pop scene, a step into Berniland. "Eleanor Rigby" is also a clumsy, but moving, attempt to write about that context.

The brisk orchestral arrangement of "Eleanor Rigby" is tense and fussy, with something of Eleanor's spinsterish neatness: the strings bring to mind sewing, or sweeping the steps, one of those little daily things you do unthinkingly, or instead of thinking. They also sound a little like a horror film soundtrack, and "Eleanor Rigby" is cinematic, and it is about horror. It's Paul McCartney taking one of pop's smooth-rubbed words—"lonely"—thinking it through, and recoiling. His matter-of-fact delivery is superb: it creates a camera's-length distance ("Look at him working") that stops us taking the song as melodrama, but there's enough inflection on the song's central simple question to let us know that this isn't voyeurism, that the loneliness people end up in worries him.

(It worries him enough that on "When I'm 64" he goes and makes a gentle joke of it.)

(It worries me, too; but for a lucky meeting here or there I think I could finish up a Rigby. That's perhaps a reason I'm more sympathetic to Number 1s than records nobody knows.)

"Eleanor Rigby" remains neat to its end, so neat that you might forget that this question of the lonely people hasn't remotely been answered. For that you need the other side of the single, "Yellow Submarine".

The vocal in "Eleanor Rigby" squeezes tightly into a gap in its arrangement: "Yellow Submarine", on the other hand, is meant to be sung along to. For me, more so than "Yesterday", it's the Beatles song that feels like it's always existed, fished out of some collective unconscious in 1966. The air of antiquity comes from the marvellous wheezing production, Ringo's guileless vocals and the framing story. Of course it helped that I grew up in the 1970s when dungareed men sang "Yellow Submarine" all the time on kids' TV, though it's been adapted for football terraces too, testament to its broad appeal and basic virtues.

Intentionally or not, "Eleanor Rigby" and "Yellow Submarine" make a perfect pair. Crushing isolation as the flip of a song that values limitless community—"And my friends are all aboard / Many more of them live next door". The one set in a drably recognizable town, the other in a fantasy utopia. Recital and singalong. It strikes me that the idea of singing along—with friends, or in costume, or to mantras, or on a worldwide satellite link—is a thread in much later Beatles music. For me though, this big-hearted single is the best expression of what made them great.

GEOFFREY O'BRIEN

"Will You Love Me Tomorrow"

Always Magic in the Air:
The Bomp and Brilliance of the Brill Building Era
BY KEN EMERSON
Viking, 334 pp., $25.95

The relatively brief phase of pop music history entertainingly memorialized in Ken Emerson's *Always Magic in the Air* has been seen as a lull between two more notorious upheavals in taste. The music that took over America in the mid-1950s, whether billed as rock and roll, rhythm and blues, or under some other rubric, came overwhelmingly from the South—Georgia (Ray Charles, Little Richard, James Brown); Mississippi (Elvis Presley, Bo Diddley); Louisiana (Fats Domino, Jerry Lee Lewis); Texas (Buddy Holly, Roy Orbison); Missouri (Chuck Berry)—and represented a fusion of all those strains of blues and country and gospel that had been kept at bay by mainstream pop. This was the first wave of the heroic breakthrough that histories of rock love to celebrate; the second came in the mid-1960s with the near-simultaneous surge of the Beatles and the rest of the British Invasion, the Detroit sound of Motown and the Memphis sound of Stax-Volt, and the one-man revolution represented by Bob Dylan.

Ken Emerson's chosen moment falls in that interregnum during the late fifties and early sixties when New York City was the primary hit factory for the pop universe, when teenage romance still provided the essential theme for performers like the Drifters, the Shirelles, the Cookies, and Dion and the Belmonts, and when in somewhat mutated form the songwriting methods of Tin Pan Alley enjoyed a last moment of glory. Emerson focuses on a cluster of songwriters (among them Carole King, Burt Bacharach, Jerry Leiber, and Mike Stoller) who stood out among the many others who toiled in the Brill Building at 1619 Broadway between 49th and 50th Streets and its somewhat "more progressive" neighbor two blocks to the north, 1650 Broadway. These were long-established hives of music business activity high and low. The Brill Building housed ninety music publishers in 1958, in accommodations ranging from plush office suites to cubicles separated from each other by walls of frosted glass; 1650 Broadway had sixty-six. "Among its warren of offices," writes Emerson of the latter,

> you could find publishers to buy a song, arrangers to arrange it, and musicians and singers to record on cheap acetate in a bare-bones studio a "demo," or demonstration record, that served as the song's calling card and blueprint.[1]

The Brill Building world was the somewhat less opulent descendant of the original Tin Pan Alley described by Theodore Dreiser in his 1900 sketch "Whence the Song":

> In Twenty-seventh or Twenty-eighth Street, or anywhere along Broadway from Madison to Greeley Squares, are the parlors of a score of publishers, gentlemen who coordinate this divided world for song publishing purposes. There is an office and a reception-room; a music-chamber, where songs are tried, and a stock

room. . . . A salaried pianist or two wait to run over pieces which the singer may desire to hear. Arrangers wait to make orchestrations or take down newly schemed out melodies which the popular composer himself cannot play.[2]

There are scenes in Dreiser's compressed and eloquent account—one of the best things ever written about the music business—that would fit right into Ken Emerson's book, from dubious accounting practices and the exploitation of black performers discouraged from examining their royalties situation too closely to the desperate search for a hit on the part of once-successful songwriters. Emerson presents a further stage of the same centralizing process that had created Tin Pan Alley in the first place, with song pluggers and sheet music replaced by record promoters and demos, and with the "gentlemen who coordinate this divided world for song publishing purposes" becoming ever more enmeshed in the strategies of large entertainment corporations.

Even though rock and roll made popular music a much bigger business, in the late fifties and early sixties it was still a network of cottage industries. Because the major labels had mostly missed the boat at the outset, a host of smaller outfits quickly moved in to feed a teenage market that grew by the year. Mass culture was undeniably getting more corporate all the time, but rock was far from a monolithic machine; market research consisted of putting out a record and seeing what happened when it got played on the radio, with or without some greasing of the wheels by record promoters. By comparison with what was to come it was almost pastoral, if your idea of pastoral allows room for a good number of gangsters and con men to ply their trade. One of the fascinations of the Brill Building era is that the scale was still small enough and the relevant technologies still sufficiently rudimentary that one can survey, in retrospect, the whole process of how songs entered the culture as if it were happening in the backyard.

For New Yorkers, of course, it did happen in the backyard. The geography of *Always Magic in the Air* extends from its outposts on Broadway to encompass such vital spots as the Rivoli Theater ("the Parthenon of Times Square"); the Winter Garden, where *West Side Story* opened in 1957 to exercise its subliminal influence on youth culture; Lindy's; Jack Dempsey's Restaurant and Bar; the old Juilliard on 122nd Street, where Neil Sedaka studied Chopin études before he studied the Penguins' "Earth Angel"; the Apollo, where black music offered its challenge to the strictures of Top 40 teen pop; and the Palladium Ballroom, where songwriters picked up the subliminal Latin flavoring of records like the Drifters' "This Magic Moment" and "Sweets for My Sweet." (The geography spills over into lyrics: "Uptown," "On Broadway," "Up on the Roof," "Under the Boardwalk," "Spanish Harlem," and others ground these songs in the city of their making.)

Perhaps the publishers should have included a subway map to enable out-of-towners to track the songwriters and producers to their early homes in Williamsburg (Doc Pomus), Brighton Beach (Mort Shuman), Coney Island (Neil Sedaka and Howard Greenfield), East New York (Hal David), Flatbush (Barry Mann), East Flatbush (Ellie Greenwich), Washington Heights (Don Kirshner), Jamaica (Gerry Goffin), Forest Hills (Burt Bacharach), and Manhattan's Upper West Side (Cynthia Weil). All of them were Jewish, from backgrounds that ranged from that of Burt Bacharach, whose father was a nationally known authority on men's grooming, to that of Gerry Goffin, who as a child worked in the family basement helping to prepare mink stoles for his grandfather, a Russian furrier; some went to high school together; three of the major teams (King-Goffin, Mann-Weil, Barry-Greenwich) were married to each other.

This becomes very local history, with Neil Sedaka teaming up with his high school classmate Howard Greenfield and going out with Carol Klein (the future Carole King), whom he saw performing at a synagogue with her band (the indelibly named Co-Sines) and whom he eventually introduced—after she had already recorded a few demos with her Queens College classmate Paul Simon—to publishing whiz Don Kirshner, who had started out in the music business writing jingles for furniture stores (up in remote Washington Heights) with his neighborhood friend Robert Cassotto, the future Bobby Darin, before collaborating with Darin on a song they managed to sell the teen singing sensation Connie Francis, the former Concetta Maria Franconero of Newark. So local do things get that when, for example, the vexed question arises of whether Sedaka and King actually went out together, it is like being dropped into the middle of a spat in a high school hallway, with Sedaka claiming that King was "a Neil Sedaka groupie . . . she would neglect her schoolwork to write songs and chase me from bar mitzvahs to weddings," and King responding: "I went out on *one* date with him!"

On closer examination, the musical scene breaks down into neighborhoods, white and black, Jewish and Italian and Puerto Rican. It was within the music business that these neighborhoods would meet and—not always on equal terms—collaborate. Doc Pomus called the music he wrote for the Drifters "Jewish Latin," but the Drifters themselves were an African-American group whose members changed continually at the whim of their manager. In the words of Mike Stoller, "They got no royalties. It was almost . . . slave labor." There is much more to this story, but it is not the story that Emerson has chosen to tell: *Always Magic in the Air* has enough to do keeping its eye on the songwriters. Although Emerson talks quite a bit about the ways in which writers like Doc Pomus, Mort Shuman, and Leiber and Stoller broke away from their origins to immerse themselves in black music and culture—Leiber is quoted as saying, "I felt black. I *was*, as far as I was concerned"—we get only scattered hints of how things looked to the black performers responsible for so many of their hits.

The Brill Building sound clearly had not so much to do with ethnic confrontation or ethnic self-definition as with a fusion of influences.

In part this had to do with the same kind of smoothing out of differences that turned Joel Adelberg into Jeff Barry and Robert Ridarelli into Bobby Rydell. Yet the obverse of that homogenization was the radical alchemy it took to make a dissonant mix of styles and devices—blues, gospel, doo-wop, cha-cha, mariachi, lush string arrangements, echoes of Puccini or Irving Berlin, of country and western or Broadway musical—come out sounding as if all the elements naturally belonged together.

Something quite new was being manufactured out of the collision of apparently antithetical modes, and some ears had to adjust to the noise of it. It is hard now to imagine that when Atlantic executives first heard the overpowering string section and Brazilian-inflected kettledrum part that Leiber and Stoller had added to the Drifters' "There Goes My Baby" (1959), they were so perturbed that they delayed releasing it. Even the astute Jerry Wexler thought the record—which of course proved an enormous hit—"sounded like two radio stations."

The upshot was that local music came out sounding as if it came from everywhere and nowhere. The Mystics may have been a street-corner doo-wop group of Italian-Americans from Bensonhurst, but with that name and with the rough-hewn yet ethereal harmonies on their one hit "Hushabye" (written by Doc Pomus and Mort Shuman)—the kind of song that makes yearning and fulfillment seem more or less the same thing—they might have dropped down from another planet. Or perhaps that other planet was simply the America where all the movies and songs were set, the America of beaches and beauty contests and advertising layouts that bore only a tenuous relation either to the world where the songs were made or to the various worlds for which they provided an increasingly inescapable soundtrack.

The soundtrack was being created by people who had themselves been shaped by earlier phases of it. If Pomus and the team of Leiber and Stoller represented a slightly older generation whose influences were jazz and blues—they had written songs like

Ray Charles's "Lonely Avenue" and the not-quite-blues classic "Kansas City" before aiming for the teen pop market—their younger associates were still in their teens or just out of them; they were products of rock and roll and doo-wop, graduates of high school combos with names like the Linc-Tones and the Jivettes, capable of grasping what the radio audience wanted because they were it.

Some (like Sedaka and Carole King) had musical training; Sedaka's piano playing had been complimented by Arthur Rubinstein, and a recording engineer remarked of King's skill that "it was almost like architecture. . . . She would sing and do a demo that would be better than any of the records were." Others (like Sedaka and King's boss Don Kirshner) had less tangible gifts, as sketched by Jeff Barry: "He can't sing, he can't dance . . . but he sure has ears. That's the only part of his body that works musically, and that's the only part you need."

The distinctions between writing a song, arranging it, producing it, and performing it were often blurred at the sessions where the hits were coaxed into being. What it came down to was the capacity to focus all that skill, energy, and intuition on perhaps two minutes and forty seconds' worth of monophonic sound. The singer Tony Orlando's description of how these sessions tended to be run now seems an echo of a simpler age:

> Everyone was singing live. No overdubs. One, two, three takes, and that's it. No fixing. You better be in key, and you better be singing from the heart, 'cause this is a live show, baby!

Two brilliant control freaks—Phil Spector and Burt Bacharach—were already replacing that impromptu approach with their very different brands of perfectionism, but half the power of their best records (say, the Crystals' "He's Sure the Boy I Love" or Dionne Warwick's "Walk on By") comes from what they retain of that earlier, more flung-together sound.

Always Magic in the Air is rock history without crowd scenes, without riots or orgies: there are here no gaudy meltdowns, no public exhibitions of religious conversion or political rage, no smashed guitars or trashed hotel suites. Presumably the denizens of the Brill Building and 1650 Broadway enjoyed their share of parties and love affairs and drug experiences, but we hear relatively little about all that. What is on display is not Dionysian excess but the adrenaline-fueled rhythm of the working life in an era when, even in the pop music business, women wore conservative dresses and men wore jackets and ties. No one is likely to find much sustenance here who is not prepared to parse the significance of contracts, partnership deals, personnel changes, work schedules, right down to the redecoration of offices— along with (this being the music business) payola, appropriated copyrights, retaliatory cover versions, and unpaid royalties.

As for the writers themselves, there hardly seems time to get to know them; they're too busy. Indeed, there seems scarcely to have been time for them to get to know each other, or perhaps themselves. A fellow songwriter describes meeting Barry Mann (responsible for such epochal hits as "Uptown," "On Broadway," and "Walking in the Rain") as he dashed through midtown and congratulating him on having three songs in the top ten; Mann is said to have replied, "Yeah, but they're all on the way down. I gotta go do some demos." The Great Game of breaking into the *Billboard* charts generated an atmosphere of ceaseless competition among writers who watched each other's moves as attentively as they focused on their own work.

On the most basic level this could be a matter of literal transposition. Neil Sedaka, according to a colleague, "could take a song that was already a hit and write it sideways. . . . He would literally play the song that he was copying from and then start changing the chords." With someone like Sedaka, professionalism could be almost terrifying in its exactness. To listen again to "Breaking Up Is Hard to Do"—probably the most relentlessly cheerful song ever written on the ostensible theme of misery—is at once to admire its

delicately judged textures and Swiss-watch precision and to lay one-
self open to endless involuntary reprises as the song's hooks play
over and over again in the mind, well beyond the point of any emotional effect. At this remove, a song like "Calendar Girl" (1961)
seems to belong to no particular era but rather to circulate eternally
in a parallel universe of pure artificiality, in which the upbeat banality of its roll call of months—"March! I'm gonna march you down
the aisle . . . April! You're the Easter bunny when you smile . . . "—
acquires, by virtue of its musical setting, the durable charm of some
elegant toy representing the zodiac.

At the core of all that hustling and deal-making there is the music
that everyone wanted to create, direct, and profit from; music as a
source of power, a live element surrounded by people trying to
shape and control it, yet only ever submitting to that control par-
tially and temporarily. Work that at its lower limits could be mechanical, as writers struggled on deadline to come up with a
production number for the new Elvis movie or a B-side for the next
single by the "teen idol" Bobby Vee. But this led at unpredictable
moments into the longed-for astonishment: the magic phrase, usually some thoroughly ordinary phrase that might have been overheard on the subway—"take good care of my baby" or "save the last
dance for me" or "don't say nothin' bad about my baby" or "we
gotta get out of this place"—would join with the magic cadence or
the magic chord and suddenly seem predestined. If songwriters are
in awe of their own hits, it's because with all their professionalism,
all their fabled ability to produce a "sideways" replication of any hit
sound, they still don't really know where the songs come from or
where they're going.

The process by which the songs happen remains mysterious even
when the circumstances are laid out. Consider one day in the collaboration of Carole King and Gerry Goffin, in the fall of 1960: somehow, between Carole looking after their six-month-old baby and
taking Don Kirshner's call about how he needed a song for the

Shirelles by tomorrow morning and then going out to play mah-jongg, and Gerry doing his day's work at the chemical plant and meeting up after work with the bowling league and then coming home late to find Carole's message on the tape recorder along with the rudiments of her melody, somehow—separately, and then by the end of the evening working together—the two managed by 2:00 A.M. to produce a song called "Will You Love Me Tomorrow." The Shirelles recorded it, with the violin and cello backup that had been added as an afterthought, and it went to number one, the first record by a black female singing group ever to do that. The record has not stopped playing for forty-five years; a good enough day's work. The matter-of-factness of the process is belied by the slow-burning passions that the song has continued to release.

I was twelve years old when "Will You Love Me Tomorrow" came out, and I don't recall that it made the slightest impact on me, despite the fact that my father was playing it on his morning radio show on WMCA. At the time my musical tastes ran more to the epic strains of Prokoviev's *Alexander Nevsky* suite. The way the Shirelles and other recording artists of the Brill Building era made their presence known was sheer osmosis: their records became part of you before you had even become conscious of their existence as separate songs. The "wall of sound" that Phil Spector sought to achieve with his Wagnerian overlays on "Be My Baby" or "Walking in the Rain" was itself perhaps a way of summing up in a single record the total sound that all the pop songs made as they piled up one on another. Apparently made with simple ideas, simple rhythms, simple structures, they became complicated as they colonized the world into which they had been released.

You easily absorbed a song like "Will You Love Me Tomorrow" and it never left you. In high school, only a few years after its release, my friends and I already looked at it as an artifact of an era that had become almost quaint. We savored the euphemism of the lines

> *Tonight with words unspoken*
> *You say that I'm the only one*

as if their circumspection only underscored how liberated the world had all at once become. In fact the whole situation of the woman who has surrendered her virtue agonizing over whether she will now be abandoned—

> *Tonight the light of love is in your eyes*
> *But will you love me tomorrow?*

—seemed, at callow moments, like something out of an early Joan Crawford movie, if not a Samuel Richardson novel. But that hint of skittish condescension could not protect us from being moved, even overwhelmed, by the distilled pain in Shirley Owens's singing and by the somber restraint of the string accompaniment. On closer listening we came to admire the song in every detail of its making, the way words and music seemed bound so intimately together that they forced an awareness of every syllable, the melody slowing and pausing just before the rhyme word so as to instill a real suspense over how the lyric would resolve itself:

> *Is this a lasting [pause] tre-ea-sure*
> *Or just a moment's [pause] ple-ea-sure?*

Running parallel to one's actual teenage life there was this imaginary teenage life, in sung form, that had been like a presence on the horizon throughout childhood. Or, more properly, this imaginary teenage girl's life: the world of charm bracelets, diaries, and tears on the pillow that gave way to the more savage world of passions, jealousies, rebellions, and martyrdoms both figurative and literal that occur in songs like "My Boyfriend's Back," "Leader of the Pack," and "Johnny Get Angry." All this was a far cry from the high school

world of Archie comics: the war of girl against girl suggested in
"Judy's Turn to Cry" or "Don't Say Nothin' Bad About My Baby"
("He's good, / He's good to me, / So girl you better shut your
mouth"), the fusing of sex and religiosity ("Chapel of Love"), the
gaudy masochism that flourished in lyrics like "My baby's got me
locked up in chains" or "He hit me, and it felt like a kiss."

The girl group sound is (along with the Drifters' string of early
sixties hits) the most enduring legacy of the Brill Building moment,
encompassing everything from the exquisitely delicate Bacharach-
David vehicles for the Shirelles ("Baby It's You," "It's Love That Really Counts") to the armored onslaught of the Crystals, the
Ronettes, and others under Phil Spector's command. Carole King
and Gerry Goffin wrote some of their best songs for the Shirelles,
the Cookies, and the Chiffons. At the time those songs, strung together, seemed like some compressed and mutated kind of opera; after all these years, and all that has happened since in the music
business, they still do. The best of those songs refuse to settle down
into a respectable tranquillity. Their protagonists inhabited a sphere
which was not that of my friends, or (except symbolically or accidentally) of the writers who created the songs, or of the performers
who sang them. Perhaps they were not quite like anyone at all, yet
finally they were the most real of all: figures of imagination who
sang in the middle of everyone's life.

Within a few years everything in pop music would change, again,
with the British Invasion, Motown, and Bob Dylan the primary
agents of that change, and the songs of the Brill Building era would
become instant artifacts of an era supposed to be at once more
mechanized and more naive. Dylan would remark: "Tin Pan Alley is
gone. I put an end to it." (In his memoir he refers to the songs of
that period as "empty pleasantries.") At least one Brill Building lyricist, Gerry Goffin, would come to see his own lyrics as trivial in the
light of Dylan's revelation, with demoralizing results. All was now to
become more formally daring, more serious, more open to real experience, more socially engaged. As one looks back, it is clear that

the best thirty or forty records by the artists discussed in Ken Emerson's book were all of those things, with a good deal less pretension and certainly taking up less time than much of what followed.

Notes

1. The songwriters and performers covered in Emerson's book of course represent only a sliver of what was going on at the time, in New York and elsewhere. Among others, James Brown and Sam Cooke were in the process of redefining in their different ways both the sound of black pop music and the status of black performers.

2. Collected in Theodore Dreiser, *The Colors of a Great City* (Boni and Liveright, 1923).

GEOFF BOUCHER

Ex-Door Lighting Their Ire

Bob Dylan is singing "The Times They Are A-Changin'" in a television ad for healthcare giant Kaiser Permanente these days, and who could argue? With Led Zeppelin pitching Cadillacs, the Rolling Stones strutting in an Ameriquest Mortgage ad and Paul McCartney warbling for Fidelity Investments, it's clear that the old counterculture heroes of classic rock are now firmly entrenched as the house band of corporate America.

That only makes the case of John Densmore all the more intriguing.

Once, back when rock 'n' roll still seemed dangerous, Densmore was the drummer for the Doors, the band with dark hits such as "Light My Fire" and "People Are Strange." That band more or less went into the grave with lead singer Jim Morrison in 1971, but, like all top classic-rock franchises, it now has the chance to exploit a lucrative afterlife in television commercials. Offers keep coming in, such as the $15 million dangled by Cadillac last year to lease the song "Break On Through (to the Other Side)" to hawk its luxury SUVs.

To the surprise of the corporation and the chagrin of his former bandmates, Densmore vetoed the idea. He said he did the same when Apple Computer called with a $4-million offer, and every time "some deodorant company wants to use 'Light My Fire.'"

The reason? Prepare to get a lump in your throat—or to roll your eyes.

"People lost their virginity to this music, got high for the first time to this music," Densmore said. "I've had people say kids died in Vietnam listening to this music, other people say they know someone who didn't commit suicide because of this music. . . . On stage, when we played these songs, they felt mysterious and magic. That's not for rent."

That not only sets the Doors apart from the long, long list of classic rock acts that have had their songs licensed for major U.S. commercial campaigns, it also has added considerably to Densmore's estrangement from former bandmates Ray Manzarek and Robbie Krieger, a trio that last set eyes on one another in the Los Angeles County Superior Courthouse last year.

"Everyone wanted him to do it," said John Branca, an attorney who worked on the Cadillac proposal. "I told him that, really, people don't frown on this anymore. It's considered a branding exercise for the music. He told me he just couldn't sell a song to a company that was polluting the world.

"I shook my head," Branca said, "but, hey, you have to respect that. How many of your principles would you reconsider when people start talking millions of dollars?"

Densmore relented once. Back in the 1970s, he agreed to let "Riders on the Storm" be used to sell Pirelli Tires in a TV spot in England. When he saw it, he was sick. "I gave every cent to charity. Jim's ghost was in my ear, and I felt terrible. If I needed proof that it was the wrong thing to do, I got it."

Since then, the animus between the drummer and Manzarek and Krieger has intensified, including a bitter dispute over naming rights.

In August, Los Angeles County Superior Court Judge Gregory W. Alarcon ruled that Manzarek and Krieger could no longer tour together as the "Doors of the 21st Century." The pair, with former Cult singer Ian Astbury handling Morrison's vocal duties, were in

Canada at the time and grudgingly switched their marquee to the acronym "D21C."

Densmore had filed the suit in 2003 to block the neo-Doors from using any permutation of the old band's name. In this battle, he was joined by the Morrison estate, which is the late singer's parents and the parents of his late girlfriend, Pamela Courson.

An audit is underway to determine how much money Krieger and Manzarek must turn over from their two years of touring with their old band name. The touring grossed $8 million, court documents show.

Manzarek said the view that Densmore was selflessly protecting the Doors legacy was laughable.

"John is going to get about a million dollars for doing nothing," Manzarek said. "He gets an equal share as us, and we were out there working. A free million bucks. That's a gig I'd like."

Manzarek, whose keyboards strongly contribute to the singular sound of the Doors, said his old friend should join the neo-Doors. "He should come and play drums with us," Manzarek said, "not fight us at every turn."

Even if Densmore is loath to tour and disdainful of Astbury playing the late Morrison ("Nobody can fill those leather pants"), Manzarek said his old mate should allow Doors hits to be used in tasteful commercials that could add flicker to the band's pop-culture memory. He pointed out that Zeppelin and U2 recently relented in their long holdouts against ad licensing and that there was hardly a stigma these days to the practice.

"We're all getting older," said Manzarek, the band's eldest member, now 66. "We should, the three of us, be playing these songs because, hey, the end is always near. Morrison was a poet, and above all, a poet wants his words heard."

Perhaps more years of life would have changed his view, but in 1969 it was quite clear that the poet of the Doors did not want to be a pitchman.

The Doors had formed in 1965. As the decade was ending, they were hailed in some quarters as the "Rolling Stones of America." An advertising firm came to the band with an offer: $50,000 to allow their biggest hit, "Light My Fire," to be used in a commercial for the Buick Opel.

Morrison was in Europe and his bandmates voted in his absence; Densmore, Krieger and Manzarek agreed to the deal. Morrison returned and was furious, vowing to sledgehammer a Buick on stage at every concert if the commercial went forward. It did not.

In November 1970, the lesson learned from the Buick fiasco was put in writing. The Doors members agreed that any licensing agreement would require a unanimous vote. Even before that, the band had agreed that the members would share equally in all music publishing rights, an arrangement that set them apart from most bands.

Those agreements also set the stage for Densmore to be a human handbrake that again and again stops the Doors profit machine from speeding down new avenues.

"There's a lot of pressure, from everyone," Densmore said recently with a weary sigh. "Pressure from the guys, the manager, the [Morrison] estate."

He was sitting in the back-house office of his Santa Monica home. The walls are covered with photos and newspaper clippings, among them a framed Morrison poem about the vantage point of man beyond the grave. Among the lines:

> No more money
> no more fancy dress
> This other kingdom seems by far the best. . . .

Morrison is dead but hardly forgotten. Just the opposite, his popularity has surged in the years since his heart gave out.

There was the one-two punch of the 1979 release of the film "Apocalypse Now," with its signature moments using the band's music, and the 1980 publication of the band tell-all book "No One Here Gets Out Alive" by Jerry Hopkins and Danny Sugerman. In 1991, another revival was stirred by Oliver Stone's movie "The Doors." Since that film's release, 14 million Doors albums have been sold in the United States alone.

Those album sales combine with the money generated by radio airplay, merchandising and the other royalty streams to put steady deposits into the bank accounts of the surviving members and the Morrison estate.

Densmore said that the money coming in should relieve pressure on the band to drift into areas that would trample the legacy. "When Ray calls, I always ask him, 'What is it you want to buy?'"

Still, there are no bigger paydays these days available for classic-rock outfits than the low-sweat licensing deals for television commercials and the warm embrace of the concert road tour. That was underscored last year when Manzarek and Krieger alleged that Densmore had committed a "breach of fiduciary duty" to the Doors partnership. Basically, the argument was that the money now was so good that Densmore couldn't reasonably say no.

When Cadillac offered $15 million last year, the money made Densmore dizzy ("More money than any of us have made on anything we've ever done," he said), but he was resolute. "Robbie was on the fence; Ray wanted to do it," Densmore said. "All of it made me think about this book I want to write. It's about greed."

Manzarek, on the other hand, describes the car commercial in tie-dyed hues. "Cadillac said we could all fly out to Detroit and give input as they start putting together their hybrid models and the way they would be presented to the public. . . . Artists and corporations working together, that's the 21st century. That's the true Age of Aquarius. But John's ego wouldn't let him see it was a good thing to do."

In the end, Cadillac held on to the motto "Break Through" but used a different dark anthem—the commercial, now in heavy rotation, features Zeppelin's frenetic 1972 single "Rock and Roll."

Cadillac's eight-figure offer was enough to coax the band to plunge into the advertising profit stream.

When Nike used the Beatles' recording of "Revolution" for a sneaker ad two decades ago, there was widespread criticism. The hubbub quieted when the commercial was retired after one year. Nowadays, the debate is largely muted. The new take? Holding out is bad for music.

"Using your music in the modern landscape is not selling out; if it's done right, it's giving it new life," said Amy Kavanaugh, an executive vice president at Edelman, the Los Angeles public relations and marketing firm that has worked with Starbucks on the coffee merchant's extensive branding efforts with music.

Even among the classic-rock purist audience, there is a shift in expectation. Pete Howard, editor in chief of *Ice* magazine, a music publication tailored to audiophiles and intense rock music collectors, not only thinks that the Doors should take money for the songs of the past, he believes that they are risking their future if they don't.

"They get a gold star for integrity, but they are missing a train that is leaving the station," Howard said. "Advertising is no longer a dirty word to the Woodstock generation, and in fact, in this landscape, the band will find that if it relies on people who hear the music in films, on radio in prerecorded formats, that with each decade their niche among music fans will narrow. It's advertising—with its broad audience and ubiquity—that gets new ears."

If Densmore is a dinosaur, he is not the last surviving one. Bruce Springsteen and the Eagles continue to say no to commercials. So do Neil Young and Carlos Santana. But all of them still pull in concert revenues that make that choice far easier. Densmore himself points out that if he were poor he might make a different choice.

But his stance against commercialization has won a chorus of support from the true believers of rock. In the *Nation*, Tom Waits wrote a letter in praise of Densmore: Corporations "suck the life and meaning from the songs and impregnate them with promises of a better life with their product. Eventually, artists will be going onstage like racecar drivers covered in hundreds of logos."

Waits has since learned that holding out isn't necessarily effective: He is suing General Motors for using what he describes as a Waits sound-alike in its European car commercials. Which make and model is involved? The Buick Opel, the same car that led Morrison to slam shut the band's corporate flirtations.

"Is it that they just didn't learn or they just don't care? I don't know," Densmore said, shaking his head. "Maybe I'm the one who is just out of touch with the times."

Now he waits to see if his old bandmates will appeal the court decision banning the use of the Doors name for their concert tours. For the time being, Manzarek has said that the band will continue on with the name Riders on the Storm. Densmore said he would not dispute them on that. Manzarek said the fans and reviews have been great, and Astbury has the same "dark, shamanistic, powerful, Celtic-Christian, mystical" vibe as his old friend Morrison. Manzarek said the group will soon record a new studio album.

"It doesn't matter what we call it, it's still Robbie and I together playing 'Light My Fire' and 'Love Me Two Times.' John should come and play and let us celebrate and keep this music alive," Manzarek said. "Look, what do I say to the cynics? I would like to play with Jim Morrison again. But you know what? I can't call him. I'm sorry. He's dead. He's busy. He's in eternity."

Densmore said he tires of the fighting.

So what about that invitation from Manzarek?

"I would love to play with the Doors and play those songs again. I would. And I will play again as the Doors. Just as soon as Jim shows up."

DAVE TOMPKINS

Permission to 'Land

If *What the Fuck?* had a face, it'd be Jay-Z that night at New Hit Factory Studios, North Miami Beach. His disbelief is a pound on the back to Tim "Timbaland" Mosley, the producer sitting behind the Triton keyboard. Surprising Shawn Carter, who has eyes in the back of his rhymes, is a feat in itself. Next to Ghostface borrowing Slick Rick's gold for a Beyoncé duet, this is one of the most goggled scenes in Jay-Z's *Fade to Black* DVD—the birth of "Dirt Off Your Shoulders." It allows a rare glimpse at Timbaland in action—rap and pop's most sweated producer bouncing around the studio, animated and chubby, taking slugs from a plastic jug of pink Crystal Light.

If *What the Fuck?* had a face, it'd be anyone who sees Timbaland a year and some lifestyle change later, sitting in Hit Factory Studio C, 100+ pounds MIA, buff, and training for Mr. Miami, a body-building contest in South Florida where he now lives.

A new Beat Club artist, rapper John Doe, slides through the room with a crack about Timbaland action figures. Across the couch, dupa fly Atlanta singer Ms. Keri whistles the belly dance jingle from "Big Pimpin'."

The lounge-area TV shows "The Potion" video with Ludacris yawping all over Tim's drunken-owl beat, one that a confused Jigga had passed on that night in Miami. "The Potion" is followed by a

Caress soap ad featuring LL and the ladies who love him. They're giggling to "Headsprung," a Timbaland track with enough bass to vibrate the entire building down to the Florida Keys.

LL, who once put a muscle-bound man's face in the sand, was the main inspiration for Mosley's new gym habit. That and Mosley seeing his former 332-pound self in Jigga's retirement DVD. Is it more of a marvel that 2004's dopest beat is on a soap commercial, or that Tim looks like he could benchpress the Beat Club studio bus sitting out in the parking lot?

"I did 'Headsprung' on the bus," says the 33-year-old from Virginia Beach. "I did it in the headphones and zoned out that way. LL was happy with it." Timbaland's beat protégé, Nate "Danja" Hills, was on the bus when "Headsprung" was first hatched. "It was hurting my chest. You thought your head was gonna pop off! That bass was crushing you, but you could hear all the other sounds too."

Costing 1.1 million dollars, the 45-foot Beat Club bus is tricked out with a fully operational studio, vocal booth, cheetah-print pillows, customized Beat Club rug, mirrors on the ceiling, and a marbleized kitchen built to specifications of Tim's personal protein chef. Catering to work and workout regime, the bus kitchen fights the late-night Denny's fat farm.

"The kitchen is as important as the studio," says Rick Frazier, Tim's manager, bus designer, and occasional bus driver. "He's on a strict diet. Before we really got stationed down here in Miami, we traveled between New York, L.A., and Virginia. We'd spend, like, four months in each city and keep moving. Tim would go back there, sleep, do a new track, and before you know it, it's on somebody's album. Tim would get a room at the Trump Hotel but stay on the bus. Only go into the hotel to shower. That's how much he was working at one time."

Sprawled on the couch, Tim nods "mm-hmm," exhausted after his two daily workouts.

He feels the move to Miami, a town known for hedonism, scams, and ghetto bass, has done wonders for his well-being. "I never really moved, I just bought a house. It made me feel better. My sound is always changing up in my head anyway. But it made me think better, by being in the sun and giving me the feel of L.A., New York, and Virginia. I love it here. I work out twice a day and then spend all night in the studio."

This tireless work ethic originated in '94, when Missy Elliot first brought Mosley to Devante Swing's mansion in Rochester, New York, where the eccentric Jodeci producer hosted an R&B commune. "They were nobodies," explains Jimmy Douglass, Timbaland's long-time engineer. "It was Timbaland, Ginuwine, Missy, Tweet, and Player. We had no place to go, so we were in the studio the whole time. Everybody else would leave and I'd start working with Tim. He had an ASR-10 all day down in the basement with headphones, collecting shit, waiting for his turn. He'd always catch me before I'd leave at 3:00 A.M. He'd go, 'Where you goin'? I wanted to do this track.'"

Having recorded Led Zeppelin and Hall & Oates, Douglass didn't take any bullshit from Devante's house of young egos. "Our arrogances were at work. One night, Tim says, 'You think you know everything, don't you? I'm gonna show you what good sound is!' I'm sitting there [*rolls eyes*] like, 'Oh really. Okay, play the damn thing!' And he played this record, two beats, and I went, '*Black Heat!*' And he goes, '*How you know that, man?!*' I said, 'See, you young guys don't bother to read who you stealing from!' Tim turns the record over. 'Produced and engineered by Jimmy Douglass.' That was the beginning. I said, 'We don't need to talk no more. Let's get to work.'"

While paying uncredited dues on various Jodeci hits, Mosley also learned to quickly hook up tracks inside headphones. "That's really a gift and an art," says Douglass. "Most kids gotta hear the big boom to create. What Tim learned in Rochester, by being deprived of studio time, was he had to go fast and put it together by himself in his headphones. When his moment came, he'd have four or five things done and he'd be hearing them on big speakers for the first time."

"When I do a beat, I usually start with my mouth," says Mosley. "I build around it. I do it then and there in the booth." Danja explains further: "I've seen him do guitar sounds with his mouth. *Weeaaarrroowww!* Like a wah-wah pedal. You'd think somebody played it, but it's him in the booth doing it with his mouth. He'd do choir sounds with his mouth, scream out effects, whatever."

Jimmy Douglass was also impressed with Tim's unique ear and avant-beatboxing. "That's a key asset—his amazing ability to reproduce sound with his mouth. Listen to [Justin Timberlake's] 'Cry Me a River.' That's no ordinary beatbox! Even when he's talking, he makes these crazy sounds. When he talks about movies, he picks up on the craziest shit. There's a movie [*A Perfect World*] with Kevin Costner and some kid. Costner's name is Butch, and the kid walks in the field and says [*real nasally*], 'Buuutch! Buuuutch!' Every time Tim hears that he cracks up. He's like, 'Listen to how the kid's saying it!'"

Timbaland's ear for subtle nuance forced beat-nerds to comply with Hot 97. There could be a horse's laugh or a burp stashed inside a platinum hook. "It's the weird stuff a lot of people don't pick up on," explains Danja. "Those little things take over. The ghosts got you."

Mindful of clearance costs, the "ghosting" technique involves playing over the original sample and then extracting it, leaving rhythmic aftereffects in the mix. "That creates that space," Timbaland shrugs. "I don't really sample. Sometimes, when somebody gives me remixes, I do it to the original beat and add another beat around the original beat. Then take the other beat out and put my beat through."

While headphone-bound in Rochester, Timbaland also stumbled upon "the double beat," the first big break of a signature that'd later be cloned all over radio. Jimmy Douglass was baffled when he first heard it, thinking someone had tripped over the drum machine. "Nothing sounded like that! I went, 'What the fuck is that?' He said, 'It's something dope. You'll see.' I was like, 'What the fuck are you doing?' It was like a skip in the record." Tim chuckles, adding, "Everybody bit the double-beat, N'SYNC, Janet. It changed the sonic tempo of radio."

The double beat would make Ginuwine's "Pony" a hit. The rattlesnake hi-hat was a perversion of the kick drum, another radio mainstay, while the voice effect mimicked a frog with indigestion. "'Pony' was made about a year before the world saw it," says Douglass. "It was sitting, done, as a demo up in Rochester. I have a couple of things he never used—the shit is *fire*. Devante kept a lot of it."

In 1996, Timbaland and Douglass left Camp Jodeci and went demo shopping. Tim was broke and Douglass figured he could get him some quick work doing remixes. "I know about him but the world doesn't," says the veteran engineer. "It's like the Manhattan Project. Nobody knows what the fuck we'd been doing!" So Douglass took Tim's bag of stutter beats, "Pony" included, to Michael Kaplan at Sony/Epic, who immediately grabbed it and got Mosley some work through an album deal with Ginuwine.

Douglass remembers the Ginuwine and Aaliyah projects happening simultaneously, an R&B double-beat double whammy. Recorded for the *Dr. Dolittle* soundtrack, Aaliyah's "Are You That Somebody?" was cut in one night. Douglass was worried. "It was getting late and we're in a rush, trying to mix it, and then Tim puts the fucking baby on there. I was like, '*What is that??*' Before the baby, it was a record. When he put the baby on, I was like, 'Oh man, that is the *stupidest* thing I ever heard!' Then Tim said, 'Wait, one more thing.' The last thing he did before finishing, he went in the booth and went, 'Dirty South, can y'all really hear me? East Coast, feel me!' I was like, 'You sure you want to ruin this record *with that?*'"

Timbaland was sure. The dance floor was sure. That summer of 1998, the ladies swooned over the baby noise and the fellas Dirty Southed themselves blind. Douglass laughs. "I'm not from the South, so I didn't get it. But once again Tim had that ability to know exactly what goes on there."

Missy Elliott, who'd worked on the Aaliyah projects, wanted some of that double bump for her breakout single, 1997's "The Rain." Suddenly, everyone from indie rock snots to the hip-hop frownies were falling for this oddball who wore hydraulic Hefty bags and used her voice percussively, placing hiccup rhymes and adlibs between Timbaland's drops and pauses. "Him and Missy were totally in the other world," marvels Danja at their chemistry. "No one can understand how they work together. It's weird and it comes out hot."

While beats for Missy and Ginuwine gave Virginia an identity distinct from New York, Timbaland's first group, Surrounded By Idiots, had Magoo sounding like Q-Tip on Dristan. "That was me, Magoo, a best friend of mine Larry, and Pharrell. It sounded more like some Tribe Called Quest stuff. Some Virginia people wanna be from New York. I'm like, 'Hell, we from the South, dude.' That's one thing that's buggin' me out. Sometimes we do ass-backwards things. People need to realize that's what we are. We borderline from New York and D.C., right down the middle, but, still, we country. We do our own interpolation."

This interpolation would go Deep South on future Timbaland collaborations with Bubba Sparxxx and Petey Pablo. The outlaw moonshine guitar on their "Gunline" duet was a slow-tempo departure from Missy's dance-floor robotics. "Dude [Petey] is the truth. I had to fool with him," says Tim. "I played that guitar. I thought about slavery when I did that. Some old-timey stuff."

Petey Pablo's North Carolina anthem "Raise Up" turned T-shirts into helicopters and took world music way out to the Southern sticks where the buses don't run. Staccato acoustic plucks, sampled from Egypt, went twang for twang with the rust-bucket South. "I had to clear that acoustic sound. That's that arpeggiation. Nobody was doing that back then. I also have a keyboard that has Arabic strings."

"You can tell by the strings on 'Raise Up,'" adds Douglass. "They use those in-between-notes that we don't use over here.

They have tones in between our tones that they find. That creates that *errrrrwwwwee.*" In Jay-Z's farewell DVD, one can find a similar *errweeee* on Tim's face, a conductor's contortion, as he tweaks yet another batch of Arabic strings.

Of course, hip-hop was familiar with dope international beats, from Bambaataa playing Japan's Yellow Magic Orchestra to Coldcut's now legendary use of Ofra Haza on Eric B. & Rakim's "Paid in Full" remix. Yet, as a devout Southern Pentecostal sampling from the Islamic faith, Timabaland took it to the bazaar. When "Big Pimpin'" blew up in summer of 2000, every jeep in New York was bumping Egyptian superstar Abdel Halim Hafez without even knowing it. Producers like Dre, Just Blaze, and DJ Quik started sprinkling pyramid dust on their tracks.

"[Tim] played me the original record," recalls Danja. "He could've made five more [hits like] 'Big Pimpin'" from that one song. There's so much goin' on in Arabic music. You don't have to sit and wait for the break." Jimmy Douglass adds, "He happened to grab it from the Elvis of Arabia or something [Elvis of Egypt, actually]. He didn't know this. He just had a bunch of records and that one hit him like that. So he had the ability to hear the good shit and this [Elvis of Egypt] is the fucking motherfucker. It's a carnival, good-time-feeling song. I was like, 'You motherfuckers are actually trying to put *pimpin'* in a hook on the radio?? Good fucking luck!'"

While "Big Pimpin'" had thieved the Pharaoh's tomb, Tweet's "Oops (Oh My)" was an African thump with digital coos, a nod to the '80s British electro of Art of Noise. A few continents over, Missy's 2001 hit "Get UR Freak On" spiked Henny with Hindu. "The Indian scale is totally different from our music," says Tim, scratching his head. "I like the tablas and all the different sounds. That style with the strings, that all came from me. People say my music sounds like jungle. I never heard it till after all that stuff came out." Jimmy Douglass laughs, adding, "I've known everything the man listens to, and he doesn't have a damn jungle record in his collection. We don't know what the fuck jungle records *are.*"

Timbaland claims to be recordless. "I don't have any records. None. All I have is a bunch of China music, Arabic music. I don't have nothing from the past. Everything—France, Brazilian music. Everything. I like all that type of music, because the way hip-hop is going now is boring. I'm about to break it out with this new Japanese sound."

As other beatsmiths tried to pimp the Punjabi vibe, Timbaland went halftime brass and mimicked a Southern marching band on Lil' Kim's "The Jump Off." "Of course, I do something first then everybody wants to come out and bite. Then you had Destiny's Child—can't keep up. Try do what I do. Can't do it. 'The Jump Off' was a hot record. I just wasn't too fond of the hook. I think she was careless. It worked though."

"Timbaland loves marching bands," smiles Douglass. "He keeps talking about the big bass drum from the schools. If you listen to all the beats—*bomp-boom-boom*—if you think about it and listen to what he's doing. That's what he's emulating, but he's emulating it in hip-hop. It also creates all that space. Our records have bottom. That's what we do."

"I changed the sound of radio three different times," Tim says. "I had everybody biting me. I changed the whole sonic tempo. Only three people did that. Dre and Teddy Riley."

While Timbaland idolizes Dre, it's Pharrell Williams with whom he shares an affinity for '80s new wave and Prince. "I like Pharrell. We think alike. I like all that ['80s music]. Prince had the style and the music. Prince walks out with his butt cheeks out. People didn't know how to take this guy because he had the girls too. I like Devo and that Human League shit."

Heavy-lidded on the couch at the New Hit Factory, Tim hums the warbled synth riff from Human League's 1982 hit "Keep Feeling (Fascination)." Another potential candidate for the Beat Club chop shop. And while he wants to collaborate with Coldplay, Maroon 5, and Ricky Martin, rather than Ja-Rule, heads will be relieved to know that Timbaland has something nasty in store for the new Redman album as well as longtime colluder Missy Elliot.

"Everybody can't rhyme on my beats. My rhythm is different from what people hear. There's this one girl I'm dying to work with that's from London. Her name is M.I.A. She's hard, boy. She's so dope. I need to get with her bad. I'm into all that type of stuff. That brings somethin' out of me."

At the Hit Factory, Juvenile then pops his head in the door and asks Tim when can he get some of that heat? Not that he's in the middle of a Scott Storch session next door or anything. Heh. In saunters a quiet Texan named 6Two, a vet who appeared on Dre's *Chronic 2001*. 6Two and Attitude are another Beat Club project on deck. They swig 22s of beer while Timbaland's chef Rafael gives advice on a strict protein diet that does not include 22s of beer.

Gym memberships are now a Beat Club requirement. Fortunately, no one is expected to bench press 406 and take out 50 Cent in a man-boob battle. Timbaland, however, is 14 weeks away from a Speedo and the Mr. Miami Contest. His trainer Jose Garcia thinks the Front Double Bicep is the winning pose. Of course, Timbaland will be producing the music for his routine. Maybe with a beatbox flex.

KEVIN WHITEHEAD

Chops: Upstairs, Downstairs with Art Tatum (and Monk)

Chops—technique, that is, in jazz parlance—a term singular in concept, but plural in construction. As in, "Her chops are up." Or, "He'd better get his chops together." Or—more to the point of this discussion—"They're too chopsy for me," that is, drunk on their own technique.

Jazz is a technical music, whose early development was marked by steady improvements in instrumental prowess—measured in terms of range, speed, articulation, tonal nuance and the like. But musicians can acquire too much technique, become chopsbound the way a weightlifter can become musclebound. Think of your least favorite '70s fusion guitarist playing some superfast solo crammed with synthetic scales and ever-shifting odd meters and signifying nothing.

Still, it's exhilarating to hear a musician with fantastic chops who manages to keep all that technique in check. Take, for instance, the restlessly flashy Art Tatum (1909–1956), the vision-impaired wizard of Toledo who made all the other piano greats nervous, and even now can lead keen admirers to the brink of overstimulation. As the gleefully chopsy Dutch keyboardist Guus Janssen has commented, "If I put on an Art Tatum record, I'm knocked out as a piano player after one second. We go upstairs, downstairs, then we go up again. It's beautiful, but it must have been exhausting to spend all night in a club listening to Tatum." Pick some quick solo performance by Tatum—it barely matters which, but you could try his "Limehouse Blues" from *Gene Norman Presents* or "Indiana" from *Solo Masterpieces Vol. 3* for starters—and you can hear what Janssen means. (Not that Tatum's slow and medium pieces don't afford him plenty of chances to leap into ear-popping double-time.) Tatum's key inspiration was pianist Fats Waller, with whom he shared a few virtues: buoyant rhythm, ceaseless momentum and a bright keyboard attack, all of which reinforce a feeling that nothing made him happier than taming the wild piano. And behind all that, explicitly or fleetingly glimpsed, was the left hand's bobbing eighth notes, shuttling between the bass jabs and mid-keyboard chords that gave the stride piano style its name.

Stride had its roots in ragtime's left-right-left-right oompah, but Tatum (like Waller) had entered the modern world, leaving ragtime's regular patterns far behind. His substitute harmonies and interpolated extra chords (on, say, "Tenderly") look ahead to Charlie Parker's bebop. As saxophonist Sean Bergin once put it, "Ideas are chops, too."

Tatum's always in motion. A downward glissando from the right hand might meet a southpaw gliss coming the other way. Crashing chords bump up against wild scalar runs. He may pop between frantic stride patterns and a looser, more open bass line, a favorite gambit of Earl Hines. (You can hear a lot of Hines, and Waller, in Tatum's "Moonglow," from his epic series of solos recorded for Norman Granz in the early '50s: a trove for chops freaks.) And for someone who could make the strings ring, Tatum also deployed a light touch that could let him fly across the ivories. His style's a riot of varied ploys competing for your attention, an approach somewhere between T. S. Eliot's shard-like poetry and vintage *Mad* magazine strips, spilling out of their panels.

It's the kaleidoscopic nature of a Tatum showpiece that bowls you over: the three-ring circus for two hands. He keeps up a driving rhythm even as he tinkers with the tempo and radically alters the texture from one phrase to the next, while somehow keeping the melody before your ears. What some folks resist in Tatum is the same thing novice jazz fans sometimes hold against Charlie Parker: he makes all the hoopla sound too easy—as if the giddy joy of indulging in sheer virtuosity was a bad thing.

Curiously, Tatum's heirs include not only show-horses like the dazzling-but-rarely-deep Oscar Peterson, but also the stubborn anti-virtuoso Thelonious Monk, whose flat-fingered keyboard attack is all wrong for fast frilly flights, but whose music can resemble an X-ray photo of a Tatum solo: just the bare bones. Monk makes the same evocative, fitful use of stride bass figures, and (on solo pieces especially) frequent recourse to a pet Tatum move, a skittering, broken-field descent spanning several octaves. You can hear their kinship on some of Tatum's ballads: in the plodding pace of "Someone to Watch Over Me," and the impacted chords that kick off Ellington's "Just A-Sittin' and A-Rockin'." But compare Tatum's take on "Just a Gigolo" with any of Monk's several solo versions. Next to Tatum, his stammering momentum is even more striking: a clue to why many folks who heard Monk early on decided he couldn't really play.

Why would Monk pointedly evoke a pianist whose monster chops highlight his own shortcomings, in a tradition where tribute-by-imitation is often a loser's game? Partly, I'd say, it was the delight Monk took in confounding expectations about virtuosity by making harmonically dense and advanced playing sound like an endless series of ham-fingered flubs: his deliberate hammering is a critique of gratuitous flash. But close inspection of Monk's stripped-down solos reveals his own homemade technical innovations, like his ability to "bend" notes on piano: he'd strike one key and, while holding it, quickly strike and release the next highest note. The lower one will appear to swerve toward and away from it. ("Reflections" from *Alone in San Francisco* makes pivotal use of that technique.)

Monk's klutzy, anti-chops persona works as an aesthetic choice, through a curious process of subtraction: he throws traditional technical baggage over the side, the better to float above everyday stylists. Somewhere in there is an implicit appreciation of Tatum's piano style: the bounce under all the filigree is what counts. Fancy is fine, but momentum is all.

ROBERT CHRISTGAU

The First Lady of Song

As with Frank Sinatra, as with Aretha Franklin, as with Elvis Presley, as with George Jones, as with Nat King Cole, as with Sarah Vaughan, as with Johnny Cash, as with Al Green, as with Kurt Cobain, as with—unfortunately, but it must be said—Snoop Dogg, coming to terms with Billie Holiday means penetrating an unfathomable mystery: her voice. To one extent or another this holds for most good singers, and my list—while politely making room for Vaughan and her gravitas in addition to the odious Dogg—is limited by age, happenstance and personal bias as well as the need to stop somewhere. For instance, it excludes the "classical" tradition, whereas Roland Barthes's seminal 1972 essay "The Grain of the Voice" was inspired by lieder specialist Dietrich Fischer-Dieskau, who, Barthes reported, "reigns more or less unchallenged over the recording of vocal music," as if Billie Holiday, Frank Sinatra and, for that matter, Edith Piaf had never existed. Nevertheless, it is in popular music, so much less stringent as to technical standards and so much more invested in performer mystique, that grain reigns.

That Billie Holiday was blessed with an extraordinary instrument isn't immediately apparent even to those who admire her. As Henry Pleasants put it, she had "a meager voice—small, hoarse at the bottom and thinly shrill on top, with top and bottom never very far apart." And what little she had she wrecked. When I discovered her in 1959, she had died a few months earlier at 43, so like most of my contemporaries, I formed my bond with the Holiday the rock critic Carol Cooper calls "our lady of perpetual suffering." By the mid-1950s, her timbre often cracked and her melodies sometimes staggered, especially on off-label live recordings like the one I bought. If you'd asked me why I liked her, I would have cited her ability to contain pain (only then I would have made the verb a bald and inaccurate "express"), her sly improvisations (which often prove less radical than that truism implies) and her "swing," a concept that like "flow" in hip-hop covers up a myriad of inexactitudes—Holiday's time in particular is a wonder that resists analysis as unflappably as her sound. These were and continue to be the standard answers, and they're all essential to her matchless achievement. But they don't nearly explain her fascination.

Julia Blackburn's fascination with Billie Holiday began when she was 14, at a party thrown by her mother that featured two prostitutes and two people dancing around with their clothes off and an old man giving her the eye and her mother giving the old man the eye. Blackburn "escaped to a far corner" and spent the night playing a 1975 compilation called *A Billie Holiday Memorial*—most of it from the 1930s, the finale from the lush, lost 1958 *Lady in Satin*. Next day she bought the LP, which she's kept ever since. A quarter of a century later, still entranced by "the way her voice could chase out my fears," Blackburn decided to write a book about Holiday. The author of two well-regarded novels and several works of history, she elected to focus not on Holiday's voice but on her life, which for many feels like the closest thing they can get to it. So she contracted with promoter Toby Byron to examine the Linda Kuehl archive: a trove of taped interviews, laborious and sometimes inaccurate transcripts of those tapes, documents, artifacts and slivers of biography previously accessed by Holiday chroniclers Robert O'Meally and Donald Clarke, although Blackburn is the first to examine more than the transcripts. Kuehl assembled this material over many years; her plan to write a definitive biography died when she committed suicide in 1979.

Strangely, Blackburn couldn't write a biography either. Instead, in something like desperation, she assembled portraits of Kuehl's interviewees, and these, added together in all their contradictory subjectivity, constitute her portrait of Holiday. Fortunately for Blackburn, the ploy worked. *With Billie* is a compelling and intelligent book, less in its exposition than in the way it's conceived and assembled. But so are O'Meally's coffee-table "biographical essay" *Lady Day* and Clarke's biography *Wishing on the Moon* and Farah Jasmine Griffin's 2001 *If You Can't Be Free, Be a Mystery: In Search of Billie Holiday*, written without Kuehl because Griffin couldn't afford the fee. All are worth reading, and that is a credit to Holiday's profundity—she's inexhaustible.

Lady Day is where to start. O'Meally, a professor of jazz studies and African-American literature at Columbia, concentrates on music and musters the sanest and fullest overview, detailed and perceptive critically and sympathetic psychologically; he never brushes past her personal faults because he believes they're subsumed by her aesthetic virtues. Clarke, a popular-music historian, brings immense factual resources to bear on the most complete picture of Holiday we have. But he's a militant middlebrow, and his confident assertions regarding Holiday's sexuality—she was a "masochist," he avers in a more clinical tone than he has any right to—tempt one to reciprocate ("male chauvinist" who likes the ladies more than they like him). Griffin's polemically black feminist perspective is far less mechanistic than Angela Davis's in *Blues Legacies and Black Feminism*, and welcome in a field of discourse where, as recently as 1997, Leslie Gourse's twenty-five-contributor *The Billie Holiday Companion* included just one black and two women, including Gourse herself. Griffin is both open-minded and hardheaded, as when she observes that the widely disparaged Diana Ross vehicle *Lady Sings the Blues*, based in theory on Holiday's notoriously inaccurate 1956 as-told-to with William Dufty, inspired a boom in Holiday scholarship extending well beyond the works just cited, thus vastly enriching our understanding of Holiday and her art.

Blackburn's principal contribution to that understanding is a sense of who Holiday's friends were. The interviews about her Baltimore girlhood constitute an oral history of a 1920s ghetto, not such an easy thing to come by; the later materials, which predominate, do the same for the jazz life, which is better documented, and also the sporting life, which is less so. But it's the sum of the documentation that's so impressive. Billie Holiday was a difficult, profane and sometimes imperious woman. She was a junkie and an alcoholic; she had sex with many men and women; she was hot-tempered and ready to clock anyone who gave her grief. Yet the love emanating from these interviews flows never-ending. Holiday wasn't just adored by her fans (to an unusual degree for a nonsuperstar, although not for what today we call a cult artist); she was adored by her friends and colleagues, and the paucity of backbiting is a clue to her greatness. Most artists are selfish as a way of life, and Holiday would always take what was offered her, especially if it would get her high. But she was also great fun to be around, certainly up till her miserable end and often then, and generous by nature, by which I mean something less showy and manipulative than the impulsive largesse of a Presley or Sinatra. She attracted her circle not with her power or charisma but with her spirit.

To Blackburn's credit, the sporting lifers come through as remarkable individuals: the stepfather who cherished Billie and the stepmother who envied her; the dancer who was her mother's confidante and the good-time girl who was her pharmacist's wife; the pimp and the madam; the two comedians and the five pianists; the white Southern bisexual woman who froze her out and the white Southern homosexual man who propped her up; John Levy the Good who played bass as opposed to John Levy the Evil who played her; the mousy secretary and the slick lawyer who shared her last days; the narc who busted her and still thought he was her friend. Holiday's last husband, Louis McKay, is captured in a brutal taped phone call, and Blackburn adds to Kuehl's roster portraits of spaced-out sweetheart Lester Young and people-collecting bitch Tallulah

Bankhead. She also goes on about the irrationality of US narcotics policy, although she argues cogently that Holiday's heroin addiction was less severe than myth would have it—she seemed to kick at will, and even the chief witness for the prosecution, accompanist Carl Drinkard, who clearly wanted to believe Holiday was as hopeless a junkie as he was, allows that unlike him she didn't shoot up to get straight: "It was not just to keep from getting sick; she actually enjoyed using drugs." Although many claimed she was only happy singing (and many claimed she didn't believe she could sing), Blackburn's Holiday is a woman who enjoyed a lot of things. As O'Meally concludes, she chose very young to reject the straight world, and she had a ball doing it.

"People don't think I like laughing. They don't think I lead any kind of normal life," Holiday complained to secretary Alice Vrbsky. And she had a right. By 1957 or so, Holiday's circumstances were bleak. She'd lost friends, she hated McKay as she'd come to hate all the other toughs who'd turned her on, and with no manager and an unearned reputation as a no-show, she wasn't getting enough club work, although Norman Granz had been overseeing some of her greatest sessions. But as Blackburn and Griffin insist, our lady of perpetual suffering was a reductive sensationalization based on her 1947 heroin conviction, which was probably a setup. Not that Holiday resisted the cliché the way she might have. Her autobiography cashed in on her notoriety, and because hard living—especially alcohol—had roughed up her instrument and sapped her sass, her late recordings often foreground her pain. Nevertheless, musically and personally, the transmutation of suffering was never all or even most of what Billie Holiday was about. Coming up when I did, I used to share O'Meally's view that the late recordings old-timers disparage were markedly superior to the music of her 20s—in O'Meally's words, "more nuanced and evocative." But listening intensively as I've read these books, I've come to feel not that their vocal attractions are somehow lacking, because her voice almost always comes through, but that they don't laugh enough—even if, as O'Meally makes clear, they laugh more than I could once discern.

An illegitimate child shunned by the striving family that never fully accepted her, Holiday was a bad girl on principle. She was singing for money before she left Baltimore at 13, but for much of her adolescence she also worked as a prostitute. The scant evidence is tantalizingly complex, but from Blackburn and the others it would seem that these two vocations overlapped—that the pimps and players she liked to hang with dug her because she could sing, because she took no shit and because she was a real party girl, none of which meant she didn't need to earn cash on her back. Speaking from the naïve perspective of someone who's never known or patronized a prostitute, I connect this to the mystery of Holiday's voice—a voice that gives its most exquisite pleasure by taking pleasure, just as what defines a quality hooker is her ability to convince her johns that they get her hot (and, who knows, maybe sometimes they do). There's something so casually delighted yet so hip and cool about Holiday's timing, tone and timbre—so willing, yet so impossible to fool.

The willing part wasn't merely a function of Holiday's soft-edged croon but of her musical attitude. It's invariably said that Holiday torpedoes the banality of the Tin Pan Alley dross she was compelled to sing in the 1930s by transforming the songs' melodies, and one way O'Meally argues for the late work is by laying out how extreme these revisions became. But as Clarke points out more than once, many of the songs were expertly crafted, and as O'Meally emphasizes, Holiday was generally given several to choose from. More-over, the assumption that to reconceive a melody is to improve it is among other things a rejection of the satisfying structural certitudes in which pop composers specialize—a rejection, that is, of the square world in which things resolve almost but not quite as you'd dreamed. In the 1930s, when she was an optimistic kid—before she turned 25 in 1940, she'd already put in stints with Count Basie and Artie Shaw and altered the course of her career by starting to sing (and climax her sets with) Abel Meeropol's antilynching song-poem

"Strange Fruit"—Holiday showed a more nuanced sense of how to keep her johns coming back for more.

Compilations are the efficient way to access a singer in history, and Columbia has cherry-picked a bunch of fine ones, starting with *Lady Day: The Best of Billie Holiday* and *A Fine Romance*. But dip anywhere into the ten-CD *Lady Day: The Complete Billie Holiday on Columbia 1933–1944*—the outtakes, the air checks, the near crap, anywhere—and you will hear first of all not one of the twentieth century's consummate jazz artists but a dynamite pop singer. Zoom in whenever the fancy strikes you and Holiday will certainly be personalizing the tune with her compliant cunning as she enunciates the lyric in her crystalline drawl. Usually the lyric will be faring better than all those accounts of how she undercuts moon-June clichés would have you believe, and usually the tune will be the thing yet not the thing, a crucial pop mode that long preceded Holiday and has been ascendant since the 1970s. But definitely there will be art going on, and definitely it will make your mind go pitter-pat. Lose concentration, however, and your aesthetic emotions will still get a proper workout. Massaged by the unfathomable, they'll give it up to background music.

Please don't think I'm trying to drag Billie Holiday by the gardenia into some quotidian realm she long ago transcended. Every realm is hers, and every good thing people say about her is true. I've learned to love the 1940s Deccas, wish their strings and big bands had gained her the hits she coveted, and I adore the Verves. *The Lady in Autumn* set is the pinnacle of her jazz artistry—evocative and nuanced, breath of my youth and intimation of my mortality. Yet it too shows off Holiday's capacity to give pleasure by taking pleasure. In the 1950s, with narcotics and inebriants eating away at her immense vitality and John Levy the Evil replaced by Big Handsome Spousal Abuser Louis McKay, it's hard to say whether she was an old whore whose skills were second nature or a dedicated artist whose best self emerged in song. Probably both, and whatever the explanation, her spirit remains a gift to anyone who'll let it in.

But her spirit couldn't have soared or penetrated without her voice. Throughout her life this was a feel-good voice, easy to listen to in the sense that 1930s guys used to say a doll was easy to look at. Early on its signal virtue is that, despite the thinness Pleasants is right to cite, it's also round, firm, even plump and gorgeous—which by an odd coincidence is pretty much how people recall her beauty in those days. Later on it's started to sag, that burnished glow coarsened a little. Yet what's underneath the skin—the nerve endings, the musculature, the living flesh itself—remains intact. And always it remains a mystery.

ANNE MIDGETTE

The End of The Great Big American Voice

In March, Jennifer Wilson, an unknown 39-year-old soprano, suddenly burst onto the international opera scene by jumping in for Jane Eaglen as Brunnhilde in Wagner's "Gotterdammerung" at the Lyric Opera of Chicago, just a day after singing the same character in a rehearsal of "Die Walkure." Artistry aside, this is a stunning athletic feat. Few people today have the vocal heft and stamina to get through even one of these roles, let alone take on both back to back.

Ms. Wilson not only sang the killer leading role of the five-hour "Gotterdammerung," she also sang it so well, with a huge, beautiful sound and dramatic nuance, that she brought down the house. It was as if a pitcher were called up from the minor leagues and threw two perfect games on two consecutive days.

A baseball-like farm system has developed in American opera in recent decades, as more and more young-artist programs have sprouted up around the country. Aspiring singers now follow a career path from a music degree and graduate school to a residency with a smaller house to, ideally, a place in one of the top programs for young artists: the Metropolitan Opera's Lindeman program, the Chicago Lyric Opera's center for American artists, San Francisco's

Merola program or the Houston Grand Opera Studio. From there they are theoretically ready for the big leagues.

But Ms. Wilson didn't go through the "minors." She auditioned dozens of times over 10 or 15 years, but she couldn't even get in. Either her big voice was deemed unwieldy, or she didn't fit people's physical standards, or perhaps they just didn't think she had the goods. So she had been singing in the Washington Opera Chorus.

American vocal training has long been bruited as the best in the world and is supposed to be better than ever. Yet there has been no commensurate rise in great new talents. One clear measure of the problem is the system's inability to deal effectively with large voices and talents like Ms. Wilson's. It seems to favor lighter, flexible voices that can perform a wide range of material accurately, rather than the powerful, thrilling, concert-hall-filling voices on which live opera ultimately relies for its survival.

"We want interesting artists," said Marlena Malas, who teaches at the Juilliard School and the Manhattan School of Music and is widely regarded as one of the finest teachers in the country. "Where are they? There must be something wrong with what we're doing that doesn't allow that to come forth."

Gayletha Nichols, who runs the Metropolitan Opera National Council Auditions, concurs. "I think it's us, somehow," she said, speaking not of her organization but of the field in general. "Even in our trying to be more helpful, we're not."

What exactly is being done? It can be hard to talk about. For one thing, talking to singers about vocal technique is like talking to the faithful about religion: views are dearly held, highly charged and difficult to prove. There are fairly objective standards to measure the performance of a young pianist or violinist. But a singer's instrument has to be built at the same time the singer learns to use it, and each teacher might have different criteria for how it is supposed to sound.

"How can you teach voice without talking about the tongue?" asked Sheri Greenawald, a former singer who now runs the Merola program in San Francisco.

"How can you teach singing without talking about elasticity?" asked Ruth Falcon, a New York teacher whose students include the soprano Deborah Voigt. (You can do both, and many teachers do.)

Yet in the upper echelons of this fractious field, the one thing people seem to agree on is what's going wrong. In dozens of interviews with singers, teachers and administrators around the country, the same complaints emerged again and again. Young singers are not being taught the fundamentals, in particular, the proper use of breath. Breath support, the coordination of lungs and diaphragm, has long been regarded as the key to singing, the thing that sustains powerful voices in huge auditoriums without a microphone. Without it, it's difficult to hit the proper pitches (particularly the top notes), modulate from soft singing to loud, or even be heard beyond the footlights.

The conservatory system where most students start out is self-perpetuating; many of its instructors went right from graduating to teaching without acquiring any stage experience. Many teachers are therefore less accustomed to the acoustics of a big opera house than to the intimacy of a voice studio, where sheer volume can sound alarming—not at all like the smaller-scaled, lighter voices on contemporary CDs (like Cecilia Bartoli's or, worse, Andrea Bocelli's). Big voices also take longer to mature, and by the time they do, those lucky enough to possess them may be considered too old to get a foot in the door. Many competitions, for example, are open only to those in their early 30s or younger.

"A lot of teachers don't understand that big voices don't settle until 35," said Speight Jenkins, the general manager of the Seattle Opera, which has a reputation in the opera world as a haven for large-scale voices. "Voice teachers in general do not encourage the unique, the original voice." Instead, he said, they encourage "the voice that can hit all the notes and do what is supposed to be done," but without any particular flair, artistry or distinction.

But voice teachers are not solely to blame. Young singers, too, are impatient, and in our "American Idol" culture, quick fame is more appealing than slow maturation. What's more, the vaunted apprentice programs tend to look for singers they can actually use, in small roles, rather than simply train.

However these factors are combined, the result is a preponderance of light, agile voices in young, attractive bodies. They may be pretty to listen to—and certainly to look at—but they are not ultimately as interesting as bigger, more mature voices. Nor do they have the same staying power. Plenty of young American singers have sprung onto the scene only to fizzle within a few years.

"I worry that today many of the people judging singers judge on accomplishment as opposed to talent," said Stephen Lord, the music director of the Opera Theater of St. Louis and the Boston Lyric Opera, known for his careful work with young artists. "If someone walks in and can sing every note of 'Marten aller Arten,'"—a virtuosic soprano aria from Mozart's "Abduction from the Seraglio"—"this is seen as the next coming, as opposed to someone young, struggling with physiology, but with more talent. What you see in front of you isn't really the person with the potential for the biggest career."

Big voices may even be actively discouraged. Take the star mezzo-soprano Dolora Zajick, who said she "grew up in isolation" studying at the University of Nevada. "Whenever I ventured out into competitions," she added, "people would say: 'Oh, no, you're singing too loud. You're going to ruin your voice.' Well, I've been ruining my voice for almost 30 years." Encouraged, by contrast, was Sylvia McNair, a light soprano a few years younger than Ms. Zacik, who won the Met audition at 26 and went on to a big career. Today, she is no longer singing opera.

Patricia McCaffrey, a former singer now among New York's elite voice teachers, scorns the American conventional wisdom that puts all young singers on a diet of Mozart arias to cultivate lightness and agility. To master those high-lying and florid vocal lines, some singers may have to compress their voices. "I send my bigger voices to Europe," she said, "where they seem not to demand that every singer sing light repertory when they are young. Believe it or not, Mozart is actually bad for some voices."

Vocal training is not only difficult, it is also expensive—for a New York student paying $150 for a private lesson or for a music school trying to provide a full-service vocal program with courses not needed by violinists or trombonists, including language instruction and fully staged opera performance. Richard Elder Adams, the dean of faculty and performance at the Manhattan School, described vocal training as "the biggest challenge at any music school."

And the schools are dealing with students who came to music relatively late. A concert pianist begins studying the instrument in early childhood; a baritone has to wait until his voice changes. Many gifted young singers first come to music in high school; a gifted violinist the same age may already have performed professionally.

"And yet we expect them in four years to be at the same level," Mr. Adams said. "There's no way in an undergraduate program to master everything that needs to be mastered."

But there's a lot of demand, and the more students you accept, the more tuition you take in. "A lot of conservatories use the vocal department as a cash cow," Ms. Greenawald said. And so there are large populations of young singers who can't get the individual attention they need.

"They feel lucky that they're in a school of music," said Diana Hossack, the managing director of the service organization Opera America. "Too often students just take whatever voice teacher is given to them."

In the past, young singers often worked with their chosen teachers every day. Today, students often choose a school rather than a teacher, or they go to a big-name teacher whose particular method might not be right for them. And the weekly voice lesson is only one component of a schedule that is overfilled with classes, rehearsals, mandatory chorus and other activities.

"One lesson a week is not enough," said Marilyn Horne, the star mezzo-soprano who now mentors young artists. "They don't remember."

So the most important component of vocal training, the student-teacher relationship, is often the most arbitrary, or neglected.

"My junior and senior year at the University of Southern California I had three teachers in two years," said Cynthia Jansen, a mezzo-soprano who is starting a two-year contract with the Bavarian State Opera in Munich. "If you're not somebody who really stands out, you kind of get shuffled through the system. I finished my degree with a decent education and no idea how to sing." Ms. Jansen found another teacher who, over many years, was able to help her undo the damage.

Whether or not one sustains actual vocal harm, it takes a highly self-motivated person to negotiate the conservatory process successfully. Then again, some argue, it takes a highly motivated person to become an artist.

"What's important is for singers to get their feet wet and survive bad teaching," Ms. Zajick said. "But that is part of the ability to have a career. People say we're ruining all these voices, but the people that have the ability are not going to let their voices be ruined."

Still, all the help available to young singers today has not made the process any easier. Even the apprentice programs, designed to help develop young professionals, create a sink-or-swim environment. Ms. Jansen, who took part in prestigious programs like the Glimmerglass Opera's and Merola, described Glimmerglass as both "artistically a wonderful experience" and an "opera boot camp."

"Those programs squeeze as much out of you as they possibly can," she said. "You start at 9 in the morning and are finished when they say you're finished. It's a survival program. You go through something like that, and you're definitely going to learn about yourself."

Part of the process is input from dozens of different people: directors and voice theaters, coaches and movement teachers, and a new category of professionals, breathing coaches, a field that has sprung up in recent years as voice teachers have ceased to tackle the subject themselves. All of this feedback is designed to help foster individuality, and yet any group program by its very nature places a certain emphasis on conformity.

"Sometimes the black sheep, the odd man out, could very well be the most talented one in the group," Mr. Lord said. "They don't fit into a particular mold. That means that perhaps when they get onstage, they won't be like anyone else either."

To their credit, the administrators of the top programs, like Ms. Greenawald in San Francisco, Richard Pearlman and Gianna Rolandi in Chicago, Lenore Rosenberg in New York, or Diane Zola in Houston, recognize the problems and are trying to find ways to accommodate singers with larger voices and less polish. One example is Marjorie Owens, a young soprano who stayed in the Houston Grand Opera program for three years and is moving on to the Chicago Lyric program, part of a deliberate plan on the part of administrators to give her time to develop further.

In the past, some singers did perform big roles at an early age. Regina Resnik, another retired star mezzo-soprano who now teaches, made her debut at 20 as a soprano, singing Verdi's Lady Macbeth, a powerhouse role. "Her voice was pure, steady, easily produced and of lovely quality," wrote the *New York Times* critic. "But I was prepared," Ms. Resnik said. "We had more time." Ms. Resnik had been trained under the watchful eye of a teacher who sent her to intense acting lessons and took her to performances. Before she sang her first "Fidelio" at the Met, at 22, the conductor Bruno Walter worked with her three times a week for two months to make sure she was ready. That kind of sustained, intense and highly personal attention from a world-class artist simply isn't available to young singers today, despite the best efforts of the farm-team system to provide it.

The system isn't even a prerequisite. Mr. Jenkins and Ms. Mc-Caffrey advise young singers to skip the conservatory and get a liberal arts degree, learn languages and study voice on the side. Morris Robinson was an English major and a football star at the Citadel, a military college; today, he sings bass roles at the Met. Some older talents who are deemed to be ready for a career, like Isabel Leonard, a mezzo-soprano currently getting her master's degree from Juilliard, are encouraged to skip the apprentice programs and start performing. For the most important element in learning to be an opera singer is something no training program can offer: on-the-job experience.

"Merola is one of the finest programs in the country," said Thomas Stewart, the retired star bass-baritone. "Even if they go into that, what have they got? They still come out unproven."

Mr. Stewart and his equally celebrated wife, the soprano Evelyn Lear, have established the Emerging Singers Program in Washington, specifically devoted to the bigger voices that are often overlooked by the standard system. It was at a master class that they discovered Jennifer Wilson, who looked "unprepossessing," Ms. Lear said, until she opened her mouth and sang "Dich, teure Halle" from Wagner's "Tannhauser."

"We couldn't believe our ears," Ms. Lear said. "We said, 'Where have you been?'" They quickly helped her get New York management, leading to her professional debut in 2002, in the title role in "Turandot" at the Connecticut Opera in Hartford, and on to the understudy contracts that led to her star-is-born moment in "Gotterdammerung."

How are artists made? Ms. Wilson was a pre-law student who chose to attend Cornell because she liked the voice teacher there, then dropped out after that teacher's sudden death. She worked a range of jobs in the Washington area: at Radio Free Europe, singing in a church and finally in the opera chorus. She lived with her mother; learned languages; took lessons in piano, dance and acting; and never stopped studying voice with any teacher she thought could help her. "I have the equivalent training to someone with a conservatory degree," she said, calling her Chicago Lyric debut "the overnight success that took 20 years."

In the end, artistic success depends, as it always has, on intangible factors that no training program can provide. One is luck. Another is stubbornness.

"People who really persevere," Ms. Zajick said, "find themselves in lucky places."

Bettye LaVette

The pair of tracks that open *I've Got My Own Hell to Raise*, the transfixing new album by soul singer Bettye LaVette, vividly map the record's prickly yet fecund emotional terrain. The first is an *a cappella* reading of Sinéad O'Connor's flinty assertion of self-reliance, "I Do Not Want What I Haven't Got." The second is a devastating reinterpretation of Lucinda Williams' "Joy," a borderline-metaphysical jeremiad about what it feels like to be robbed of your innermost self.

LaVette's remake of "I Do Not Want" sounds nothing like the original. Distilling O'Connor's prolix test to its essentials, she moans the remaining lines unhurriedly and with staggering self-possession, stretching out the vowels as if intoning a field holler. Bereft of accompaniment—and, presumably, of the comfort such company affords—LaVette sings in a craggy rasp of passing through a searing desert. The material and spiritual sustenance she takes with her, she assures us, is enough to fortify her, even though she doesn't know where her solitary road might lead.

Fuzz-toned guitar barbs rend the parched silence that follows, igniting "Joy," in which LaVette recounts a much less dignified sojourn than her trek through the desert. "Jo-o-oy," she bawls to the juking cadence of the opening chorus, wrenching the word back and forth as if trying to get it to taste right in her mouth again. "Oh-oh, my jo-oy / I don't like it no more," she goes on, the notes convulsing in her throat. "They took my joy."

The offending party here isn't an individual like it is in Williams' original. LaVette casts her nemesis as a more nebulous and aggregate force—some mix of the happenstance and indifference that has plagued her in city after city where she's recorded over the years.

Detroit, New York, Memphis, Muscle Shoals: All have proven barren places for LaVette, each a "desert" where she made sublime music, including some two dozen singles for labels ranging from Atlantic to Motown, only to watch her hopes of reaching a wider audience wither. "They had no right to take my joy," she roars each time the chorus rolls around. "I want it back."

The emotional extremes that LaVette traverses in "Joy" and "I Do Not Want What I Haven't Got" strike at the embattled yet resilient heart of her new CD—and, for that matter, at that of her more than 40-year career.

LaVette's record, which came out on the Anti- label in late September, is an inadvertent concept album, or at least one that she arrived at intuitively. LaVette selected each of its ten songs from a pool of a hundred or so that people involved with the project, including producer Joe Henry, played for her. All were written or co-written by women. Each speaks in some way to what Billie Holiday, with as pregnant a claim about the intersection of self-determination and self-worth as any, was getting at with the line "God bless the child who's got [her] own."

LaVette's performances on the album inhabit Holiday's assertion with knowing and womanly resolve. She transforms Dolly Parton's cautionary "Little Sparrow," a surreal, sisterly derivative of the Appalachian ballad "The Coo Coo Bird," into a harrowing oracle from the Delta. She reimagines the proto-feminist woolgathering of Joy of Cooking's "Only Time Will Tell" as a funked-up monument to liberation. And she method-acts Aimee Mann's snarling kiss-off "How Am I Different" as if the part had been written for her. "One

more question before I pack," she seethes over the record's implaca-
ble backing track: "When you fuck it up later, do I get my money
back?"

LaVette seldom writes the songs she sings, but as her bracing
performances on *I've Got My Own Hell* attest, she is no mere cover
artist. The lines from "How Am I Different" cited above just as easily could apply to record companies LaVette has dealt with as to
Mann's faithless lover. So intensely does LaVette personalize the
material on the album, in fact, that even those familiar with its ten
songs doubtless will feel compelled to consult its liner notes to confirm a couple of the writing credits.

Indeed, neither LaVette's swampy take on "Little Sparrow" nor
her sobbing redemption of Bobbie Cryner's "Just Say So" registered
with one of this magazine's longtime contributors when I played the
album for him this summer. The writer in question was well acquainted in each case with the original.

LaVette, in other words, has plenty of her own to say, even when
she's using someone else's words to say it. "You can't stifle my
dreams, my body, my mind, *this voice*," she avers, by way of Fiona
Apple, on the album's imperious closing track, biting down on the
final two words before delivering the payoff: "I've got my own hell
to raise."

It's not surprising LaVette would gravitate toward material that un-
tangles the knot of autonomy and self-esteem plumbed so evoca-
tively in "God Bless the Child." She's spent more than four decades
making riveting music, both on record and onstage, yet until the release of 2003's exquisite soul-blues testament, *A Woman Like Me*, she
languished in considerable obscurity. As if to underscore this persis-
tent marginalization, LaVette has long been a darling of aficionados
of northern soul, a de facto sub-genre of '60s soul music consisting
largely of titles that flopped in the United States but later became
the toast of the clubs in northern England. (Geno Washington,
Jimmy James & the Vagabonds, and Candy & the Kisses are among

the other artists, some obscure, others better known, who became northern soul favorites.)

A Woman Like Me earned LaVette a W. C. Handy Award for Best Blues Comeback Album in 2004. Yet even it—just her second official studio album in a four-decade career that included tours with Clyde McPhatter and James Brown and a run on Broadway with Cab Calloway—didn't exactly afford her mainstream cultural exposure.

Child of the Seventies, the omnivorous album she made for Atlantic's Atco subsidiary with producer Brad Shapiro in 1972, might have done so, though. The record, which after three decades has yet to be issued in the United States, is a wondrous amalgamation of southern-style pop, rock and soul akin to those that Howard Tate, Delaney & Bonnie, and Arthur Alexander were making at the time. Inexplicably, the otherwise perspicacious Jerry Wexler, who at that point was overseeing operations for Atlantic, shelved the project.

Child of the Seventies would have marked LaVette's debut on LP— and after a decade of extensive touring and recording, no less. "It liked to kill me," she told me, speaking by telephone this summer from her home in West Orange, New Jersey, where her husband Kevin has an antique business. "I'm not sure, but I may not be over that yet. I had many days when all I did was sit and drink and cry. But if I wanted it eventually to work, I couldn't keep doing that."

As one might expect, given LaVette's place in the northern soul pantheon, *Child of the Seventies* has been out in England and the rest of Europe for several years now, and to overwhelming critical acclaim. "It's been so well received," she said. "I just wish, even now, that it were on a really big label."

Meanwhile, LaVette is selling copies out of the trunk of the car at shows as fast as she can.

Unusual perhaps for a soul singer who summons such a vast well of emotion, LaVette, who was born Betty Haskin in 1946, didn't grow up singing in church like so many of her postwar counterparts did. LaVette's parents sold corn liquor out of their home in Muskegon,

Michigan, and Saturday night, as the well-worn cliché would have it, typically bled over into Sunday morning, precluding any real chance of getting to church. As if to compensate, LaVette's mother, a Louisiana-born Catholic whom Bettye describes as mulatto, was forever making her sing the rosary.

More than anything else, the blues and boogie that blared from LaVette's parents' home-turned-roadhouse is what nurtured their daughter's gifts as a singer and entertainer. "There was a jukebox in my living room where there was a couch in other people's living rooms," LaVette recalled with a husky laugh. "They would stand me on top of the jukebox and I could roll my stomach over into three rolls going down and three coming back up. I have no idea how I did that. I wish I could do it now, it would make my stomach muscles so tight. But I did that and people would give me dollars and 50-cent pieces.

"I was like 18 months old then, so I've just always done this. I've always been willing to pull my dress up and sing songs," she went on, revealing herself not only to be a child who had her own, but one who, as the title of her new record puts it, had plenty of hell to raise as well. Indeed, LaVette's comment is reminiscent, of all things, of Kathleen Hanna's declaration of grrrl power in Bikini Kill's 1993 single "New Radio": "I'm the little girl at the picnic who won't stop pulling up her dress / It doesn't matter who's in control now, it doesn't matter 'cause this is the new radio."

Among the patrons who frequented the Haskin home were electrifying gospel quartets such as the Soul Stirrers, the Pilgrim Travelers, and the Blind Boys of Mississippi. "They came to my house on Sundays after their 'singings,' as they used to call them," LaVette said. "That's where they ate barbecue sandwiches and drank and just got up and challenged each other. Maybe the whole group wouldn't be there. Maybe it'd be one person (from a group) and three from another, but they always sang."

LaVette's exposure to the pressing gospel of these vaunted quartets, though, didn't make much of an impression on her, at least not on any conscious level. "Young people weren't into that," she explained. "As I got older I never even mentioned or thought about the fact that I met those people. It's only since they have become popular again that it's come to my mind, 'Well, gosh, I knew them as a child!'"

Making a much deeper mark were a couple of female R&B stars LaVette heard on the radio and saw on television in the mid-to-late 1950s. "There were only two women, Ruth Brown and LaVern Baker—black women—who sang songs that people who were my age—kids, I mean, pre-teens—could dance to," she said. "There was Sarah Vaughan and Ella Fitzgerald and that whole group, but we didn't like their music because it was too slow. The only two women who sung songs that I liked were LaVern Baker and Ruth Brown. Then later, when 1960 came, there was Baby Washington and Etta James. But before that there was just Ruth Brown and LaVern Baker.

"Of course everybody had a local TV show, you know, a dance-party type show, and I saw them on those," LaVette continued, adding that she also has vivid memories of tuning in to see Jackie Wilson and Little Willie John, both of whom still lived in Detroit at the time.

"But you didn't see a lot of women doing a lot, period. As far as black women were concerned, Ruth Brown and LaVern Baker were the only two that I ever saw stand up and sing in a gown or whatever. That was who I wanted to be exactly like when I thought in terms of singing."

The influence of self-possessed black women like Baker and Brown, and especially the brassy attitude and pinched, keening wail of the latter, certainly is evident in LaVette's earliest recordings. Foremost among them was the single "My Man—He's a Lovin' Man" LaVette made for Detroit's small Lupine label in 1962; Atlantic soon snatched it up and began distributing it nationally. LaVette was barely 16 at the time, but her ravaged vocals, along with the track's serpentine groove and spiky guitar lines, conveyed enough adult sensuality to land the single at #7 on the R&B chart.

"When 'My Man' came out in 1962, there were not any black stations that went all over the country," LaVette recalled. "WLAC in Nashville wasn't a black station, but it had that black program that came on at night and we could get it, even in Muskegon, Michigan, because it came on so late.

"You can't imagine how it felt on the road the very first time, on the road with Clyde McPhatter and Ben E. King and traveling down this two-lane highway going south and trying to get WLAC, which was playing all the hit records. To hear the deejay say, 'Now we gonna listen to a little filly named Bettye La-*Vitt*,' I was just, oh, honey, wow."

Wow, indeed. Trouble is, "My Man" has had the distinction of being LaVette's highest charting single, R&B or pop (#101), ever since. She churned out a series of terrific sides with a variety of producers and sessions players, and for various labels, as the '60s progressed, all of them to little commercial avail. The most successful was "Let Me Down Easy," a gloriously anguished record aggravated by nagging syncopation, astringent strings, and a stinging blues guitar break that went to #20 R&B in 1965.

LaVette recorded the hit version of "Let Me Down Easy" for New York's Calla label, but her 1969 remake of the song for Karen, another New York indie, is a completely different yet equally enthralling record. The reconstituted take is an incantatory funk workout replete with "Cosmic Slop" guitar redolent of the sound that George Clinton and Funkadelic were honing in LaVette's native Detroit at the time.

LaVette's recording of "He Made a Woman Out of Me" is another of her '60s sides that did reasonably well, this one cut in Memphis for Shelby Singleton's Nashville-based Silver Fox label. The single rose as high as #25 on the R&B chart in 1969, despite being banned from numerous radio stations, presumably for its exultant take on what amounted to statutory rape. LaVette's unhinged performance likely prompted some of this censure as well. (Bobbie Gentry would reach a much wider audience with a steamy, somewhat more contained remake on *Fancy*, the terrific but largely forgotten LP she recorded for Capitol in 1970.)

Ironically perhaps, the man who robs the girl of her innocence in "He Made a Woman Out of Me" was named Joe Henry, a coincidence not lost on LaVette. "I took that as an omen," she said, alluding to her decision to have Joe Henry produce her current album. "I took it as a definite omen."

LaVette toured throughout the '60s, and with fabulous revues that included Otis Redding and Barbara Lynn, the criminally unsung singer and left-handed guitarist from Beaumont, Texas, among other luminaries. The small independents for which she recorded—evanescent imprints including Lupine, Scepter, Calla, Karen, and SSS—nevertheless lacked the promotional muscle or the confidence in LaVette to put her over beyond the era's chitlin and supper-club circuits.

"No one ever did any promo," LaVette said. "There was never enough faith in the front office, in any of the situations I was in, to have that extra push that [a record] needed.

"People now say how great those records were, but do you know the live CD that I did for the Dutch in 1999 called *Let Me Down Easy*? Before I did that show that night, I had never sung 'You'll Never Change' live before. I had never done 'Right in the Middle,' I had never done 'Your Turn To Cry.' I had never done (a lot of my early singles) because all those things flopped so fast I didn't realize they were good songs. I was convinced they weren't any good, and I didn't do any of them on my show."

To get gigs back then, LaVette relied on her instincts, which meant performing the hits of some of the most successful pop, rock and soul singers of the day. "I'd sing whatever was selling," she explained, "and I did those well, so I was able to work all the time, but my show was based on my interpretation of other people's songs. I felt so bad that my records were not selling. I would try to do things to other people's records. And that helped me. That helped me work all the time. I've worked (constantly throughout my career), sometimes for $50, sometimes for $50,000, but I've worked all the time."

Singing other people's songs did more than just secure LaVette work; it helped her become the bravura interpretive singer that she is today—and, for that matter, that she's been for the better part of four decades. For every knockoff of a hit by Janis Joplin or Kenny Rogers & the First Edition that she's recorded over the years, all of them worth hearing, there's an astonishing remake of something like "With a Little Help from My Friends." Her reinvention of that Beatles classic, a 1969 single for Karen, is an epiphany, a rampaging shuffle galvanized by wah-wah flourishes and quicksilver guitar runs that is utterly different from, but just as thrilling as, Joe Cocker's gloriously histrionic performance of the song at Woodstock.

LaVette's as-yet-unreleased retrieval of Morris Albert's treacly 1975 smash "Feelings" is an even more dramatic case in point. Singing in an aggrieved wail, she transforms the bathos of the original into an expression of spiritual and emotional abandonment of seemingly cosmic proportions, something more akin to Robert Johnson's harrowing "Stones in My Passway" than to any Top 40 hit. LaVette has worked similar, if less astonishing, wonders with the well-traveled likes of Joe South's "Games People Play," Charlie Rich's "Behind Closed Doors," and The Association's "Never My Love," among numerous others.

"It's a very difficult thing to do," LaVette said, referring to the art of interpretation. "I know what I can sing and what I can't sing. All songs start off, for example, as Fiona Apple songs, as words on a piece of paper. But they can be anybody's songs, anybody who feels a different way about them. If I sang ['Sleep to Dream'] Fiona Apple's way, then it would still be a Fiona Apple song. But when I say songs that I can sing, I mean songs that *I* can sing.

"It took me 30 years to learn to interpret songs. I think I could always sing, if you call what I do singing. I mean, I've always been able to attack rhythm & blues songs. But it took me 30 years to learn to interpret and learn to *sing*. Not only that, what I've had to do, to make things interesting, is to make my show entertaining as well.

"It's awful," LaVette went on, "but a Sarah Vaughan probably could not make it now, because you would have to be still and listen to her. I have to tell jokes and stand on my head and *then* interpret a song. But I'm glad in a way. The things that happened to me in this 44-year struggle made me a more rounded entertainer. I could not rely on a hit record, or I did not have a hit record to rely on, or anything else to lean on, so I had to do what the situation called for."

In some respects, LaVette, who turned 59 this year, still feels like she's trying to prove herself as a singer and entertainer. "I'm still introducing myself," she said without hesitation. "Hopefully, this new record will cause people to go back and listen to *A Woman Like Me*, and then listen to the earlier stuff I did and see how I got to where I am now."

A Woman Like Me certainly set that process of discovery in motion. Produced by Robert Cray collaborator Dennis Walker, the album, which compares favorably to Cray's *Strong Persuader*, is an out-and-out wonder, a witness to the blues as live—and with it, to the possibility of transcending them.

With raves in papers ranging from the *New York Times* to the *Village Voice*, *A Woman Like Me* also exposed LaVette to rock and pop audiences, or at least to discerning segments among them who likely didn't know she existed. (A perennial singles artist—the only other album she released prior to *A Woman Like Me* was a fine disco-soul set titled *Tell Me a Lie* that came out on Motown in 1982—LaVette's name is nowhere to be found in the album-oriented rock and pop guides published over the past quarter-century.)

Fred Wilhelms, LaVette's Nashville-based attorney, recounts a particularly vivid epiphany from a fete in Mill Valley toward the end of 2002, just as *A Woman Like Me* was about to come out. The celebration, which took place at the famous Sweetwater club the night before LaVette's first date in San Francisco in 30 years, was held by John Goddard, the owner of Village Music in Mill Valley. Goddard's guest list drew heavily from his hip and celebrity-rich customer list, which for this occasion included Elvis Costello, Huey Lewis, Maria Muldaur, the eminent pop and soul producer Jerry Ragovoy, and Bonnie Raitt.

"Bonnie, who had never heard Bettye before, spent a lot of the show with her head on the table, just moaning in delight," Wilhelms recalled. "The rest of the time, she was shouting for more.

"Watching Bonnie in the audience is almost as good as watching her onstage," Wilhelms continued. "After Bettye did 'Let Me Down Easy,' Bonnie grabbed me by the neck and asked, 'Where the fuck has she been?'" At the club to see the renascent Howard Tate, Raitt didn't even know LaVette would be performing.

A Woman Like Me forged other propitious connections for LaVette as well, including the chance to renew ties with some of the musicians with whom she'd worked earlier in her career. "When I was down [in Memphis] for the Handys," she began, referring to the 2004 blues awards ceremony, "Jim Dickinson came up to me and said, 'I just wanted to introduce myself. My name is Jim Dickinson and I played [piano] on "You Made a Woman Out of Me."'

"I just broke into more tears," LaVette added, alluding to the up-welling of emotion she'd felt after accepting the award for Best Blues Comeback Album at the Handy Awards that year. "That was a wonderful night. All of those guys have done so much better than I have. The Memphis Horns were just the guys who played the horns on my records. None of those people were names then and they've all just gone on to be so much bigger than I have. But I'm so glad that I'm being acknowledged by them now. I was just so, so grateful to Jim for coming over and telling me that."

All of which does nothing to gainsay the deep sense of abandonment, the palpable grief over what might have been that pervades
the version of Lucinda Williams' "Joy" which galvanizes the opening six minutes of *I've Got My Own Hell to Raise*. LaVette nevertheless has recovered a measure of the joy of which she's been robbed
over the years, as well as a good bit of the satisfaction that goes with
it. Best of all, perhaps, she still has the vision and chops as a performer to enjoy it—in fact, to exult in it.

LaVette has taken astonishingly good care of her gruff, powerful
alto, especially when you consider that she's been shouting over
crowds in loud, smoky rooms since she was a teenager. *A Woman
Like Me* and *I've Got My Own Hell* reveal that she's singing with as
much nuance and command as ever, roaring like a lioness one
minute and weeping in the midnight hour the next.

"I've had to learn to take care of my voice, and to be very conscious of everything I do," she said. "But because of my size
[LaVette is maybe 5'3" and weighs a hundred pounds, tops], it's as
much my body as it is my voice. It takes every muscle in my frame to
sing that loud, and so I have to take care of my body. I know that I
can't sing drunk, and I know that if I were up on cocaine, I'm subject
to have my heart burst, like Philippe Wynne's [of the Spinners] did.
And I know that if I were on heroin I'd go into a deep nod and never
come out. So I have to do things in a certain way."

LaVette also is fiercely invested in what she's doing musically
these days—not just in singing, but in song selection and arranging,
and just about every aspect of recording. When I asked her about
working with Joe Henry, I mentioned that upon learning they were
going into the studio together, I feared Henry might embalm the
proceedings with a preponderance of tasteful yet monochromatic,
midtempo arrangements like those he used on the album he produced for Solomon Burke.

"No, *I* put all of those tempos there," LaVette responded,
promptly setting the record straight. "And I did many of those
arrangements.

"He, he, he let me . . . ," LaVette went on, before pausing and thinking better of her choice of the verb "let." "What Joe did was put everything together for me and explain to everybody what I meant.

"I think that if Solomon had taken more interest in his record, it wouldn't have come out the way it did. When I went into the studio to do my record, I said, 'I'm really not gonna sweat too much of anything else, but no one can tell me what to sing or how to sing it.'"

Her stamp certainly is evident on the album's majestic take of Joan Armatrading's "Down to Zero," and even more so after hearing LaVette talk about how she re-envisioned the song with her voice in mind. "When I figured out what she was talking about, it tickled me," LaVette said, referring to Armatrading's lyrics. "Here's a woman telling a guy off pretty much, but she's not American, so it doesn't even sound like she's telling him off. So I said, 'I've got to put a little more attitude in it, a little bit of bitch, and a little more "American woman" in it and make it a little snappier and sassier.'"

Once again, and as the previous comments and the entirety of *I've Got My Own Hell to Raise* attest, LaVette is no mere cover artist. When she reimagines a song—and she hadn't heard any of those that were pitched to her for the album—she in effect rewrites it, thereby elevating the art of interpretation, an art form that's often devalued by those who insist, in rockist fashion, that artists have to write the songs they sing to be "authentic."

"Everybody gets hung up on writing new songs when there's so many great things out there already," LaVette said. "I wish to God I could hear Aretha Franklin or Gladys Knight or Bill Withers do some of those old songs, especially some of the country songs.

"I'd love to do a country album," she went on. (LaVette has recorded country material through the years, and she made her 1982

LP *Tell Me a Lie* in Nashville with producer Steve Buckingham, but she's never done an album consisting entirely of country material.)

"Not a country album [per se], but something like *Songs by George Jones on William Bell*, you know. I just think they would be so great, and the songs are so good. And if the songs are good and you don't mess 'em up with too much strange sounds . . . God, I just wish that some of these people would do some of those songs. A song being done by just one person, one time—I just don't believe songs are disposable like that."

Take for example, LaVette's heart-rending resurrection—just the singer backed by a nylon-string guitar—of the Bobby Cryner ballad "Just Say So."

"My husband found that tune," LaVette began, "and when I heard it, I immediately knew what I wanted to do with it. We recorded it down about three times, and I said, 'No, there's something wrong.' So we were eating lunch and I called my husband and said, 'I think we've lost "Just Say So." We've done it three times and I don't like it.' So he said, 'Well, why don't you just get the keyboard player [Lisa Coleman, formerly of Prince's band the Revolution], just take her in the studio and sit down on the floor the way you do it here at home and just sing it with her?'

"So I said, 'Lisa, let's just you and I try it.' So we started doodling with it, I in my little cubicle and her out in the studio. Then the guitarist came in and he started doodling with it. I had a control board in my room, so I took Lisa out, so I could just hear the guitar.

"I realized that with the two women, we were telling the story, actually a woman's song from a woman's point of view. But when Chris [Bruce] started to play it on guitar, I could sing it *to* him, and the whole thing felt better to me. I liked what Lisa was playing, but she was mimicking in music what I was playing, whereas Chris was more or less standing there quietly letting me be pitiful the way it probably would be if I were talking to a man. So I knew then, this is all I want, just me and him.

"I just had ideas about everything," LaVette went on, talking about what was clearly a liberating recording process for her. "I had no idea where they came from. They've never come to me before, but on *A Woman Like Me*, and on this one, I think all the things that I've never said over the years I've just started to say. And because I can't say them musically, because I don't play anything, I've always felt apprehensive about saying them. But now I fall all over the floor and have fits and say I want it to go like this here. And because I'm able to defend it vocally, they tend to listen to me. So I'm getting braver. I'm getting braver and braver."

And how. And spoken like a child, or rather a grown woman, who's got her own—and then some.

SUSAN ALCORN

The Road, the Radio, and the Full Moon

Houston

Houston, black hole, geographical epicenter of American culture. It is the farthest point southwest for the prototypical "Southern" culture. In the 1950s thousands upon thousands of rural farmers from East Texas moved south in search of jobs and found them, many working in the oil industry. Houston is the farthest northeast of the established Mexican-American, or "Chicano," culture—corridos, norteño mixed with r&b and country; accordions gave way to keyboards to form the music now known as "Tejano."

Houston is also the farthest point west of the indigenous cajun and zydeco cultures. The white Cajuns still meet every Saturday and Sunday at Pe Te's Cajun restaurant to eat crawfish, gumbo, and boudin and dance to the (mostly white) cajun bands from Louisiana. Similarly, the Creoles every Friday go to Jax or St. Mary's Catholic Church to dance to Marcus Ardoin, L'il Brian Terry and the Zydeco Travelers, Chris Ardoin, Step Rideaux, or Roy Carrier. Zydeco—the propulsive beat, the washboards, the black (and white) people all in Western clothes doing a dance that is something like a jitterbug.

The band leader is usually the accordion player, and a washboard player is mandatory.

And Houston has always had a healthy blues scene highlighted by luminaries such as Lightnin' Hopkins, Pete Mayes, Joe "Guitar" Hughes, Martha Turner, and Trudy Lynn.

There is a jazz tradition in Houston. Saxophonist Arnett Cobb, a Houston native, known for his swaggering "Texas Tenor" style, lived and played here for years (when he could find work), as did Joe Sample and the Crusaders. Houston jazz, however, developed differently than it did in the North—the energy was different. The musicianship was often as good as it was in New York, Chicago, and other northern bastions of bebop and the avant-garde, and in a way just as innovative, but the jazz musicians in Houston channeled their creativity in a more down-home way—a soul jazz deeply rooted in the blues, funk, Creole, and country of the culture they grew up in.

There is a thriving rap scene in Houston, which has given the world groups like the Geto Boys and South Park Mexican, though I know little about it.

Houston had its share of rockers, too. In the sixties and early seventies, bands like the 13th Floor Elevators and ZZ Top would play at Liberty Hall in lower Montrose, while in the surrounding small towns, blue-eyed soul singers BJ Thomas and Roy Head with their horn bands performed for dances at ballrooms. The 13th Floor Elevators split up; Roy Head and BJ Thomas both achieved a modest success in pop music and then later as country-western singers. ZZ Top is still around and still in Houston.

Country singers like George Jones, Freddie Fender, and Gatemouth Brown used to record at Sugar Hill studios off Wayside Drive near the Old Spanish Trail. The producer was the legendary Hughey Meaux, the "Crazy Cajun" who did time in prison in the early seventies for payola and again in the nineties for rape. A room in the back of Sugar Hill was where he brought teenage girls and plied them with drugs and alcohol.

Elvis used to perform at Magnolia Gardens on the banks of the San Jacinto River as it widened before emptying itself into the Gulf of Mexico and at the Harbor Lights club near the Ship Channel, which, before closing in the mid-nineties, was a popular watering hole for Norwegian and Greek sailors, drug addicts, motorcycle gangs, and prostitutes. When I played there, the piano player kept a loaded pistol on top of his keyboard, and the musicians openly smoked pot on the bandstand. This was one bar the police never entered.

And then there was western swing, which in Houston had a Dixieland flair to it with steel guitar, hot fiddles, horns, guitar, and piano all improvising simultaneously. As far as I know, this was unique to western swing in this part of the state. Twenty-five years ago all the old western swing musicians and those few (like me) who wanted to be around, play with, and learn from the masters used to congregate every Sunday afternoon at Frank's Ice House, an old beer joint in Houston's "Heights" district overlooking Buffalo Bayou. Frankie V, the owner, was once a singer with the original River Road Boys (one of Houston's more popular western swing ensembles) and was a lover of western swing. It was an open jam session, and the musicians got free drinks. Musicians in blue jeans, white shirts, and cowboy hats, with grey hair and beer bellies would pull up in old pickup trucks, broken-down Fords or Chevys, and new Mercedes with their instruments in hand for these weekly gatherings. Herb Remington and Bucky Meadows would play twin parts on the steel guitar and the guitar, and Ernie Hunter, a rancher from Bryan, Texas, played fiddle rides that would be the envy of Joe Venuti. Once I thought I heard three fiddles playing harmony; I looked up and saw only Cliff Bruner, one of the founders of western swing, and then still playing in his eighties. Frank's Ice House has long since closed down. Frankie, Cliff Bruner, Ernie Hunter, and Bucky Meadows are all dead. The building was used as a Mexican ice house for several years, and is now a yuppie bar.

Country music in Houston, as in most of Texas, is first and foremost for dancing, and it was usually performed in huge ballrooms with eight- to ten-piece bands. When I came to Houston in 1981, the current local stars were people like Randy Cornor, Kenny Dale, Mundo Earwood, and Kelly Schoppa. But this was the beginning of the end for live country music in the city. The stars of the eighties, most with only a fraction of the creativity and originality of the previous generation, wasted their time, money, and talent on liquor, gambling, and cocaine. They spent everything they had as if it would never end, but it all came crashing down in the mid-eighties when the price of oil dropped, turning Houston's boomtown mentality into its polar opposite. And it never recovered. Nowadays, there is very little country music played in the city itself, and Houston's musicians are only recognized if they leave town (which most do) and then become famous.

This is the Houston I remember, though it is long gone, by now only a shadow in this oil-driven megalopolis of heat, humidity, and glass skyscrapers, that exists mainly in bits of conversations shared by the older musicians and the people they once played for, sitting in their now-stuffy wood-paneled living rooms, showing off their old 45s and long-playing records, eager to share in the old stories filled with names now gone. People who used to go whip dancing to white Houston bluesman Joey Long now talk about how he died. The heroin king of white Texas blues, always with a lit cigarette stuck between the tuning keys of his guitar. Playing a lick, taking a puff, and then blowing out the smoke in ringlets while he sustained and bent the note. They say he was playing at the Cedar Lounge one night, and during break time, he went outside and sat on the curb and closed his eyes. It was twenty minutes before anyone realized that he was dead. However, according to his son, Jimmy Joe Long, he actually died of a massive heart attack while walking home from the store. And they talk about Tommy Williams, the drummer who used to have a bowl of goldfish in his bass drum, but by the end of the night the fish were always floating belly up at the top. Still older voices will tell of the times when they went to Dance Town USA up on Airline Drive to dance to Bob Wills, and Tommy Duncan was singing. Willie

Nelson played there, too, and his steel player Jimmy Day (one of my musical heroes) gave his steel guitar bar to an admirer who gave it to me, and I in turn eventually gave it to someone else whom I'll most likely never see again. I remember the last time I saw Arnett Cobb playing on Allen's Landing with an organ trio. He needed a cane to stand up, but stand he did all night. He died six months later.

Friday

It is early Friday evening. I start loading my equipment into my van and get ready to make the 90-minute drive down to Rosenberg, Texas, to play at my first country-western gig this year. It is April. While I load my van, my next door neighbor Juan, a 70-year-old immigrant from Mexico, walks over to tell me, in a mix of Spanish and English, that last night someone broke into his car and tried to steal it. His car is usually parked on the street right in front of my van, so I'm a little nervous, both at the prospect of the van being broken into and at the prospect of having to come home late at night and unload my equipment when these people may be roaming the neighborhood. We talk and commiserate for a few minutes, then I start driving down Interstate 10, to the Loop 610, and then onto Highway 59 southwest towards Rosenberg. I pass through the Galleria area, an upscale shopping center surrounded by the large apartment complexes that are home to extremely poor, illegal, and sometimes desperate recent immigrants from Mexico and Central America. Past the Galleria, the scenery is more suburban. Apartment complexes giving way to ranch-style houses built in the seventies and eighties, each one identical to the other—a large percentage of them owned by those who could eventually leave the Galleria ghettos. Forty years ago this was all rice paddies.

I'm driving past Wal-Marts, Targets, McDonalds, and chain stores of an unlimited variety of names and a numbing sameness of concept.

Eventually, the chain stores become fewer and farther between. The sun starts to set, and I now feel more relaxed. The land is flat and green with few trees.

As I pass the prison at Sugarland, the sign says, "Do Not Pick Up Hitchhikers."

I pass Crabb River Road and the ancient, meandering, red-banked Brazos River.

Through Richmond, former home of BJ Thomas.

The next exit is Rosenberg.

There's a sign for the Rosenberg Opry (in the last twenty years or so, opries have spread up all over Southeast Texas to give people an opportunity to see live country music without the corrupting influences of alcohol, cigarette smoke, and foul language). Ed Junot, the left-handed Cajun fiddler, used to play there. Then he had a heart attack and a quadruple bypass operation. His doctor told him that he needed to stop playing music, but Ed continued to perform at the opry every Saturday singing in French, dancing, and playing the fiddle all at the same time. He had another heart attack and dropped dead on stage. His funeral was held in El Campo, Texas. Frenchie Burke, with shaking hands, played "Amazing Grace" as they laid him in the ground.

I gaze to my right to see the mist is rising above Rabbs Bayou. It's been years since I was here. I take the State Highway 36 exit. There's a huge Wal-Mart on the corner, a billboard says "Bud Light." On the other corner is a Toyota dealership with acres of cars. Rosenberg is not as rural as I remember it. An old Silver Eagle Bus with a sign on it that says "Los Chaves" is parked at the McDonalds. I go south on Highway 36, and finally for a few miles there is nothing but country. In the fields I can see mounds of fire ant hills. When there is a flood, these hardy creatures will all lock their bodies together and form a miniature boat. I pass the American Legion Hall, which is having a bingo tournament. A minute later on the right is the Fort Bend County Fairgrounds. It has a new sign. Twenty years ago I played here with James Casey and the Texas

Swing Band. Bucky Meadows was playing guitar. Going south, there is nothing but cotton fields for twenty miles.

At last I reach the corrugated metal building with a big neon sign that says "Chelsea's."

Twenty years ago this place would have been called something like "Silver Wings Ballroom" or "Larry Joe's Dance City," or "Cowboy Country," but times have changed. I get out of my van and walk inside. There is a full moon overhead, and a dead possum next to the back door. On the wall facing the bandstand is a large painting of the Texas flag. On the wall to the left is an equally large and somewhat menacing looking bald eagle. The audience, the club owners, and the band are, I'm sure, very conservative, so I am careful not to talk about politics (which is difficult to avoid at this time in America).

It's a Friday night, so there are not too many people in the building; perhaps they will all come later. After setting up my equipment, I look for a place to sit where I won't be conspicuous sitting alone.

Everyone in the band is dressed in blue jeans and "Brooks and Dunn" style western shirts. Before we start the first song, the singer shouts out, "Are there any rednecks out there?" A tepid response. He tries again, "I said, ARE THERE ANY REDNECKS OUT THERE?" A slightly better response. Then he yells, "Can I hear a 'Yee Haw'?" A few people shout out "Yee Haw" and the band begins to play. They play the current Top 40 country hits as much like the record as they can. This band, made up of weekend warriors, gets through the first set. The bass player, playing an old fretless bass (a big no no in c&w), is hopelessly and blissfully out of tune. Annoyed, I look over at him while we're playing, and he just smiles and nods as if everything is going great. This is a bit frustrating for me because as the player of a different fretless instrument, the pedal steel guitar, I am unable to find a pitch to lock in to. During break time I broach the subject with him, but my advice to him to check his tuning falls on deaf ears. "Well, I think that *everybody* should check their tuning." The next set he smiles at me less. The night seems to be going OK even though I don't know the tunes. I try to play what seems to me appropriate, and the band seems to appreciate it.

Third set—the band goes into "Old Time Rock and Roll." If you have not had the distinct misfortune to watch drunken middle-aged rednecks try to dance to rock and roll, I'll spare you the details.

Fourth set—they play some Merle Haggard, and I feel more comfortable. At the end of the last song, the singer announces, "Last Call for Alcohol," and then tones into the microphone, "You don't have to go home, but you can't stay here." The club owner starts flashing the lights. At 2:00 A.M. we are finished and begin the fun part, tearing down. The guitar player, who is the bandleader, leans over to me and announces that I play so well that he's in love and wants to marry me. I ask him what his wife would think of that. He shouts to his wife (the drummer) standing behind him, "Rita, you heard me, get lost!" I chuckled all the way home.

Saturday

My Saturday night gig is in Cleveland, Texas, with my old friend Brian (brother of a famous country singer) who until 4:30 Saturday afternoon owed me money from a gig I did with him back in November. He had to pay me in cash, plus the amount for that night's gig before I would leave my house. He tells me, "Sound check is at 5:30." I leave home at 6:00 P.M. and drive again on Highway 59, this time in the other direction, northeast, into the Piney Woods of East Texas. Along 59 North through Houston are peppered dozens of tire shops, discount furniture stores, and also what are euphemistically called "Gentlemen's Clubs."

After Houston comes Montgomery County, and I pass through Kingwood, Houston's last suburb to the northeast. After Kingwood, there is nothing on either side of the road but the towering pines, their presence not entirely benevolent. I feel as if they are watching and harboring a silent dislike for anything human, including me. Their old enemies the timber companies are fading away (I remember playing at dances in East Texas twenty years ago for loggers who were missing fingers from their work at the saw mill and missing teeth from god knows what else), being replaced by bulldozers, housing subdivisions, and outlet malls.

The sun is beginning to set.

Twenty minutes later, I become bored. I fish out a disk and put it into the CD player. Albert Ayler, "Ghosts."

Up ahead I cross the San Jacinto River where my daughter Rose and I once saw a four-year-old girl drown. It was twenty-two years ago at a party/benefit for the victims of a tornado that had recently passed through the outskirts of Houston. The girl's parents were hosting the event and, like most of the people there, were so drunk they could hardly walk. Roy Head, a neighbor of the organizers, was the main entertainment. Rose and I watched as they dragged her limp body out of the muddy river, and, a minute later, when a fight broke out over whether the mouth-to-mouth resuscitation was being done correctly, we walked away. The girl's mother, held by two women, was screaming. Roy Head, wearing a black T-shirt and black shorts, his hair dyed purple, was standing behind a barbecue pit and sobbing. The next time I saw him was a year ago on the bandstand. While I was playing, he whispered into my ear, "Play something sexy," and while I played, he did something slightly unnatural with his microphone.

On the left is a billboard for a tent revival. This, as they like to say, is the buckle of the Bible Belt. My mind flashes back to my old friends Ronnie Mack and Bucky Meadows. Ronnie grew up playing at these revivals while his father preached, his family traveling from town to town through the Piney Woods. In the seventies, Ronnie wound up playing piano with Mel Tillis and writing several of his big hits. But Ronnie had a drinking problem. One morning he woke up, and his wife was lying next to him dead. The police asked him if he had killed her, and he answered, honestly, that he didn't remember. I don't think he ever recovered from that, and it gnawed on him for the rest of his life. He would go on binges, get fired from his country gigs, or just disappear for weeks or months at a time. Then he would reappear with some Pentecostalist friends of his driving him to the gigs. He would play beautifully and between sets he would drink coffee. Then a few weeks later he'd be drinking beer, and then whiskey. Then he would disappear again, this pattern repeating itself for years. At his funeral, the Holy Rollers sat on one side of the church, and the country musicians sat on the other. Both claimed him as their own. The owner of a local beer joint had paid for his funeral, which did not, however, include an expert embalming job. I remember it was quiet in the chapel (provided by the Pentecostalists) and very serious. I was crying, and even the most hardened men were getting tearful, then someone blurted out, "Ronnie looks like a god damned wooden Indian." We all busted out laughing.

Bucky Meadows came from Livingston, down the road from Cleveland. When he was seventeen, in the early fifties, he hit the road with Hank Thompson and the Brazos Valley Boys playing piano and later guitar. In the sixties, he wound up playing with Willie Nelson (he did the guitar ride on "Remember Me" in Willie's acclaimed "Red Headed Stranger" album). When I knew Bucky he owned two pairs of pants, a couple shirts, a small black-and-white TV, a dog named "PJ" (Pure Jazz—the dog before PJ was named Tal) and two old Gibson Super 400 guitars. He could barely write his own name, couldn't drive a car, and couldn't play the same lick twice if his life depended on it, but he could play "What's New" for three hours straight without repeating himself. Ronnie Mack said that Bucky had "seen something really bad" when he was a boy, and he had never been the same since. In the 1980s, Bucky could not hold down a job playing in Houston—they wanted copy musicians playing the same exact things night after night. When he got evicted from his apartment and his friends got tired of taking him in, Willie Nelson gave him a condo on his property outside of Austin and a job as mayor of his Western town. Bucky lived there until he died.

I cross Caney Creek and pass Porter, Texas.

A billboard for a right-wing "Christian" radio station announces, "*He* loves you, yeah yeah, yeah."

New Caney, Texas, where a drummer I knew, Jack Fielder, a soft-spoken man with shoulder-length blond hair, a mustache, and a beard, was shot in the chest point blank by his wife, Tara. His last word was "Why?"

As much as this part of Texas repulses me and sometimes scares me, I don't for a minute forget that this forgotten murky backwoods is a Cradle of American culture both black and white. Perhaps it was the forest that shielded East Texas from the passing of time, allowing culture, both black and white, sheltered in some way from the stifling influences of racism, fundamentalism, and political conservatism, to stew and mix in its own way, producing a mix of blues and country that to a small extent still exists today. If you've seen the movie "Deliverance," that is East Texas, too, and perhaps more appropriately, "O Brother Where Art Thou." In Texas we chuckle quite a bit at that movie because those archetypal characters actually exist here. We all know people here who are exactly like the characters in the film—the same wide-eyed wonder, superstitiousness, but mixed with a certain anger and resentment, and a profound suspicion of outsiders.

On the left, a billboard announces "Cleveland Chili Cookoff."

Patton Village—speed trap. I slow down.

An old shack by the side of the road. The sign says, "Granny's Country Antiques."

I pass through Splendora, Texas, which used to be (and maybe still is) a stronghold of the Texas KKK. Years ago, I visited a middle school in Splendora, and the principal, wearing a black cowboy hat and chewing tobacco, tried to recruit me to teach special education. "Yup," he said, "there was a little problem with, um, inbreedin' several years ago, so we have a lot of special ed kids now. Know what I mean?"

I drive on.

The last of the Texas spring wildflowers—Indian paintbrushes, pink buttercups. The bluebonnets (the state flower) have probably been gone for a few weeks.

I enter Liberty County.

On the right, a tent with a big sign that says "Swords and Knives."

Another sign—"Hog Processing."

Cold Spring—Kent Morrison, a guitar player who had played briefly with Barbara Mandrell in the sixties, used to be the county judge up here until he was convicted of taking bribes. I had played a few gigs with him—always very proud, very stubborn, and very serious. Kent died late one night on his way home from a gig when his car struck a tree. Everyone said it was suicide.

Huge building on the left—"Bethel Assembly of God."

Sign on the right—"East Texas Drug Screening and Consortium."

My directions say to go past the Cleveland cutoff and take a left at the first gravel road after "Joy Juice." Most of East Texas is still dry, so the liquor stores are located just outside the city limits. I drive twenty feet, and there it is, another large corrugated steel building; the sign on the building says "Reno." By now it's dark outside. I get out of my van, open the door, and immediately, I'm struck by the scent of pine needles, dirt, and barbecue smoke. I walk across the parking lot and into the door. There's a grey-haired man standing next to a woman sitting at a table who tells me to pay seven dollars. I tell them I'm in the band. They don't want to let me in—a girl playing steel guitar? Finally someone recognizes me and they tell me to come in, but first I need to have a membership. It is illegal to sell alcohol in a public place, so all night clubs and dance halls are private clubs, most of them selling memberships at the door. I fill out the card.

It is 7:30 and there is no sound check. Another band is playing. I sit around for three hours while this band plays. Inside it is dark, smoky, and loud. Drunks are falling down on the dance floor. The singer introduces a song that he dedicates to "our fighting men in

Iraq who are dying so that we can be free at home." A man in a cowboy hat, missing a couple teeth and carrying a longneck bottle of beer in his hand, runs up to the dance floor and shouts, "You god damned right! You god damned right!" As I walk to the rest rooms, I notice there is fresh blood on the floor. Two women in front of the mirror fixing their makeup, "Yeah, it wuz somethin' else. Did you see it? Billy Ray told Justin to back off, but he wouldn't listen." "Well, he really messed up Justin's face. I just hope he'll be all right." I walk out and toward the bandstand. The cigarette smoke is starting to bother me, and I wipe my eyes, which only makes it worse.

Finally we start playing. Brian's reputation with money is such that he has a difficult time keeping a steady band, so this gig is done with hired guns—some of the better country musicians from Houston, but instead of gelling, the feeling becomes somewhat stiff as the musicians try to prove themselves to each other by over-playing. The sound from the vocal monitors is so loud that I can barely hear my own instrument. Brian tells the drummer to "rock it more." The drummer, misinterpreting this comment as an instruction to turn up, starts banging so hard and so loud that he breaks the head on his snare drum. Then the guitar player turns up. People on the dance floor are feverishly two-stepping to the music; occasionally someone falls down.

During the break when I tell the drummer that he really didn't need to play that loud, he replies, "Well, if you want me to turn down, you should have *Brian* talk to me." As you can see, my frank and opinionated nature usually gets me nowhere.

As I walk back up to the bandstand, I notice a sign for a Bobbie Blue Bland concert, "Live at Reno's." During the second set, Brian leaves the stage after the first song to dance with his new girlfriend, and his brother Kevin comes up to sing. His voice blares through the monitor, ". . . I'm proud to be an A-me-ri-can where at least I know I'm free. Where the fighting men who died . . . blah blah blah," the Lee Greenwood's song. I try turning my head to different angles so that the volume won't hurt my ears, but nothing works. The smoke is now so thick that I am playing with my eyes closed.

At 2:00 A.M., we are finally finished. I pack up and load my equipment as fast as I can, then say good-bye to the other musicians sitting around the empty bandstand waiting to get paid. I walk out the door, get into my van, put the key in the ignition, start the engine, and pull out onto the gravel road that leads to the highway. My ears are ringing. Later, I turn on the radio to help me stay awake. Art Bell's late-night talk show is on. A woman from Phoenix is talking about a UFO she has just seen. As I drive, there is nothing but the road, the sound of the radio, and the full moon reflected dimly through the pines.

JOHN JEREMIAH SULLIVAN

Upon This Rock

It is wrong to boast, but in the beginning, my plan was perfect.

I was assigned to cover the Cross-Over Festival in Lake of the Ozarks, Missouri, three days of the top Christian bands and their backers at an isolated Midwestern fairground or something. I'd stand at the edge of the crowd and take notes on the scene, chat up the occasional audience member ("What's harder—homeschooling or regular schooling?"), then flash my pass to get backstage, where I'd rap with the artists themselves: "This Christian music—it's a phenomenon. What do you tell your fans when they ask you why God let Creed break up?" The singer could feed me his bit about how all music glorifies Him, when it's performed with a loving spirit, and I'd jot down every tenth word, inwardly smiling. Later that night, I might sneak some hooch in my rental car and invite myself to lie with a prayer group by their fire, for the fellowship of it. Fly home, stir in statistics. Paycheck.

But as my breakfast-time mantra says, I am a professional. And they don't give out awards for that sort of toe-tap, J-school foolishness. I wanted to know what these people are, who claim to love this music, who drive hundreds of miles, traversing states, to hear it live. Then it came, my epiphany: I would go with them. Or rather, they would go with me. I would rent a van, a plush one, and we would travel there together, I and three or four hard-core buffs, all the way from the East Coast to the implausibly named Lake of the Ozarks. We'd talk through the night, they'd proselytize at me, and I'd keep my little tape machine working all the while. Somehow I knew we'd grow to like and pity one another. What a story that would make— for future generations.

The only remaining question was: how to recruit the willing? But it was hardly even a question, because everyone knows that damaged types who are down for whatever's clever gather in "chat rooms" every night. And among the Jesusy, there's plenty who are super f'd up. He preferred it that way, evidently.

So I published my invitation, anonymously, at youthontherock. com, and on two Internet forums devoted to the good-looking Christian pop-punk band Relient K, which had been booked to appear at Cross-Over. I pictured that guy or girl out there who'd been dreaming in an attic room of seeing, with his or her own eyes, the men of Relient K perform their song "Gibberish" from *Two Lefts Don't Make a Right . . . but Three Do*. How could he or she get there, though? Gas prices won't drop, and Relient K never plays North Florida. Please, Lord, make it happen. Suddenly, here my posting came, like a great light. We could help each other. "I'm looking for a few serious fans of Christian rock to ride to the festival with me," I wrote. "Male/female doesn't matter, though you shouldn't be older than, say, 28, since I'm looking at this primarily as a youth phenomenon."

They seem like harmless words. Turns out, though, I had failed to grasp how "youth" the phenomenon is. Most of the people hanging out in these chat rooms were teens, and I don't mean 19, friends, I mean 14. Some of them, I was about to learn, were mere tweens. I had just traipsed out onto the World Wide Web—which, if we can believe what we read, is essentially a giant Tron-world for unregenerate child-diddlers—and asked a bunch of 12-year-old Christians if they wanted to come for a ride in my van.

It wasn't long before the little fuckers rounded on me. "Nice job cutting off your email address," wrote "mathgeek29," in a tone that seemed not at all Christlike. "I doubt if anybody would give a full

set of contact information to some complete stranger on the Internet. . . . Aren't there any Christian teens in Manhattan who would
be willing to do this?"

"Oh, I should hope not," I blubbered.

A few of the children were credulous. "Riathamus" said, "i am 14
and live in indiana plus my parents might not let me considering it is
a stranger over the Internet. but that would really be awsome." A
girl by the name of "LilLoser" even tried to be a friend:

> I doubt my parents would allow their baby girl to go with some
> guy they don't and I don't know except through email, especially
> for the amount of time you're asking and like driving around
> everywhere with ya. . . . I'm not saying you're a creepy petifile, lol,
> but i just don't think you'll get too many people interested . . . cuz
> like i said, it spells out "creepy" . . . but hey—good luck to you in
> your questy missiony thing. lol.

The luck that she wished me I sought in vain. The Christians
stopped chatting with me and started chatting among themselves,
warning one another about me. Finally one poster on the official
Relient K site hissed at the others to stay away from my scheme, as I
was in all likelihood "a 40 year old kidnapper." Soon I logged on and
found that the moderators of the site had removed my post and its
lengthening thread of accusations altogether, offering no explanation. Doubtless at that moment they were faxing alerts to a network
of moms. I recoiled in dread. I called my lawyer, in Boston, who told
me to "stop using computers."

In the end, the experience inspired in me a distaste for the whole
Cross-Over Festival, and I resolved to refuse the assignment. I
withdrew.

The problem with a flash mag like the *Gentlemen's Quarterly* is that
there's always some overachieving assistant, sometimes called Greg,
whom the world hasn't beaten down yet and who, when you phone

him, out of courtesy, just to let him know that "the Cross-Over thing fell through" and that you'll be in touch when you "figure out what to do next," hops on that mystical boon the Internet and finds out that the festival you were planning to attend was in fact not "the biggest one in the country," as you'd alleged. The biggest one in the country—indeed, in Christendom—is the Creation Festival, inaugurated in 1979, a regular Godstock. And it happens not in Missouri but in ruralmost Pennsylvania, in a green valley, on a farm called Agape. This festival did not end a month ago; it starts the day after tomorrow. Already they are assembling, many tens of thousands strong. *But hey—good luck to you in your questy missiony thing. lol.*

I made one demand: that I not be forced to camp. I'd be given some sort of vehicle with a mattress in it, one of these pop-ups, maybe. "Right," said Greg. "Here's the deal. I've called around. There are no vans left within a hundred miles of Philly. We got you an RV, though. It's a twenty-nine-footer." Once I reached the place, we agreed (for he led me to think he agreed), I would certainly be able to downgrade to something more manageable.

The reason twenty-nine feet is such a common length for RVs, I presume, is that once a vehicle gets much longer, you need a special permit to drive it. That would mean forms and fees, possibly even background checks. But show up at any RV joint with your thigh stumps lashed to a skateboard, crazily waving your hooks-for-hands, screaming you want that twenty-nine-footer out back for a trip to you *ain't sayin' where*, and all they want to know is: Credit or debit, tiny sir?

Two days later, I stood in a parking lot, suitcase at my feet. Debbie came toward me. She was a lot to love, with a face as sweet as a birthday cake beneath spray-hardened bangs. She raised a meaty arm and pointed, before either of us spoke. The thing she pointed at was the object about which I'd just been saying, "Not that one, Jesus, okay?" It was like something the ancient Egyptians might have left behind in the desert.

"Hi, there," I said. "Listen, all I need is, like, a camper van or whatever. It's just me, and I'm going 500 miles . . . "

She considered me. "Where ya headed?"

"To this thing called Creation. It's, like, a Christian-rock festival."

"You and everybody!" she chirped. "The people who got our vans are going to that same thing. There's a *bunch o' ya.*"

Her coworker Jack emerged—tattooed, squat, gray-mulleted, spouting open contempt for MapQuest. He'd be giving me real directions. "But first let's check 'er out."

We toured the outskirts of my soon-to-be mausoleum. It took time. Every single thing Jack said, somehow, was the only thing I'd need to remember. White water, gray water, black water (drinking, showering, *le devoir*). Here's your this, never ever that. Grumbling about "weekend warriors." I couldn't listen, because listening would mean accepting it as real, though his casual mention of the vast blind spot in the passenger-side mirror squeaked through, as did his description of the "extra two feet on each side"—the bulge of my living quarters—which I wouldn't be able to see but would want to "be conscious of" out there. Debbie followed us with a video camera, for insurance purposes. I saw my loved ones gathered in a mahogany-paneled room to watch this footage; them being forced to hear me say, "What if I never use the toilet—do I still have to switch on the water?"

Mike pulled down the step and climbed aboard. It was really happening. The interior smelled of spoiled vacations and amateur porn shoots wrapped in motel shower curtains and left in the sun. I was physically halted at the threshold for a moment. Jesus had never been in this RV.

What should I tell you about my voyage to Creation? Do you want to know what it's like to drive a windmill with tires down the Pennsylvania Turnpike at rush hour by your lonesome, with darting bug-eyes and shaking hands; or about Greg's laughing phone call "to see how it's going"; about hearing yourself say "no No NO NO!" every time you try to merge; or about thinking you detect—beneath the mysteriously comforting blare of the radio—faint honking sounds, then checking your passenger-side mirror only to find you've been straddling the lanes for an unknown number of miles (those two extra feet!) and that the line of traffic you've kept pinned stretches back farther than you can see; or about stopping at Target to buy sheets and a pillow and peanut butter but then practicing your golf swing in the sporting-goods aisle for a solid twenty-five minutes, unable to stop, knowing that when you do, the twenty-nine-footer will be where you left her, alone in the side lot, hulking and malevolent, waiting for you to take her the rest of the way to your shared destiny?

She got me there, as Debbie and Jack had promised, not possibly believing it themselves. Seven miles from Mount Union, a sign read CREATION AHEAD. The sun was setting; it floated above the valley like a fiery gold balloon. I fell in with a long line of cars and trucks and vans—not many RVs. Here they were, all about me: the born again. On my right was a pickup truck, its bed full of teenage girls in matching powder blue T-shirts; they were screaming at a Mohawked kid who was walking beside the road. I took care not to meet their eyes—who knew but they weren't the same fillies I had solicited days before? Their line of traffic lurched ahead, and an old orange Datsun came up beside me. I watched as the driver rolled down her window, leaned halfway out, and blew a long, clear note on a ram's horn.

Oh, I understand where you are coming from. But that is what she did. I have it on tape. She blew a ram's horn. Quite capably. Twice. A yearly rite, perhaps, to announce her arrival at Creation.

My turn at the gate. The woman looked at me, then past me to the empty passenger seat, then down the whole length of the twenty-nine-footer. "How many people in your group?" she asked.

I pulled away in awe, permitting the twenty-nine-footer to float. My path was thronged with excited Christians, most younger than 18. The adults looked like parents or pastors, not here on their own. Twilight was well along, and the still valley air was sharp with campfire smoke. A great roar shot up to my left—something had happened onstage. The sound bespoke a multitude. It filled the valley and lingered.

I thought I might enter unnoticed—that the RV might even offer a kind of cover—but I was already turning heads. Two separate kids said, "I feel sorry for him" as I passed. Another leaped up on the driver's-side step and said, "Jesus Christ, man," then fell away running. I kept braking—even idling was too fast. Whatever spectacle had provoked the roar was over now: The roads were choked. The youngsters were streaming around me in both directions, back to their campsites, like a line of ants around some petty obstruction. They had a disconcerting way of stepping aside for the RV only when its front fender was just about to graze their backs. From my elevated vantage, it looked as if they were waiting just a tenth of a second too long, and that I was gently, forcibly parting them in slow motion.

The Evangelical strata were more or less recognizable from my high school days, though everyone, I observed, had gotten better looking. Lots were dressed like skate punks or in last season's East Village couture (nondenominationals); others were fairly trailer (rural Baptists or Church of God); there were preps (Young Life, Fellowship of Christian Athletes—these were the ones who'd have the pot). You could spot the stricter sectarians right away, their unchanging antifashion and pale glum faces. When I asked one woman, later, how many she reckoned were white, she said, "Roughly 100 percent." I did see some Asians and three or four blacks. They gave the distinct impression of having been adopted.

I drove so far. You wouldn't have thought this thing could go on so far. Every other bend in the road opened onto a whole new cove full of tents and cars; the encampment had expanded to its physiographic limits, pushing right up to the feet of the ridges. It's hard to put across the sensory effect of that many people living and moving around in the open: part family reunion, part refugee camp. A tad militia, but cheerful.

The roads turned dirt and none too wide: Hallelujah Highway, Street Called Straight. I'd been told to go to "H," but when I reached H, two teenage kids in orange vests came out of the shadows and told me the spots were all reserved. "Help me out here, guys," I said, jerking my thumb, pitifully indicating my mobile home. They pulled out their walkie-talkies. Some time went by. It got darker. Then an even younger boy rode up on a bike and winked a flashlight at me, motioning I should follow.

It was such a comfort to yield up my will to this kid. All I had to do was not lose him. His vest radiated a warm, reassuring officialdom in my headlights. Which may be why I failed to comprehend in time that he was leading me up an almost vertical incline—"the Hill Above D."

I'm not sure which was first: the little bell in my spine warning me that the RV had reached a degree of tilt she was not engineered to handle, or the sickening knowledge that we had begun to slip back. I bowed up off the seat and crouched on the gas. I heard yelling. I kicked at the brake. With my left hand and foot I groped, like a person drowning, for the emergency brake (had Jack's comprehensive how-to sesh not touched on its whereabouts?). We were losing purchase; she started to shudder. My little guide's eyes looked scared.

I'd known this moment would come, of course, that the twenty-nine-footer would turn on me. We had both of us understood it from the start. But I must confess, I never imagined her hunger for death could prove so extreme. Laid out below and behind me was a literal field of Christians, toasting buns and playing guitars, fellowshipping. The aerial shot in the papers would show a long scar, a swath through their peaceful tent village. And that this gigantic psychopath had worked her vile design through the agency of a child—an innocent, albeit impossibly stupid, child . . .

My memory of the next five seconds is smeared, but logic tells me that a large and perfectly square male head appeared in the windshield. It was blond and wearing glasses. It had wide-open eyes and a Chaucerian West Virginia accent and said rapidly that I should "JACK THE WILL TO THE ROT" while applying the

brakes. Some branch of my motor cortex obeyed. The RV skidded
briefly and was still. Then the same voice said, "All right, hit the gas
on three: one, two . . . "

She began to climb—slowly, as if on a pulley. Some freakishly
powerful beings were pushing. Soon we had leveled out at the top of
the hill.

There were five of them, all in their early twenties. I remained in
the twenty-nine-footer; they gathered below.

"Thank you," I said.

"Aw, hey," shot back Darius, the one who'd given the orders. He
talked very fast. "We've been doing this all day—I don't know why
that kid keeps bringing people up here—we're from West Virginia—listen, he's retarded—there's an *empty field* right there."

I looked back and down at what he was pointing to: pastureland.

Jake stepped forward. He was also blond, but slender. And handsome in a feral way. His face was covered in stubble as pale as his
hair. He said he was from West Virginia and wanted to know where
I was from.

"I was born in Louisville," I said.

"Really?" said Jake. "Is that on the Ohio River?" Like Darius, he
both responded and spoke very quickly. I said that in fact it was.

"Well, I know a dude that died who was from Ohio. I'm a volunteer fireman, see. Well, he flipped a Chevy Blazer nine times. He
was spread out from here to that ridge over there. He was dead as
four o'clock."

"Who are you guys?" I said.

Ritter answered. He was big, one of those fat men who don't really have any fat, a corrections officer—as I was soon to learn—and
a former heavyweight wrestler. He could burst a pineapple in his
armpit and chuckle about it (or so I assume). Haircut: military. Mustache: faint. "We're just a bunch of West Virginia guys on fire for
Christ," he said. "I'm Ritter, and this is Darius, Jake, Bub, and that's
Jake's brother, Josh. Pee Wee's around here somewhere."

"Chasin' tail," said Darius disdainfully.

"So you guys have just been hanging out here, saving lives?"

"We're from West Virginia," said Darius again, like maybe he thought I was thick. It was he who most often spoke for the group. The projection of his jaw from the lump of snuff he kept there made him come off a bit contentious, but I felt sure he was just high-strung.

"See," Jake said, "well, our campsite is right over there." With a cock of his head he identified a car, a truck, a tent, a fire, and a tall cross made of logs. And that other thing was . . . a PA system?

"We had this spot last year," Darius said. "I prayed about it. I said, 'God, I'd just really like to have that spot again—you know, if it's Your will.'"

I'd assumed that my days at Creation would be fairly lonely and end with my ritual murder. But these West Virginia guys had such warmth. It flowed out of them. They asked me what I did and whether I liked sassafras tea and how many others I'd brought with me in the RV. Plus they knew a dude who died horribly and was from a state with the same name as the river I grew up by, and I'm not the type who questions that sort of thing.

"What are you guys doing later?" I said.

Bub was short and solid; each of his hands looked as strong as a trash compactor. He had darker skin than the rest—an olive cast—with brown hair under a camouflage hat and brown eyes and a full-fledged dark mustache. Later he would share with me that friends often told him he must be "part N-word." He was shy and always looked like he must be thinking hard about something. "Me and Ritter's going to hear some music," he said.

"What band is it?"

Ritter said, "Jars of Clay."

I had read about them; they were big. "Why don't you guys stop by my trailer and get me on your way?" I said. "I'll be in that totally empty field."

Ritter said, "We just might do that." Then they all lined up to shake my hand.

While I waited for Ritter and Bub, I lay in bed and read *The Silenced Times* by lantern light. This was a thin newsletter that had come with my festival packet. It wasn't really a newsletter; it was publisher's flackery for *Silenced*, a new novel by Jerry Jenkins, one of the minds behind the multi-hundred-million-dollar *Left Behind* series— twelve books so far, all about what happens after the Rapture, to people like me. His new book was a futuristic job, set in 2047. The dateline on the newsletter read: "March 2, 38." You get it? Thirty-seven years have passed since they wiped Jesus from history. *The Silenced Times* was laid out to look like a newspaper from that coming age.

It was pretty grim stuff. In the year 38, an ancient death cult has spread like a virus and taken over the "United Seven States of America." Adherents meet in "cell groups" (nice touch: a bit of old Commie lingo); they enlist the young and hunger for global hegemony while striving to hasten the end of the world. By the year 34— the time of the last census—44 percent of the population had professed membership in the group; by now the figure is closer to half. This dwarfs any other surviving religious movement in the land. Even the president (whom they mobilized to elect) has been converted. The most popular news channel in the country openly backs him and his policies; and the year's most talked-about film is naked propaganda for the cult, but in a darkly brilliant twist, much of the population has been convinced that the media are in fact controlled by . . .

I'm sorry! That's all happening now. That's Evangelicalism. *The Silenced Times* describes Christians being thrown into jail, driven underground, their pamphlets confiscated. A dude wins an award for ratting out his sister, who was leading a campus Bible study (you know how we do). Jerry Jenkins must blow his royalties on crack. I especially liked the part in *The Silenced Times* where it reports that antireligion forces have finally rounded up Jenkins himself—in a cave. He's 97 years old but has never stopped typing, and as they drag him away, he's bellowing Scripture.

Ritter beat on the door. He and Bub were ready to hear some Jars of Clay. Now that it was night, more fires were going; the whole valley was aromatic. And the sky looked like a tin punch lantern—thousands of stars were out. There were so many souls headed toward the stage, it was hard to walk, though I noticed the crowd tended to give Ritter a wider berth. He kind of leaned back, looking over people's heads, as if he expected to spot a friend. I asked about his church in West Virginia. He said he and the rest of the guys were Pentecostal, speaking in tongues and all that—except for Jake, who was a Baptist. But they all went to the same "sing"—a weekly Bible study at somebody's house with food and guitars. Did Ritter think everyone here was a Christian? "No, there's some who probably aren't saved. With this many people, there has to be." What were his feelings on that? "It just opens up opportunities for witnessing," he said.

Bub stopped suddenly—a signal that he wished to speak. The crowd flowed on around us for a minute while he chose his words. "There's Jewish people here," he said.

"Really?" I said. "You mean, Jew Jews?"

"Yeah," Bub said. "These girls Pee Wee brung around. I mean, they're Jewish. That's pretty awesome." He laughed without moving his face; Bub's laugh was a purely vocal phenomenon. Were his eyes moist?

We commenced walking.

I suspect that on some level—say, the conscious one—I didn't want to be noticing what I noticed as we went. But I've been to a lot of huge public events in this country during the past five years, writing about sports or whatever, and one thing they all had in common was this weird implicit enmity that American males, in particular, seem to carry around with them much of the time. Call it a laughable generalization, fine, but if you spend enough late afternoons in stadium concourses, you feel it, something darker than machismo. Something a little wounded, and a little sneering, and just plain ready for bad things to happen. It wasn't here. It was just . . . not. I looked for it, and I couldn't find it. In the three days I spent at Creation, I saw not one fight, heard not one word spoken in anger, felt at no time even mildly harassed, and in fact met many people who were exceptionally kind. I realize they were all of the same race, all believed the same stuff, and weren't drinking, but there were also 100,000 of them. What's that about?

We were walking past a row of portable toilets, by the food stands. As we came around the corner, I saw the stage, from off to the side. And the crowd on the hill that faced the stage. Their bodies rose till they merged with the dark. "Holy crap," I said.

Ritter waved his arm like an impresario. He said, "This, my friend, is Creation."

For their encore, Jars of Clay did a cover of U2's "All I Want Is You." It was bluesy.

That's the last thing I'll be saying about the bands.

Or, no, wait, there's this: The fact that I didn't think I heard a single interesting bar of music from the forty or so acts I caught or overheard at Creation shouldn't be read as a knock on the acts themselves, much less as contempt for the underlying notion of Christians playing rock. These were not Christian bands, you see; these were Christian-rock bands. The key to digging this scene lies in that one-syllable distinction. Christian rock is a genre that exists to edify and make money off of evangelical Christians. It's message music for listeners who know the message cold, and, what's more, it operates under a perceived *responsibility*—one the artists embrace—to "reach people." As such, it rewards both obviousness and maximum palatability (the artists would say *clarity*), which in turn means *parasitism*. Remember those perfume dispensers they used to have in pharmacies—"If you like Drakkar Noir, you'll love Sexy Musk"? Well, Christian rock works like that. Every successful crappy secular group has its Christian off-brand, and that's proper, because culturally speaking, it's supposed to serve as a stand-in for, not an alternative to or an improvement on, those very groups. In this it succeeds wonderfully. If you think it profoundly sucks, that's because your priorities are not its priorities; you want to hear something cool and new, it needs to play something proven to please . . . while praising Jesus Christ. That's Christian rock. A Christian band, on the other hand, is just a band that has more than one Christian in it. U2 is the exemplar, held aloft by believers and nonbelievers alike, but there have been others through the years, bands about which people would say, "Did you know those guys were Christians? I know—it's freaky. They're still fuckin' good, though." The Call was like that; Lone Justice was like that. These days you hear it about indie acts like Pedro the Lion and Damien Jurado (or P.O.D. and Evanescence—de gustibus). In most cases, bands like these make a very, very careful effort not to be seen as playing "Christian rock." It's largely a matter of phrasing: Don't tell the interviewer you're born-again; say faith is a very important part of your life. And here, if I can drop the open-minded pretense real quick, is where the stickier problem of *actually being any good* comes in, because a question that must be asked is whether a hard-core Christian who turns 19 and finds he or she can write first-rate songs (someone like Damien Jurado) would ever have anything whatsoever to do with Christian rock. Talent tends to come hand in hand with a certain base level of subtlety. And believe it or not, the Christian-rock establishment sometimes expresses a kind of resigned *approval* of the way groups like U2 or Switchfoot (who played Creation while I was there and had a monster secular–radio hit at the time with "Meant to Live" but whose management wouldn't allow them to be photographed onstage) take quiet pains to distance themselves from any unambiguous Jesus-loving, recognizing that this is the surest way to connect with the world (you know that's how they refer to us, right? We're "of the world"). So it's possible—and indeed seems likely—that Christian rock is a musical genre, the only one I can think of, that has excellence-proofed itself.

It was late, and the Jews had sown discord. What Bub had said was true: There were Jews at Creation. These were Jews for Jesus, it emerged, two startlingly pretty high school girls from Richmond. They'd been sitting by the fire—one of them mingling fingers with Pee Wee—when Bub and Ritter and I returned from seeing Jars of Clay. Pee Wee was younger than the other guys, and cute, and he gazed at the girls admiringly when they spoke. At a certain point, they mentioned to Ritter that he would writhe in hell for having tattoos (he had a couple); it was what their people believed. Ritter had not taken the news all that well. He was fairly confident about his position among the elect. There was debate; Pee Wee was forced to escort the girls back to their tents, while Darius worked to calm Ritter. "They may have weird ideas," he said, "but we worship the same God."

The fire had burned to glowing coals, and now it was just we men, sitting on coolers, talking late-night hermeneutics blues. Bub didn't see how God could change His mind, how He could say all that crazy shit in the Old Testament—like don't get tattoos and don't look at your uncle naked—then take it back in the New.

"Think about it this way," I said. "If you do something that really makes Darius mad, and he's pissed at you, but then you do something to make it up to him, and he forgives you, that isn't him changing his mind. The situation has changed. It's the same with the old and new covenants, except Jesus did the making up."

Bub seemed pleased with this explanation. "I never heard anyone say it like that," he said. But Darius stared at me gimlet-eyed across the fire. He knew my gloss was theologically sound, and he wondered where I'd gotten it. The guys had been gracefully dancing around the question of what I believed—"where my walk was at," as they would have put it—all night.

We knew one another fairly well by now. Once Pee Wee had returned, they'd eagerly shown me around their camp. Most of their tents were back in the forest, where they weren't supposed to be; the air was cooler there. Darius had located a small stream about thirty yards away and, using his hands, dug out a basin. This was supplying their drinking water.

It came out that these guys spent much if not most of each year in the woods. They lived off game—as folks do, they said, in their section of Braxton County. They knew all the plants of the forest, which were edible, which cured what. Darius pulled out a large piece of cardboard folded in half. He opened it under my face: a mess of sassafras roots. He wafted their scent of black licorice into my face and made me eat one.

Then he remarked that he bet I liked weed. I allowed as how I might not *not* like it. "I used to love that stuff," he told me. Seeing that I was taken aback, he said, "Man, to tell you the truth, I wasn't even convicted about it. But it's socially unacceptable, and that was getting in the way of my Christian growth."

The guys had put together what I did for a living—though, to their credit, they didn't seem to take this as a reasonable explanation for my being there—and they gradually got the sense that I found them exotic (though it was more than that). Slowly, their talk became an ecstasy of self-definition. They were passionate to make me see *what kind of guys they were.* This might have grown tedious, had they been any old kind of guys. But they were the kind of guys who believed that God had personally interceded and made it possible for four of them to fit into Ritter's silver Chevrolet Cavalier for the trip to Creation.

"Look," Bub said, "I'm a pretty big boy, right? I mean, I'm stout. And Darius is a big boy"—here Darius broke in and made me look at his calves, which were muscled to a degree that hinted at deformity; "I'm a freak," he said; Bub sighed and went on without breaking eye contact—"and you *know* Ritter is a big boy. Plus we had two coolers, guitars, an electric piano, our tents and stuff, all"—he turned and pointed, turned back, paused—"in that Chevy." He had the same look in his eyes as earlier, when he'd told me there were Jews. "I think that might be a miracle," he said.

In their lives, they had known terrific violence. Ritter and Darius met, in fact, when each was beating the shit out of the other in middle-school math class. Who won? Ritter looked at Darius, as if to

clear his answer, and said, "Nobody." Jake once took a fishing pole
that Darius had accidentally stepped on and broken and beat him to
the ground with it. "I told him, 'Well, watch where you're stepping.'"
Jake said. (This memory made Darius laugh so hard he removed
his glasses.) Half of their childhood friends had been murdered—
shot or stabbed over drugs or nothing. Others had killed themselves. Darius's grandfather, great-uncle, and onetime best friend
had all committed suicide. When Darius was growing up, his father
was in and out of jail; at least once, his father had done hard time. In
Ohio he stabbed a man in the chest (the man had refused to stop
"pounding on" Darius's grandfather). Darius caught a lot of grief—
"Your daddy's a jailbird!"—during those years. He'd carried a chip
on his shoulder from that.

"You came up pretty rough," I said.

"Not really," Darius said. "Some people ain't got hands and feet."
He talked about how much he loved his father. "With all my
heart—he's the best. He's brought me up the way that I am."

"And anyway," he added, "I gave all that to God—all that anger
and stuff. He took it away."

God had left him enough to get by on. Earlier in the evening, the
guys had roughed up Pee Wee a little and tied him to a tree with
ratchet straps. Some other Christians must have reported his
screams to the staff because a guy in an orange vest came stomping
up the hill. Pee Wee hadn't been hurt much, but he put on a show of
tears, to be funny. "They always do me like that," he said. "Save me,
mister!"

The guy was unamused. "It's not them you got to worry about,"
he said. "It's me."

Those were such foolish words! Darius came forward like some
hideously fast-moving lizard on a nature show. "I'd watch it, man,"
he said. "You don't know who you're talking to. This'n here's as like
to shoot you as shake your hand."

The guy somehow appeared to move back without actually taking a step. "You're not allowed to have weapons," he said.

"Is that right?" Darius said. "We got a conceal 'n' carry right there in the glove box. Mister, I'm from West Virginia—I know the law."

"I think you're lying," said the guy. His voice had gone a bit warbly.

Darius leaned forward, as if to hear better. His eyes were leaving his skull. "How would you know that?" he said. "Are you a prophet?"

"I'm Creation staff!" the guy said.

All of a sudden, Jake stood up—he'd been watching this scene from his seat by the fire. The fixed polite smile on his face was indistinguishable from a leer. "Well," he said, "why don't you go somewhere and *create* your own problems?"

I realize that these tales of the West Virginia guys' occasional truculence might appear to gainsay what I claimed earlier about "not one word spoken in anger," etc. But look, it was playful. Darius, at least, was performing a bit for me. And if you take into account what the guys have to be on guard for all the time back home, the notable thing becomes how effectively they checked their instincts at Creation.

In any case, we operated with more or less perfect impunity from then on.

This included a lot of very loud, live music between two and three o'clock in the morning. The guys were running their large PA off the battery in Jake's truck. Ritter and Darius had a band of their own back home, First Verse. They were responsible for the music at their church. Ritter had an angelic tenor that seemed to be coming out of a body other than his own. And Josh was a good guitar player; he had a Les Paul and an effects board. We passed around the acoustic. I had to dig to come up with Christian tunes. I did "Jesus," by Lou Reed, which they liked okay. But they really enjoyed "Redemption Song." When I finished, Bub said, "Man, that's really Christian. It really is." Darius made me teach it to him; he said he would take it home and "do it at worship."

Then he jumped up and jogged to the electric piano, which was on a stand ten feet away. He closed his eyes and began to play. I know enough piano to know what good technique sounds like, and Darius played very, very well. He improvised for an hour. At one point, Bub went and stood beside him with his hands in his pockets, facing the rest of us, as if guarding his friend while the latter was in this vulnerable trance state. Ritter whispered to me that Darius had been offered a music scholarship to a college in West Virginia; he went to visit a friend, and a professor heard him messing around on the school's piano. The dude offered him a full ride then and there. Ritter couldn't really explain why Darius had turned it down. "He's kind of our Rain Man," Ritter said.

At some juncture, I must have taken up my lantern and crept back down the hill, since I sat up straight the next morning, fully dressed in the twenty-nine-footer. The sound that woke me was a barbaric moan, like that of an army about to charge. Early mornings at Creation were about "Praise and Worship," a new form of Christian rock in which the band and the audience sing, all together, as loud as they can, directly to God. It gets rather intense.

The guys had told me they meant to spend most of today at the main stage, checking out bands. But hey, fuck that. I'd already checked out a band. Mine was to stay in this trailer, jotting impressions.

It was hot, though. As it got hotter, the light brown carpet started to give off fumes from under its plastic hide. I tumbled out the side hatch and went after Darius, Ritter, and Bub. In the light of day, one could see there were pretty accomplished freaks at this thing: a guy in a skirt wearing lace on his arms; a strange little androgynous creature dressed in full cardboard armor, carrying a sword. They knew they were in a safe place, I guess.

The guys left me standing in line at a lemonade booth; they didn't want to miss Skillet, one of Ritter's favorite bands. I got my drink and drifted slowly toward where I thought they'd be standing.

Lack of food, my filthiness, impending sunstroke: These were ganging up on me. Plus the air down here smelled faintly of poo. There were a lot of blazing-hot portable toilets wafting miasma whenever the doors were opened.

I stood in the center of a gravel patch between the food and the crowd, sort of gumming the straw, quadriplegically probing with it for stubborn pockets of meltwater. I was a ways from the stage, but I could see well enough. Something started to happen to me. The guys in the band were middle-aged. They had blousy shirts and half-hearted arena-rock moves from the mid-'80s.

What was . . . this feeling? The singer kept grinning between lines, like if he didn't, he might collapse. I could just make out the words:

> *There's a higher place to go*
> *(beyond belief, beyond belief),*
> *Where we reach the next plateau,*
> *(beyond belief, beyond belief) . . .*

The straw slipped from my mouth.
"Oh, shit. It's Petra."

It was 1988. The guy who brought me in we called Verm (I'll use people's nicknames here; they don't deserve to be dragooned into my memory-voyage). He was a short, good-looking guy with a dark ponytail and a devilish laugh, a skater and an ex-pothead, which had got him kicked out of his house a year or so before we met. His folks belonged to this nondenominational church in Ohio, where I went to high school. It was a movement more than a church—thousands of members, even then. I hear it's bigger now. "Central meeting" took place in an empty warehouse, for reasons of space, but the smaller meetings were where it was at: home church (fifty people or so), cell group (maybe a dozen). Verm's dad said, Look, go with us once a week and you can move back in.

Verm got saved. And since he was brilliant (he became something of a legend at our school because whenever a new foreign student enrolled, he'd sit with her every day at lunch and make her give him language lessons till he was proficient), and since he was about the most artlessly gregarious human being I've ever known, and since he knew loads of lost souls from his druggie days, he became a champion evangelizer, a golden child.

I was new and nurturing a transcendent hatred of Ohio. Verm found out I liked the Smiths, and we started swapping tapes. Before long, we were hanging out after school. Then the moment came that always comes when you make friends with a born-again: "Listen, I go to this thing on Wednesday nights. It's like a Bible study— no, listen, it's cool. The people are actually really cool."

They were, that's the thing. In fifteen minutes, all my ideas about Christians were put to flight. They were smarter than any bunch I'd been exposed to (I didn't grow up in Cambridge or anything, but even so), they were accepting of every kind of weirdness, and they had that light that people who are pursuing something higher give off. It's attractive, to say the least. I started asking questions, lots of questions. And they loved that, because they had answers. That's one of the ways Evangelicalism works. Your average agnostic doesn't go through life just *primed* to offer a clear, considered defense of, say, intratextual Scriptural inconsistency. But born-agains train for that chance encounter with the inquisitive stranger. And when you're a 14-year-old carting around some fairly undernourished intellectual ambitions, and a charismatic adult sits you down and explains that if you transpose this span of years onto the Hebrew calendar, and multiply that times seven, and plug in a date from the reign of King Howsomever, then you plainly see that this passage predicts the birth of Christ almost to the hour, despite the fact that the Gospel writers didn't have access to this information! I, for one, was dazzled.

But also powerfully stirred on a level that didn't depend on my naïveté. The sheer passionate engagement of it caught my imagination: Nobody had told me there were Christians like this. They went at the Bible with grad-seminar intensity, week after week. Mole was their leader (short for Moloch; he had started the whole thing, back in the '70s). He had a wiry, dark beard and a pair of nail-gun cobalt eyes. My Russian-novel fantasies of underground gatherings—shared subversive fervor—were flattered and, it seemed, embodied. Here was counterculture, without sad hippie trappings.

Verm hugged me when I said to him, in the hallway after a meeting, "I think I might believe." When it came time for me to go all the way—to "accept Jesus into my heart" (in that time-honored formulation)—we prayed the prayer together.

Three years passed. I waxed strong in spirit. Verm and I were sort of heading up the high school end of the operation now. Mole had discovered (I had discovered, too) that I was good with words, that I could talk in front of people; Verm and I started leading Bible study once a month. We were saving souls like mad, laying up treasure for ourselves in heaven. I was never the recruiter he was, but I grasped subtlety; Verm would get them there, and together we'd start on their heads. Witnessing, it's called. I had made some progress socially at school, which gave us access to the popular crowd; in this way, many were brought to the Lord. Verm and I went to conferences and on "study retreats"; we started taking classes in theology, which the group offered—free of charge—for promising young leaders. And always, underneath but suffusing it all, there were the cell-group meetings, every week, on Friday or Saturday nights, which meant I could stay out till morning. (My Episcopalian parents were thoroughly mortified by the whole business, but it's not easy telling your kid to *stop spending so much time at church*.)

Cell group was typically held in somebody's dining room, somebody pretty high up in the group. You have to understand what an honor it was to be in a cell with Mole. People would see me at central meeting and be like, "How is that, getting to rap with him every week?" It was awesome. He really got down with the Word (he had a wonderful old hippie way of talking; everything was something *action:* "time for some fellowship action . . . let's get some chips 'n' salsa action"). He carried a heavy "study Bible"—no King James for the nondenominationals; too many inaccuracies. When he cracked open its hand-tooled leather cover, you knew it was on. And no joke: The brother was gifted. Even handicapped by the relatively pedestrian style of the New American Standard version, he could twist a verse into your conscience like a bone screw, make you think Christ was standing there nodding approval. The prayer session alone would last an hour. Afterward, there was always a fire in the backyard. Mole would sit and whack a machete into a chopping block. He smoked cheap cigars; he let us smoke cigarettes. The guitar went around. We'd talk about which brother was struggling with sin—did he need counsel? Or about the end of the world: It'd be soon. We had to save as many as we could.

I won't inflict on you all my reasons for drawing away from the fold. They were clichéd, anyway, and not altogether innocent. Enough to say I started reading books Mole hadn't recommended. Some of them seemed pretty smart—and didn't jibe with the Bible. The defensive theodicy he'd drilled into me during those nights of heady exegesis developed cracks. The hell stuff: I never made peace with it. Human beings were capable of forgiving those who'd done them terrible wrongs, and we all agreed that human beings were maggots compared with God, so what was His trouble, again? I looked around and saw people who'd never have a chance to come to Jesus; they were too badly crippled. Didn't they deserve—more than the rest of us, even—to find His succor, after this life?

Belief and nonbelief are two giant planets, the orbits of which don't touch. Everything about Christianity can be justified *within the context of Christian belief.* That is, if you accept its terms. Once you do, your belief starts modifying the data (in ways that are themselves defensible, see?), until eventually the data begin to reinforce belief. The precise moment of illogic can never be isolated and may not exist. Like holding a magnifying glass at arm's length and bringing it toward your eye: Things are upside down, they're upside

down, they're right side up. What lay between? If there was something, it passed too quickly to be observed. This is why you can
never reason true Christians out of the faith. It's not, as the adage
has it, because they were never reasoned into it—many were—it's
that faith is a logical door which locks behind you. What looks like a
line of thought is steadily warping into a circle, one that closes with
you inside. If this seems to imply that no apostate was ever a true
Christian and that therefore, I was never one, I think I'd stand by
both of those statements. Doesn't the fact that I can't write about
my old friends without an apologetic tone just show that I never deserved to be one of them?

The break came during the winter of my junior year. I got a call
from Verm late one afternoon. He'd promised Mole he would do
this thing, and now he felt sick. Sinus infection (he always had sinus
infections). Had I ever heard of Petra? Well, they're a Christian-
rock band, and they're playing the arena downtown. After their
shows, the singer invites anybody who wants to know more about
Jesus to come backstage, and they have people, like, waiting to talk
to them.

The promoter had called up Mole, and Mole had volunteered
Verm, and now Verm wanted to know if I'd help him out. I couldn't
say no.

The concert was upsetting from the start; it was one of my first
encounters with the other kinds of Evangelicals, the hand-wavers
and the weepers and all (we liked to keep things "sober" in the
group). The girl in front of me was signing all the words to the
songs, but she wasn't deaf. It was just horrifying.

Verm had read me, over the phone, the pamphlet he got. After
the first encore, we were to head for the witnessing zone and wait
there. I went. I sat on the ground.

Soon they came filing in, the seekers.

I don't know what was up with the ones I got. I think they may
have gone looking for the restroom and been swept up by the
stampede. They were about my age and wearing hooded brown

sweatshirts—mouths agape, eyes empty. I asked them the questions: What did they think about all they'd heard? Were they curious about anything Petra talked about? (There'd been lots of "talks" between songs.)

I couldn't get them to speak. They stared at me like they were waiting for me to slap them.

This was my opening. They were either rapt or retarded, and whichever it was, Christ called on me to lay down my testimony.

The sentences wouldn't form. I flipped through the list of dogmas, searching for one I didn't essentially think was crap, and came up with nothing.

There might have ensued a nauseating silence, but I acted with an odd decisiveness to end the whole experience. I asked them if they wanted to leave—it was an all but rhetorical question—and said I did, too. We walked out together.

I took Mole and Verm aside a few nights later and told them my doubts had overtaken me. If I kept showing up at meetings, I'd be faking it. That was an insult to them, to God, to the group. Verm was silent; he hugged me. Mole said he respected my reasons, that I'd have to explore my doubts before my walk could be strong again. He said he'd pray for me. Unless he's undergone some radical change in character, he's still praying.

Statistically speaking, my bout with Evangelicalism was probably unremarkable. For white Americans with my socioeconomic background (middle to upper-middle class), it's an experience commonly linked to one's teens and moved beyond before one reaches 20. These kids around me at Creation—a lot of them were like that. How many even knew who Darwin was? They'd learn. At least once a year since college, I'll be getting to know someone, and it comes out that we have in common a high school "Jesus phase." That's always an excellent laugh. Except a phase is supposed to end—or at least give way to other phases—not simply expand into a long preoccupation.

Bless those who've been brainwashed by cults and sent off for de-programming. That makes it simple: You put it behind you. But this group was no cult. They persuaded; they never pressured, much less threatened. Nor did they punish. A guy I brought into the group—we called him Goog—is still a close friend. He leads meetings now and spends part of each year doing pro bono dental work in Cambodia. He's never asked me when I'm coming back.

My problem is not that I dream I'm in hell or that Mole is at the window. It isn't that I feel psychologically harmed. It isn't even that I feel like a sucker for having bought it all. It's that I love Jesus Christ.

"The latchet of whose shoes I am not worthy to unloose." I can barely write that. He was the most beautiful dude. Forget the Epistles, forget all the bullying stuff that came later. Look at what He said. Read *The Jefferson Bible*. Or better yet, read *The Logia of Yeshua*, by Guy Davenport and Benjamin Urrutia, an unadorned translation of all the sayings ascribed to Jesus that modern scholars deem authentic. There's your man. His breakthrough was the aestheticization of weakness. Not in what conquers, not in glory, but in what's fragile and what suffers—there lies sanity. And salvation. "Let anyone who has power renounce it," He said. "Your father is compassionate to all, as you should be." That's how He talked, to those who knew Him.

Why should He vex me? Why is His ghost not friendlier? Why can't I just be a good Enlightenment child and see in His life a sustaining example of what we can be, as a species?

Because once you've known Him as God, it's hard to find comfort in the man. The sheer sensation of life that comes with a total, all-pervading notion of being—the pulse of consequence one projects onto even the humblest things—the pull of that won't slacken.

And one has doubts about one's doubts.

"D'ye hear that mountain lion last night?"

It was dark, and Jake was standing over me, dressed in camouflage. I'd been hunched over on a cooler by the ashes for a number of hours, waiting on the guys to get back from wherever they'd gone.

I told him I hadn't heard anything. Bub came up from behind, also in camo. "In the middle of the night," he said. "It woke me up."

Jake said, "It sounded like a baby crying."

"Like a little bitty baby," Bub said.

Jake was messing with something at my feet, in the shadows, something that looked alive. Bub dropped a few logs onto the fire and went to the Chevy for matches.

I sat there trying to see what Jake was doing. "You got that lantern?" he said. It was by my feet; I switched it on.

He started pulling frogs out of a poke. One after another. They strained in his grip and lashed at the air.

"Where'd you get those?" I asked.

"About half a mile that way," he said. "It ain't private property if you're in the middle of the creek." Bub laughed his high expressionless laugh.

"These ain't too big," Jake said. "In West Virginia, well, we got ones the size of chickens."

Jake started chopping their bodies in half. He'd lean forward and center his weight on the hand that held the knife, to get a clean cut, tossing the legs into a frying pan. Then he'd stab each frog in the brain and flip the upper parts into a separate pile. They kept twitching, of course—their nerves. Some were a little less dead than that. One in particular stared up at me, gulping for air, though his lungs were beside him, in the grass.

"Could you do that one in the brain again?" I said. Jake spiked it, expertly, and grabbed for the next frog.

"Why don't you stab their brains before you take off the legs?" I asked.

He laughed. He said I cracked him up.

Darius, when he got back, made me a cup of hot sassafras tea. "Drink this, it'll make you feel better," he told me. I'd never said I felt bad. Jake lightly sautéed the legs in butter and served them to me warm. "Eat this," he said. The meat was so tender, it all but dissolved on my tongue.

Pee Wee came back with the Jews, who were forced to tell us a second time that we were damned. (Leviticus 11:12, "Whatsoever hath no fins nor scales in the waters, that shall be an abomination unto you.") Jake, when he heard this, put on a show, making the demi-frogs talk like puppets, chewing the legs with his mouth wide open so all could see the meat.

The girls ran off again. Pee Wee went after them, calling, "Come on, they're just playin'!"

Darius peered at Jake. He looked not angry but saddened. Jake said, "Well, if he wants to bring them girls around here, they oughtn't to be telling us what we can eat."

"Wherefore, if meat make my brother to offend," Darius said, "I will eat no flesh while the world standeth."

"First Corinthians," I said.

"8:13," Darius said.

I woke without having slept—that evil feeling—and lay there steeling myself for the strains of Praise and Worship. When it became too much to wait, I boiled water and made instant coffee and drank it scalding from the lid of the peanut butter jar. My body smelled like stale campfire. My hair had leaves and ash and things in it. I thought about taking a shower, but I'd made it two days without so much as acknowledging any of the twenty-nine-footer's systems; it would have been stupid to give in now.

I sat in the driver's seat and watched, through tinted glass, little clusters of Christians pass. They looked like people anywhere, only gladder, more self-contained. Or maybe they just looked like people anywhere. I don't know. I had no pseudo-anthropological moxie left. I got out and wandered. I sat with the crowd in front of the stage. There was a redheaded Christian speaker up there, pacing back and forth. Out of nowhere, he shrieked, "MAY YOU BE COVERED IN THE ASHES OF YOUR RABBI JESUS!" If I were to try to convey to you how loudly he shrieked this, you'd think I was playing wordy games.

I was staggering through the food stands when a man died at my feet. He was standing in front of the funnel-cake window. He was big, in his early sixties, wearing shorts and a short-sleeve button-down shirt. He just . . . died. Massive heart attack. I was standing there, and he fell, and I don't know whether there's some primitive zone in the brain that registers these things, but the second he landed, I knew he was gone. The paramedics jumped on him so fast, it was weird—it was like they'd been waiting. They pumped and pumped on his chest, blew into his mouth, ran IVs. The ambulance showed up, and more equipment appeared. The man's broad face had that slightly disgruntled look you see on the newly dead.

Others had gathered around; some thought it was all a show. A woman standing next to me said bitterly, "It's not a show. A man has died." She started crying. She took my hand. She was small with silver hair and black eyebrows. "He's fine, he's fine," she said. I looked at the side of her face. "Just pray for his family," she said. "He's fine."

I went back to the trailer and had, as the ladies say where I'm from, a colossal fucking go-to-pieces. I kept starting to cry and then stopping myself, for some reason. I felt nonsensically raw and lonely. What a dickhead I'd been, thinking the trip would be a lark. There were too many ghosts here. Everyone seemed so strange and so familiar. Plus I suppose I was starving. The frog meat was superb but meager—even Jake had said as much.

In the midst of all this, I began to hear, through the shell of the twenty-nine-footer, Stephen Baldwin giving a talk on the Fringe Stage—that's where the "edgier" acts are put on at Creation. If you're shaky on your Baldwin brothers, he's the vaguely troglodytic one who used to comb his bangs straight down and wear dusters. He's come to the Lord—I don't know if you knew. I caught him on cable a few months ago, some religious talk show. Him and Gary Busey. I don't remember what Baldwin said, because Busey was saying shit so weird the host got nervous. Busey's into "generational curses." If you're wondering what those are, too bad. I was born-again, not raised on meth.

Baldwin said many things; the things he said got stranger and stranger. He said his Brazilian nanny, Augusta, had converted him and his wife in Tucson, thereby fulfilling a prophecy she'd been given by her preacher back home. He said, "God allowed 9/11 to happen," that it was "the wrath of God," and that Jesus had told him to share this with us. He also said the Devil did 9/11. He said God wanted him "to make gnarly cool Christian movies." He said that in November we should vote for "the man who has the greatest faith." The crowd lost it; it seemed like the trailer might shake.

When Jake and Bub beat on the door, I'd been in there for hours, rereading *The Silenced Times* and the festival program. In the program, it said the candle-lighting ceremony was tonight. The guys had told me about it—it was one of the coolest things about Creation. Everyone gathered in front of the stage, and the staff handed out a candle to every single person there. The media handlers said there was a lookout you could hike to, on the mountain above the stage. That was the way to see it, they said.

When I opened the door, Jake was waving a newspaper. Bub stood behind him, smiling big. "Look at this," Jake said. It was Wednesday's copy of *The Valley Log*, serving Southern Huntingdon County—"It is just a rumor until you've read it in *The Valley Log*."

The headline for the week read MOUNTAIN LION NOT BE-LIEVED TO BE THREAT TO CREATION FESTIVAL CAMPERS.

"Wha'd we tell you?" Bub said.

"At least it's not a threat," I said.

"Well, not to us it ain't," Jake said.

I climbed to their campsite with them in silence. Darius was sitting on a cooler, chin in hands, scanning the horizon. He seemed meditative. Josh and Ritter were playing songs. Pee Wee was listening, by himself; he'd blown it with the Jewish girls.

"Hey, Darius," I said.

He got up. "It's fixin' to shower here in about ten minutes," he said.

I went and stood beside him, tried to look where he was looking.

"You want to know how I know?" he said.

He explained it to me, the wind, the face of the sky, how the leaves on the tops of the sycamores would curl and go white when they felt the rain coming, how the light would turn a certain "dead" color. He read the landscape to me like a children's book. "See over there," he said, "how that valley's all misty? It hasn't poured there yet. But the one in back is clear—that means it's coming our way."

Ten minutes later, it started to rain, big, soaking, percussive drops. The guys started to scramble. I suggested we all get into the trailer. They looked at each other, like maybe it was a sketchy idea. Then Ritter hollered, "Get 'er done!" We all ran down the hillside, holding guitars and—in Josh's case—a skillet wherein the fried meat of some woodland creature lay ready to eat.

There was room for everyone. I set my lantern on the dining table. We slid back the panes in the windows to let the air in. Darius did card tricks. We drank spring water. Somebody farted; the conversation about who it had been lasted a good twenty minutes. The rain on the roof made a solid drumming. The guys were impressed with my place. They said I should fence it. With the money I'd get, I could buy a nice house in Braxton County.

We played guitars. The RV rocked back and forth. Jake wasn't into Christian rock, but as a good Baptist he loved old gospel tunes, and he called for a few, God love him. Ritter sang one that killed me. Also, I don't know what changed, but the guys were up for secular stuff. It turned out that Pee Wee really loved Neil Young; I mean, he'd never heard Neil Young before, but when I played "Powderfinger" for him, he sort of curled up like a kid, then made me play it again when I was done. He said I had a pretty voice.

We all told each other how good the other ones were, how everybody else should really think about a career in music. Josh played

"Stairway to Heaven," and we got loud, singing along. Darius said, "Keep it down, man! We don't need everybody thinking this is the sin wagon."

The rain stopped. It was time to go. Two of the guys had to leave in the morning, and I needed to start walking if I meant to make the overlook in time for the candlelighting. They went with me as far as the place where the main path split off toward the stage. They each embraced me. Jake said to call them if I ever had "a situation that needs clearing up." Darius said God bless me, with meaning eyes. Then he said, "Hey, man, if you write about us, can I just ask one thing?"

"Of course," I said.

"Put in there that we love God," he said. "You can say we're crazy, but say that we love God."

The climb was long and steep. At the top was a thing that looked like a backyard deck. It jutted out over the valley, commanding an unobstructed view. Kids hung all over it like lemurs or something.

I pardoned my way to the edge, where the cliff dropped away. It was dark and then suddenly darker—pitch. They had shut off the lights at the sides of the stage. Little pinpricks appeared, moving along the aisles. We used to do candles like this at church, when I was a kid, on Christmas Eve. You light the edges, and the edges spread inward. The rate of the spread increases exponentially, and the effect is so unexpected, when, at the end, you have half the group lighting the other half's candles, it always seems like somebody flipped a switch. That's how it seemed now.

The clouds had moved off—the bright stars were out again. There were fireflies in the trees all over, and spread before me, far below, was a carpet of burning candles, tiny flames, many ten thousands. I was suspended in a black sphere full of flickering light.

And sure, I thought about Nuremberg. But mostly I thought of Darius, Jake, Josh, Bub, Ritter, and Pee Wee, whom I doubted I'd ever see again, whom I'd come to love, and who loved God—for it's true, I would have said it even if Darius hadn't asked me to, it may be the truest thing I will have written here: They were crazy, and they loved God—and I thought about the unimpeachable dignity of that love, which I never was capable of. Because knowing it isn't true doesn't mean you would be strong enough to believe if it were. Six of those glowing specks in the valley were theirs.

I was shown, in a moment of time, the ring of their faces around the fire, each one separate, each one radiant with what Paul called, strangely, "assurance of hope." It seemed wrong of reality not to reward such souls.

These are lines from a Czeslaw Milosz poem:

And if they all, kneeling with poised palms,
millions, billions of them, ended together with their illusion?
I shall never agree. I will give them the crown.
The human mind is splendid; lips powerful, and the summons
    so great it must open Paradise.

That's so exquisite. If you could just mean it. If one could only say it and mean it.

They all blew out their candles at the same instant, and the valley—the actual geographical feature—filled with smoke, there were so many.

I left at dawn, while creation slept.

The Return

It has been a long, drawn-out process to meet up with Bushwick Bill, involving scores of tactical phone calls over a period of weeks. The diminutive dreadlocked rapper has been AWOL somewhere in Tennessee on a mission to purchase a vintage trailer home that he will henceforth use to travel cross-country like some sort of madman John Madden. But at last Bill has appeared in Los Angeles, and is seated with his beautiful wife (Chuckie really did get lucky), their sleepy one-year-old daughter and a coterie of hungry handlers around an impeccably arranged dining room table in the swanky Ritz-Carlton Hotel in Marina del Rey.

I've been assigned to interview Bill—along with fellow Geto Boys Willie D and Scarface—to see what's up with one of the greatest groups in hip-hop history as they prepare to release their fourth album together, *War & Peace*.

Having grown up separately (Bill in Bushwick, Brooklyn, Willie and 'Face in rival sections of Houston's notorious 5th Ward), the Geto Boys don't hang out a lot outside the studio, and interviews are to be conducted individually. With the words of Willie D and Scarface previously recorded and transcribed, tonight's the Mr. Bill Show.

The instant a basket of dinner rolls is placed on the table, Bill attacks it, spraying breadcrumbs like sawdust from a woodchipper. He

motions to an anxious waitress for a bottle of white wine and en-
thuses about his newest acquisition: "Can't nobody tell from outside
the camper what's happening on the inside!"

You bought the camper because you prefer driving to flying?

"Right," Bill says, rotating his head like a periscope—the better
to stare at me with his one good eye. "See, driving is like stabbing
somebody, it's very personal. Whereas flying is like shooting somebody, it's more distant."

Welcome to the mind of a lunatic. This sort of gory metaphor is
a Bushwick Bill specialty, and this haughty dining room will shortly
be transformed into a place not unlike the sulfurous shore of the
River Styx. But before all hell breaks loose, I will have the great
pleasure of conversing with one of the most intelligent, verbose,
historically experienced hip-hop performers of all time—and the
owner of what ego trip's *Book of Rap Lists* deemed the "Longest rap
alias ever": Dr. Wolfgang von Bushwickin the Barbarian Mother-
Funky Stay High Dollar Billster.

The good Doctor will recall being a nine-year-old member of the
Linden Crash Crew in the Brooklyn neighborhood that gave him
his name. "Hanging out between Knickerbocker and Irving, the
first record I ever breakdanced to was Baby Huey." He will praise
the teenage season he spent in an outreach program with Redemption Ministries in Minnesota. "Otherwise I would've never seen
deer in the snow, or been to Gooseberry Falls in Duluth and experienced the coldest water in the world." He will explain the difference
between hanging with Tupac and Biggie. "With 'Pac, I could talk
everything from aphrodisiacs to Egyptology. With Big it was strictly
blunts and the block." And he will squash the supposition that he
doesn't write his own rhymes. "Willie D was calling me for weeks
on the phone while writing the new album, like, 'What would you
say here, Bill?' And asking me to repeat myself while he wrote it
down." It'll all be so engrossing that I will fail to notice that, while
devouring his broth-boiled tuna strips, Bill will be steadily rubbing a

pair of chopsticks together with such fervor that their tips become sharp as shanks. No, that fact I will fail to notice until it is too late.

One week earlier, November 3, 2004. As I deplane at George Bush Intercontinental Airport in Houston, the first sight I see is an overhead television monitor on which Democratic presidential candidate John Kerry is delivering his concession speech, effectively ending the hope that anyone other than dry-drunk smirker George W. Bush will be commander-in-chief of the United States of America for the next four years.

In my rental car, I pass a billboard advertising a talk-radio station with the slogan: *We Talk, God Listens.* I snap on my radio in time to hear a female radio jock gloating, "He did it, he did it! A mandate from God for George W. Bush." *Great.*

With a rusted gate and plain stucco facade, Rap-A-Lot Records headquarters doesn't look like much from the outside. As I pull into the underground garage, though, I spy dozens of collectible cars, everything from a stainless-steel DeLorean to a Hummer more stretch than Armstrong. These autos are the property of James Smith, a.k.a. Lil' J, a.k.a. J Prince, Rap-A-Lot CEO.

In 1987, Lil' J released "Car Freaks," a single by an unknown group, the Geto Boys—Johnny C, Juke Box, Raheem, Ready Red and dancer/hypeman Bushwick Bill. It would be another two years until the GB's sophomore LP, *Grip It! On That Other Level,* when a lineup shuffle would solidify the group around the core of DJ Ready Red and Bushwick, plus new members DJ Akshun (a.k.a. Scarface) and a headstrong boxer named Willie Dennis.

Ushered into the offices by an attendant, I'm taken into a black-marble boardroom where Willie D sits at a chrome conference table. His frame is still graced with the musculature of a pugilist, but with his shaved head and plaid shirt he looks otherwise innocuous. He speaks in measured, sober tones, without the guttural intimidation instantly recognizable on the Geto Boys' comeback single "Yes,

Yes, Y'all": "Some of y'all make me hotter than Tabasco / Mess with my money, I'ma kick you in the asshole."

"I was 19 years old, living in the Bloody Nickel, selling newspaper subscriptions door-to-door," Willie says. "Me and Lil' J were both going to Harvey's Barbershop, yet we'd never spoken with each other. Harvey had a tracheotomy and was like [*puts his finger on his throat and rasps*], 'Lil' J got the record company and you got the raps, blow this thing up and put 5th Ward on the map!' I left my number, Lil' J gave me a call a week later and I went up to Rap-A-Lot, auditioned in person. I was real raw, real edgy, real street—wasn't shit on Rap-A-Lot sounded like what I was doing."

While the Geto Boys were not the first gangsta rappers, the impact of their uppercut was intensified by the fact that at that point, Houston—in fact the entire South, save Miami—was nowhere on the hip-hop map. Sporting classics like "Do It Like a G.O.," "No Sell Out" and "Mind of a Lunatic" (where Willie promised such thorough demolition that "your dental records couldn't prove your identity"), *Grip It!* caught the ear of hip-hop's Gandalf, Rick Rubin, who put out an eponymously retitled version on his Def American label in 1990. That album's lyrical preoccupation with necrophilia and disemboweling led to the heavily documented case of Def American distributor Geffen Records' refusal to release it (a situation that prompted Rubin to switch to Warner Bros).

By 1991's *We Can't Be Stopped*, the Geto Boys were fully back on Rap-A-Lot, immortalized in the cover photograph of 'Face and Willie (dressed in a playalistic purple suit) wheeling Bushwick Bill, his eye socket freshly pulped by a bullet to the head, down a hospital hallway.

"I still have that suit jacket," says Willie. "I'm not one for keeping mementos of the past, but I kept that. The hat is in the Rock & Roll Hall of Fame."

We Can't Be Stopped spawned the timeless smash "Mind Playing Tricks on Me." The song encapsulated the GB's appeal, as over a bass-girded grid of battle drums the three MCs detail the rampant paranoia and delusional self-doubt that accompanies their homicidal urges—a million miles from the self-aggrandizement that is today's commercial norm.

"The Beat in LA was only playing R&B at that time," Willie remembers, "and R&B stations love to boast about not playing any rap. Well, 'Mind Playing Tricks' was the first rap song they ever played. We came to the station and it was packed with people wanting autographs. A 78-year-old woman called in, 'I don't listen to no rap, but that's my song!'"

The success of "Mind Playing Tricks on Me"—a staple at Halloween parties to this day—galvanized the group's audience, and granted each member some degree of financial freedom. It allowed Willie D to pursue his other passion, real estate.

"Take a look at your hood," Willie says, "and envision what it could be. Instead of buying a piece or a chain, buy a lot, build a new house where a crackhouse used to be. How about buying the block instead of shooting it up? Which is more powerful? Which has more longevity?"

Recently, Willie purchased land in the center of Baku, Azerbaijan, a city on the Caspian Sea in the former Soviet Union, neighboring Iran. In August 2004, he moved his wife, a mechanical engineer in the oil industry, and their two young children to Baku.

"Baku is going to be a tourist destination in 10 years. There are talks about the US military coming in there next year. Anytime you have oil you have money. BP has a $400 billion project there. You've got all these rich people needing somewhere to stay. So I'm going to build high-rises."

The new Geto Boys album, *War & Peace*, booms through the Rap-A-Lot playback bunker at a volume that could wake the dead. It sounds phenomenal, wise beyond the GB's gore-core glory days. If *Grip It!* was their *Niggaz4Life*, *War & Peace* is roughly analogous to *Dr. Dre's 2001*—a firestorm of Technicolor production that ranges in tone from the hood boogie hook of "1, 2, the 3" to the sweet soul confessional "I Tried"—where Bushwick raps, "Little shit drives me crazy / Then I start thinking 'bout my babies / I can't go to jail / I can't die / Who better to teach 'em about this cruel world than I?"

"We wanted to make a reunion album that didn't sound like a reunion album," says Brad Jordan, known to the world as Scarface. "Nobody trying extra to prove a point, just relax and go in there and do it." Sitting beneath a mondo Rap-A-Lot mirror mounted on the wall, casual in a Yankees cap, leather jacket and jeans, the jewelry-free 'Face is in good form. A high-watt smile frequently creases his features.

"A lot of people make music," he continues. "But not a lot of it is relevant. Music should be respected. Record companies are brainwashing the community by letting them think there's a party going on. Drive to the south side of Houston or a place like east Cleveland—I'm telling you there is no party going on. I remember a time when niggas didn't go to clubs, they'd avoid the confusion. We stayed at the crib and got ready for the morning. Living in the hood was hard enough in itself."

A multi-instrumentalist, Scarface wonders aloud what happened to the days of Black bands like the Bar-Kays, Con Funk Shun, B.T. Express. "I was telling George Clinton, 'Don't come over to us—I'm still trying to get to where you are.'"

Then there's his famed passion for rock. Scarface named his pitbull Eddie, after the hellacious cartoon ghoul that graces the album covers of the British metal band Iron Maiden. He went to see Kiss four times on their 1996 reunion tour, a fulfillment of a 20-year-old childhood dream: "In 1976, I put on my mom's Noxema to look like Kiss face paint. She gave me a serious ass-whoopin'."

It's so pleasant talking music with such an impassioned fan, it's easy to forget that this one's also the former president of Def Jam South—the man who signed Ludacris—and one of the most widely heralded MCs of all time. He's downright worshipped in the South, and during a recent TV interview on the highbrow *Charlie Rose*

Show, no less an authority than Jay-Z recently called 'Face one of the best to ever do it. He's quick to return the compliment.

"Jay-Z is a helluva lyricist and good dude," he says of his frequent collaborator. "My verses don't come quick, but Jay-Z be done with a song in eight minutes. That shit ain't fair! For 'Some How, Some Way' on *Blueprint* 2, he finished and left while I was still writing."

Like Jigga, Scarface is talking retirement. He plans to herd cattle full-time, he says, on his Texas prairie ranch, the Emancipation Plantation. "Music took my whole life from me," he says. "I got no me-time no more. Wake up, music, go to bed, music, since 1987." Scarface pounds on the table. "So this is my last trip."

If *War & Peace* is indeed the Geto Boys' swan song, how will the group be remembered? Where do they sit in the pantheon? They're certainly up there, but, as Scarface himself opines on "Yes, Yes, Y'all": "I thought the Beatles was the greatest?" Bushwick Bill responds: "I'll cut Paul, and the rest of y'all!"

This brings us back to where this story started, in the dining room of a fancy California hotel with Bushwick Bill. The past hour has been a conversational whirlwind, Bill declaiming on topics from the primal importance of Mantronix ("Dude was making beats 20 years ago, sounded like what Timbaland's doing now!") to his own appearance on *The Chronic* ("I never got a plaque or a check") to his near-victory in the 1982 Swatch Watch breakdancing competition in Times Square ("I lost to Ladyflex when she went from a windmill into a spider"). When Bill pauses to guzzle more wine, I ask him what he thinks of the way President Bush has hijacked Jesus to serve corporate special interests.

"When *hasn't* God been pimped?" Bill says. "When *hasn't* Jesus been mugged?" And then, suddenly, Bill starts rapping: *"I ain't getting my leg shot off while Bush ass on TV playing golf!"* As Bill continues, I realize it's the Geto Boys' 1991 song "Fuck A War," just as apt today: *"A nigga die for a broil, but I ain't fightin' behind no goddamn oil, against muthafuckas I don't know . . . Yo, Bush! I ain't your goddamn hoe!"*

"Really, all that crazy shit I rap is because that's what Scarface, Red and Lil' J told me to say. I'm not really like that."

I ask if he considers himself more of a gangster or prankster.

This rubs Bill the wrong way. "If you saw my arrest record," he says, angrily, "you'd know most of them are assaults!" He then hops up out of his seat and—brandishing a chopstick—says, "Really, the only way I can answer that question is physically."

The idea of being chopped and screwed right here at the table doesn't appeal to me. "Maybe I shouldn't have asked you while you have a sharp stick in your hand," I say.

"Sharp stick got nothing to do with it!" Bill is shouting now. "None of this shit does!" He suddenly begins smashing everything on the table—utensils, plates, bottles, glasses—into a broken pile, before raising his Popeye-like arms, fists clenched.

"I retract my question," I say, struggling to maintain composure.

Bill calms down. "Hey, I'm sorry, man," he says, "I'm a little drunk and emotional. I gotta go."

With that, Bill and his entourage get up and leave. I am left holding a bill for $350. I try to put it on my credit card. Card rejected.

The waitress is standing over me. I call Bill on his cell phone.

"Bill," I say, "I'm a bit embarrassed by this, but can you come back and help with the bill?"

Sure enough, seconds later, Bill returns, grabs the check, scrawls a room number and signature. The waitress, squinting, says, "What is your last name, sir?"

Bill: "Schwartz."

Skeptical waitress: "Schwartz?"

Bill: "What, you never met a nigga named Schwartz?"

Waitress: "Thank you, Mr. Schwartz."

Bill and I walk outside. As I wait for the valet to spin my clunker around, I thank Bill and say, "I hope you're not angry."

"Only dude who's gonna be angry is whoever staying in the room number I wrote on the check!" Then Dr. Wolfgang von Bushwickin cackles dementedly and disappears into the night.

MIKE McGUIRK

Frosty, *Liquor Drink*

Liquor Drink, and the band responsible for it, are some of the most abrasive, anti-social and puerile statements of outsider life ever made. Made by and for people addicted to truck stop encounters and stealing drugs from grandma, this record can't help but alienate 90 percent of the people who hear it. It may be funny, but it ain't a joke.

Thorpe's Notes on
R. Kelly's *Trapped in the Closet*

List of Characters

Sylvester: The narrator of the story, who has awakened in a strange woman's house and must deal with her angry husband.

Cathy: The unfaithful woman in whose closet Sylvester finds himself trapped.

Rufus: Cathy's husband, who is carrying on a homosexual affair with Chuck.

Chuck: Rufus's secret lover.

Gwendolyn: The wife of the narrator, who tries to disguise her own unfaithfulness through rowdy sex.

Policeman: Secret lover of Gwendolyn.

CHARACTER SEX MAP

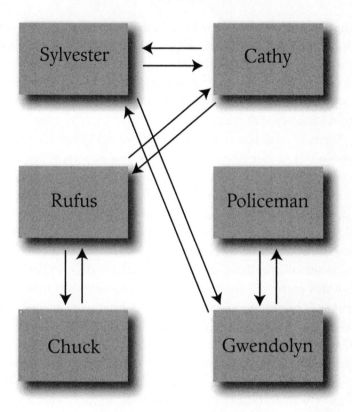

Critical Commentary

The following sections contain explanatory notes and textual insights on Trapped in the Closet. There is a summary of each chapter, as well as helpful commentary that illuminates literary motifs and stylistic elements within the narrative. Please keep in mind that there is no single correct interpretation of a complex work of literature like Trapped in the Closet, so your own interpretation of the themes and events present in the work may differ from the one presented here.

Chapter 1

Summary

The narrator awakens in a bed that he does not recognize. He hears Cathy's voice call out to him, and he is shocked that he is in the bed of a woman who is not his wife. He tries to piece together the events of the previous night, and he determines that he left a club with Cathy and only intended to stay with her for a short while, but instead fell asleep with her.

Sylvester scrambles to put on his clothes and gather his belongings so that he can go home, but Cathy tries to prevent him from leaving. Sylvester tells her that he has a wife at home, and urges her to let him leave so he can avoid trouble. She informs him that her husband is coming home, so he can't leave without being seen.

Sylvester tries to think of a way to escape the apartment, but he determines that there is no safe way to leave. He decides to hide in the closet in hopes that Cathy's husband will not discover him.

Rufus enters the apartment, and Cathy pretends that nothing strange is happening; she tries to distract Rufus with amorous advances, but Sylvester's cell phone rings, alerting Rufus that something strange is afoot in his apartment. Rufus searches the apartment, looking under the furniture and in the bathroom, until he reaches the closet. Sylvester pulls out his gun in anticipation of a conflict with Rufus. As the chapter ends, Rufus is opening the closet, about to discover Sylvester within.

Commentary

Theme: Immediately we are presented with the theme of Sylvester's mixed feelings toward infidelity. He scolds himself for being stupid and allowing himself to fall asleep at the house of his paramour, but he seems to be more concerned with the danger of getting caught than with feelings of guilt over his own infidelity. He admits to Cathy that he has a wife, but only in an attempt to make her understand that he has to leave immediately.

While we are initially led to believe that Cathy wants Sylvester to stay despite his brusque treatment of her, we soon learn that she is only trying to prevent him from walking out the door because he would be discovered by her husband, Rufus. Her decision to hide Sylvester and to distract and deceive her husband is as much for her own protection as for Sylvester's. Sylvester states that Cathy's deception "deserves an Oscar," implying that she is an expert liar. The theme of deception is prominent in this and subsequent chapters.

Character Insight: By the end of the chapter, Sylvester is prepared to threaten Rufus with a gun in order to leave the apartment. Throughout the narrative, Sylvester is presented as a thoughtless and thuggish man, set adrift on a sea of troubles of his own making. He often seems remorseless; what regrets he has stem not from the fact that he has hurt others, but from the fact that he has put himself in precarious situations. He urges God not to let Rufus open the closet, but offers no penance for his sins; seemingly, Sylvester feels as if he is owed favors by God, despite the fact that he behaves thoughtlessly, without regard for the feelings of others.

Glossary of Difficult Words and Phrases

Beretta: Refers to a brand of handgun manufactured in the USA and Italy.

Shuh, shuh: Cathy makes this sound to indicate to Sylvester that he should be quiet.

Shit is going down: Bad things are going to happen.

She deserves an Oscar: Sylvester is implying that Cathy deserves an Academy Award for her deception of her husband.

Put it on Vibrate: Silencing a cellular phone so that it vibrates instead of ringing.

Chapter 2

Summary

Rufus opens the closet door, exposing Sylvester. Rufus quickly ascertains that his wife has been unfaithful to him, despite his wife's efforts to claim that it was some sort of misunderstanding. Rufus is furious, and says that he would kill Sylvester if Sylvester weren't holding a gun.

Rufus's cell phone rings, but he continues to talk to Sylvester. Rufus explains that he is a pastor, which prompts Sylvester to suggest that they deal with the situation like Christians. However, Rufus is still furious; his wife attempts to apologize, but he rejects her apology and asserts that nobody can leave until he reveals a secret.

Rufus answers his telephone and tells the party on the other end to come back to his apartment immediately. He tells his wife that he doesn't intend to be the only broken-hearted one, so he intends to expose his own infidelity. Rufus's telephone rings and the party on the other end says, "Sweetheart, I'm downstairs."

Sylvester threatens to shoot Rufus unless he is allowed to leave, but Rufus insists that there is a shocking secret that he needs to reveal before anyone will be allowed to leave. Sylvester asserts that he will count to four and then start shooting; as he counts, Rufus and Cathy beg for their lives. When the count reaches four, Sylvester is interrupted by a man entering. Sylvester is shocked to find that Rufus's lover is not a woman; Rufus is carrying out a homosexual affair.

Commentary

Theme: Already the titular literal closet is done away with, and we see that the title of the narrative refers to broader themes. Most obviously, Rufus was "trapped in the closet" as well; he was carrying out a secret gay romance, but he has exposed it to Cathy and Sylvester so that they might see that their infidelity cannot make a fool of him. One could also see "the closet" as a metaphor for all the sneaking and deception carried out by the various adulterous characters: the metaphorical closet is the device which keeps Sylvester and Rufus's adulterous affairs hidden.

The chapter starts out with one of the narrative's most telling expositions of the themes of deception and adultery. Rufus stares at Sylvester "as if he was staring in the mirror." In Sylvester, Rufus sees himself: tricky, adulterous, and cocky. Rufus's anger at Sylvester is probably not centered upon the fact that he had relations with his wife, but is more probably a product of Rufus's own insecurities. In Sylvester, he sees his ugly reflection.

Character Insight: Sylvester's uneasy relationship with God is further illuminated in Chapter Two. Upon Rufus's revelation that he is a pastor, Sylvester once again tries to use his fair-weather faith to weasel his way out of a difficult situation. He suggests that he and Rufus work out the situation "Christian-like," but is seemingly unaware of the irony of his statement, considering that he has just committed adultery and is currently threatening a pastor with a gun.

Little insight is gained into Cathy's personality in this chapter. She seems to be overwhelmed with the situation, and her gift for trickery fails her when she is confronted with her husband's anger and Sylvester's needless and violent threats.

Glossary

Bogus shit: Unpleasant business.
Mack shit: The lies of an insincere womanizer.
Nigga: A term of endearment or derision, the use of which is limited strictly to African Americans.

Chapter 3
Summary

Sylvester stares in disbelief at Rufus, initially unwilling to believe that he's really Rufus's secret lover. Sylvester tells everyone that they are crazy, and that he is leaving. Cathy tries to persuade him to stay, but he says that he has nothing to do with the present mess, and he has to get home. Cathy persuades him to stay, suggesting that the story of how this affair came about may be an interesting one.

Sylvester agrees to stay for three minutes while Rufus and Chuck explain themselves. Cathy lashes out at Rufus, asking him how he could do such a hurtful thing to her, but he counters her volley by reminding her that she's lied to him and been adulterous as well. Cathy puts forth the opinion that a homosexual affair is much more unexpected and hurtful than her simple infidelity, but Rufus insists that since she hid a man with a gun in their closet she has no right to judge him.

Sylvester, sick of all the arguing, insists upon an explanation. Chuck explains that he and Rufus have been carrying on a secret affair for a year, sleeping in motels and doing their best to avoid discovery. This causes Cathy and Rufus to erupt into another argument, which frustrates and bewilders Sylvester. He fires a shot into the air to shock them into silence, and announces that he can't handle any more of their fighting. He uses his cellular phone to call his house, and is shocked to hear a man's voice answer.

Commentary

With Sylvester, Rufus, and Chuck now decidedly "out of the closet," the situation erupts into conflict and violence. Sylvester seems incredibly conflicted in this chapter; his initial instinct is to leave, but Cathy manages to convince him to stay by appealing to his curiosity. Sylvester is both repulsed and intrigued by Rufus's affair with Chuck; just as Rufus saw elements of himself in Sylvester, Sylvester clearly sees parallels to his own situation in Rufus and Chuck's romance.

Character Insight: While he initially agreed to stay in the hope of witnessing an interesting dramatic spectacle, he became more and more eager to leave when Rufus and Cathy began fighting. It becomes clear that Sylvester has a strange aversion to conflict. Although he could leave at any time (since he has a gun and nothing to gain by staying), he seems to be staying in Rufus and Cathy's apartment only to act as a mediator. He repeatedly demands that they stop fighting, although their affairs are truly none of his concern. This provides crucial insight into Sylvester's character: the combination of habitual infidelity and extreme distaste for arguments among couples suggests that he was the product of a dysfunctional family, probably involving an abusive and unfaithful father. This might explain why Sylvester demands to be in control at all times.

Although he is a Casanova himself, Sylvester has an obvious aversion to being played. He becomes hurt when it is revealed that Cathy didn't use her real name when she courted him at the nightclub, even though it has little bearing on his situation. Although he is unfaithful himself, he is stunned when, at the end of the chapter, a man answers the telephone at his house.

Glossary

Deep shit: A difficult situation.
Y'all ass is crazy: Your entire ass is crazy.
Bitch, please: Used to express disbelief at a woman's words.
Club hoppin': Searching for sexual encounters or cheap thrills at nightclubs.
I'ma: I am going to.

Chapter 4

Summary

Sylvester is speeding home to investigate his suspicion of his wife's infidelity. His angry stewing is interrupted when he is pulled over by a police officer who informs him that he's going sixty miles an hour in a zone with a speed limit of forty miles per hour. He tries to tell the police officer that it's an emergency, but the officer will accept no excuses.

Sylvester angrily bursts into his house and confronts Gwendolyn over hearing a man's voice on the telephone, but his fears are allayed when she reminds him that her brother Twan is visiting. He apologizes for the misunderstanding, and they exchange pleasantries and go to the bed to engage in marital intimacy. Sylvester gets a cramp in his leg right as his wife is about to reach the height of her physical excitement, and has to stop the proceedings. He turns back the bedspread to discover a prophylactic left in the bed.

Commentary

The bulk of Chapter Four is contained in the early driving scene and the later love scene, which are comparatively relaxed; there is less tension and conflict in Chapter Four, making it a much-needed interlude between the high conflict of Chapter Three and the shocking resolution provided by Chapter Five.

We are introduced to two new characters in Chapter Four: a police officer who stops Sylvester for speeding as he drives home, and Sylvester's wife Gwendolyn, who at first appears to be a calm and faithful counterpoint to Sylvester's tightly wound mania.

Literary Device: Chapter Four provides R. Kelly with a perfect vehicle to demonstrate the narrative writing that made him famous; he has always had a flair for romantic and sensual scenes, and the love scene between the narrator and his wife presented in this chapter can be placed among his finest work: "And then she looked at me / and said 'go deeper please.' / And that's when I start going crazy, / like I was trying to give her a baby."

Glossary

Climax: The fictional height of a woman's sexual experience.
Rubber: A latex sheath for the male genitalia which prevents the transmission of sperm and disease.

Chapter 5

Summary

Sylvester confronts Gwendolyn about the prophylactic he found in the bed. He berates and threatens her, and then he draws his gun again and asks if the man she slept with is still in the house. She admits that she did have a man over, but that he left shortly after Sylvester called.

As Sylvester continues his tirade against his wife, she interrupts him to tell him that she knows about his infidelity, and launches a withering counterattack. Sylvester physically menaces her until she agrees to tell him the name of the man who just left.

She explains that a friend of hers knows a fellow named Chuck who is friends with a man named Rufus, and Rufus's wife Cathy introduced her to the man with whom she was having an affair: the very policeman who stopped Sylvester in Chapter Four.

Commentary

Literary Device: In Chapter Five, the ironic underpinnings that buttress the story all come into plain view. It is revealed that not only was Sylvester's wife aware of his marital infidelity, but that she was carrying on an affair with a man who knew Cathy, the woman with whom Sylvester was having an affair. The theme of perverted religious faith comes full circle in the end, with Gwendolyn rattling off a list of names of friends-of-friends which reads like a biblical lineage.

Theme: The central morality tale of the story also comes to light once all the pieces of the puzzle are revealed. All four of the married characters in the story are furious at their spouses for their infidelity, but all of them are unfaithful themselves. The story presents a vicious circle of revenge and mistrust, in which infidelity feeds more infidelity. The married characters are still very much "trapped" in the "closet" of their own guilty consciences and frustrated relationships.

Glossary

Baby, you gonna be breathless: I am going to beat you until you are dead.

Thorpe's Notes Review

Students may find this review section beneficial in testing their own knowledge and understanding of the events and themes presented in Trapped in the Closet. We are confident that students who have a deep enough understanding of the source material to answer these questions will be equipped to understand much of the body of critical writing about Trapped in the Closet, and may even be able to meaningfully contribute to that body.

Q&A

1. What name does Cathy give Sylvester when she meets him at the club?
   A. Claude
   B. Terrence
   C. Russell
   D. Mary

2. Which of these places does Rufus check when he is looking for Sylvester?
   A. Underneath the dresser
   B. Between two opposite walls
   C. Wedged between the neighbors' brownstone and the window

    D. Sylvester's house

3. What is the main plot function of Chuck and Rufus's romance?
    A. To illustrate the pervasive infiltration of sodomites in our society
    B. To legitimize homosexuality among blacks
    C. To explore R. Kelly's bi-curious fantasies
    D. All of the above

4. Why doesn't Sylvester just leave Cathy's house?
    A. He's curious about Chuck and Rufus, even though he keeps telling them to shut up
    B. He wants to see Cathy and Chuck argue, even though he keeps telling them to stop
    C. He is physically intimidated by Chuck, even though he has a gun
    D. For some reason

5. Who survives at the end of the text?
    A. Nobody
    B. Rufus and Gwendolyn
    C. Sylvester
    D. Nobody dies

Answers: 1: d. 2: a. 3: b. 4: d. 5: d.

Identify the character who spoke each of these lines:

1. "That's right, nigger, I was there."
2. "Something is rotten in the state of Denmark."
3. "God, please don't let this man open the closet."
4. "Don't give me that mack shit please."
5. "Oh my goodness, I'm about to climax."

Answers: 1: Gwendolyn in Chapter 5. 2: Marcellus in Act 1, Scene 4. 3: Sylvester in Chapter 1. 4: Chuck in Chapter 2. 5: Gwendolyn in Chapter 4.

Essay questions:

1. Why does Chuck look for Sylvester under the dresser? How big do you imagine the dresser to be?
2. In Chapter 4, what does Sylvester mean by "a tear fell up out my eye"?
3. When Gwendolyn is describing the string of friends that led to the policeman, who is Tina and where does she fit into anything?

RAQUEL CEPEDA

Riddims by the Reggaetón

*Puerto Rico's hip-hop hybrid
takes over New York*

Tego Calderón enters stage right at Madison Square Garden. On cue, the crowd at last October's second annual Megaton concert—the largest reggaetón event in the country—erupts into a frenzy. They're drunk off the deafening riddims pulsating from the venue's enormous speakers. Midway through a medley of hits that secured Tego's position as the king of reggaetón in the U.S., Fat Joe and the Terror Squad join their Afro-Boricua counterpart to perform the year's pervasive "Lean Back" remix. And the sea of almost 20,000 screaming (and some sobbing) fans of all ages and races ripple enormous Puerto Rican, Dominican, Colombian, and Ecuadorian flags in the air. It looks like closing night at the summer Olympics.

Though he's a household name in at least 35 Spanish-speaking countries around the world, Tego—who, on Thursday, headlines the LIFEbeat Music Industry Fights AIDS benefit "Reggaetón Explosion" concert at the Manhattan club Spirit New York—is a reluctant representative. "When I got out of jail [after serving two years] for arms and assault, I resisted making reggaetón songs," he'll later say, between puffs of a Newport. "Back in the day I thought it was just a carbon copy of dancehall."

But today, the stuff is increasingly invading the U.S. rap and r&b charts, and a whole crop of stars have major releases scheduled for this spring. Last month, S.O.B.'s even kicked off its weekly "Picante Fridays: Latin Rap & Reggaetón Fiesta" at Joe's Pub. Other Megaton top-billers—Zion y Lennox, Trebol Clan, Nicky Jam, Mickey Perfecto, and the genre's next great brown hope, Julio Voltio, who is on Tego's own Jiggiri/White Lion label—blur the lines between hip-hop and reggaetón culture. Like rappers, reggaetón artists are driven by the competition of freestyle battles. And the incorporation of the DJ into sets is becoming the industry norm. "Musically, reggaetón was born in a hip-hop environment, with a little bit of Jamaican dancehall and Puerto Rico's own tropical flavor and *ritmo*," says Vico C, one of the movement's founding fathers. He's on a phone from Miami, one of the hotbeds of the culture in the States, followed by New York City, Orlando, and Chicago.

Almost single-handedly and perhaps unintentionally, the artist born Tegui Calderón Rosario, 33, steered his country's dominant youth culture out of the island and Latino neighborhoods and into the American stream of pop consciousness. "Tego is someone who represents struggle, an underdog," says Tony Touch. "He's more of an MC, a product of late-'80s hip-hop."

The DJ, also known as Tony Toca, hosts a reggaetón show on Power 104.1 in Connecticut and dropped his first reggaetón album, *Guatauba*, in 1996. He's releasing *The ReggaeTony Album*, featuring Tego, Daddy Yankee, Zion y Lennox, Don Omar, and Ivy Queen, this June. But he's not alone in his praise of Tego. "I credit Tego a lot for making reggaetón big over here," says Fat Joe, who first discovered the music through C, when visiting family in Puerto Rico about 15 years ago. "It's like hip-hop all over again, in the '70s back in the Bronx, when it was just bubbling. But it's going to be huge."

Tego's 2002 debut, *El Abayarde*, has sold an estimated 210,000 to date, and *El Enemy de Los Guasibiri*—last year's greatest-hits collection—sold at least 102,000 and left fans salivating to hear (and record labels fighting a bidding war to release) his forthcoming third joint, *The Underdog.*

Back at MSG, the fruit of Tego's crossover appeal was palpable. Not only did attendance surge by thousands from 2003, but now masses of non-Spanish-speaking gringos were bopping their heads and flailing their arms to the universal beat.

"In 2003 when we performed at MSG, [it was] in front of nine or ten thousand people," says Don Omar later, on his way back to New York for a meeting with Sean John about the possibilities of distributing his clothing line, called Do. Tego and reggaetón pioneer Daddy Yankee are also planning to release clothing and sneaker lines this year—all in a race to capitalize on their newfound stateside fame.

Though he's only been recording for four years, William Omar Landrón Rivera, a.k.a. Don Omar, is also lauded among the genre's biggest players. The former Christian minister-cum-super freak has spent time in jail for alleged arms and drug offenses, but his debut, *The Last Don,* and its *Live* version have sold over 745,000 copies combined. The 26-year-old lover boy has a set of perfectly groomed eyebrows, and he caps off the MSG show by unzipping his jeans and air-humping in the direction of the women in the front row. A Latino man standing up front consoles a hysterical Central American girlfriend, whose black mascara is running down her flushed cheeks. When the Don's humping goes into overdrive, she nearly faints.

Ivy Queen, as the first lady of the male-dominated genre, has just as much power to incite a crowd. Daddy Yankee calls her "the Celia Cruz" of reggaetón. "Ivy definitely holds her own," adds Wyclef Jean, who made a guest appearance on her *The Original Rude Girl* album in 1998. Born Martha Ivelisse Pesante in Spanish Harlem but raised in Puerto Rico, Ivy Queen has worked with Fat Joe and Swizz Beatz. Her success is owed in part to her around-the-way-girl charm (think Mary J. Blige, circa *My Life*), and rugged, almost baritone rasp (think Lauryn Hill, circa *The Score*). "When we started, our voices sounded like Alvin and the Chipmunks because the beats were really, really fast," she remembers.

"In Puerto Rico we started doing reggaetón a lot because El General and Nando Boom were hitting hard. When they came out, it wasn't called reggaetón," says Tego, taking a pull from yet another cigarette. "In Panama, there's more soca influences. It's faster and more of an emulation of dancehall. They were purists, like rudeboys," he continues. "In Puerto Rico, we slowed down the pace, sang in different tones, and sometimes shrill pitches." Now, they are taking that formula global.

At MTV's *TRL* studios in midtown Manhattan, Nas and his father, bluesman Olu Dara, are sound-checking their track "Bridging the Gap." Meanwhile, N.O.R.E. and a wolf pack of cohorts are inside the green room, trading spanking new shirts airbrushed with Big Pun and Tony Montana. Raymond Ayala, who bills himself as Daddy Yankee, is taking it all in. The 26-year-old is waiting his turn to hit the stage for the very first time on American television, unaware of the fawning women pacing up and down the studio's hallway.

At 13, Yankee became one of the forefathers of reggaetón, along with other characters like Rankin Stone, Wiso G, Blanco, Boricua Guerrero, and Michael & Manuel. Yankee's third album, *Barrio Fino*, which he released on his own El Cartel label last summer, has moved over 315,000 units. As with Tego, major labels have been vying to distribute Yankee's forthcoming greatest-hits LP, *Los Homeruns Part II*, which will also feature eight new songs. "Every major player has his own kingdom and we're economically independent," says Yankee, his large, gaudy diamond "D.Y." pendant glistening in the light. "Whoever wants to sign me has to talk to me about big money, because I already make real money."

Reggaetón artists have learned a lot about business by studying hip-hop's history. "Hip-hop had people who abused it and the first artists were taken advantage of," says Daddy Yankee. "We learned from it. And much like early hip-hop, the record labels ignored us."

A sex symbol for thug-loving *mamis* (and the antithesis to Don Omar's R. Kelly appeal), Yankee survived being shot at close range by an AK-47. And while he's never been arrested, the authorities in Puerto Rico have investigated him numerous times: All these experiences inform his lyrics and help to feed his 50 Cent–like legend. But, thanks to rap, he chooses to keep beef among his peers to a minimum. "We learned from the examples of B.I.G. and Tupac," he says. "You just can't take away someone's life over music."

Back at home, beef in reggaetón does exist between the major players and lesser-known, struggling artists. However, it hasn't escalated to the point where artists are regularly calling each other out in public. "Nobody has died yet, thank God," says Tego. "But I think that's on the way because reggaetón is getting bigger. And because I'm popular, all the cannons are aimed at me, even the police's."

While it's been widely reported that rap stars here in the States have had a Hip-Hop Task Force trailing their movements, reggaetón artists are now drawing part of the heat. Tego's last trip to New York City over the summer proved a dramatic one.

A few hours before Tego headed out to perform at a Pepsi-sponsored show, the DEA paid an impromptu visit to Tego's hotel room, looking for drugs and guns. When they failed to find anything—at one point mistaking a bar of herbal soap for heroin—the cops who were trailing Tego all day tried to befriend him. One invited him to dinner next time he was in town, another Cuban officer struck up a conversation about the Yoruba-derived Santeria religion, noticing the green and yellow *íde* of Ifa on his left wrist, which patrons wear for spiritual protection. "I know my rights were violated," says Tego, staring down at his wrists. "But then again, Biggie did say, 'more money, more problems.'"

Maybe the police have heard about the past conflicts with the law—or perhaps they are interested in monitoring the money, 'hos, and clothes content that drives much of the music. Ironically, Tego offers up a powerful proletariat image (he has a newborn son named

Malcolm X and a daughter named Ebony Nairobi). And as a guest on tracks by Cypress Hill, 50 Cent, and Wyclef Jean—and, most extraordinarily, on Tony Touch's remix of Fat Joe's "Lean Back"—he delivers uplifting messages in a laid-back, almost lazy fashion.

Since Tego mainstreamed the music, upping the ante for producers like Dominican beat tailors the Luny Tunes—reggaetón's answer to the Neptunes—the genre has spread all over radio like a virus, eclipsing salsa artists. "The music has become less underground and considerably more commercial and far better produced," says Leila Cobo, the Bureau Chief for *Billboard*'s Miami-Latin division. "Today, reggaetón very judiciously mixes tropical beats, pop beats; it uses samples, making it easier on the listener's ear, and certainly, easier on radio. Now you have many English-language rappers tapping into reggaetón acts."

One such artist is Lil Jon. "I think it has the energy of Miami bass," says the crunk impresario, who became acquainted with the sound at a strip club in Puerto Rico while hanging with his Cuban American protégé Pitbull. For his part Lil Jon produced "Culo," Pitbull's reggaetón-influenced ode to the derriere, and appeared on the remix, along with N.O.R.E., to Yankee's "Gasolina." "Reggaetón, much like Miami bass," he says, "is all about the girls dancing to it."

The rowdy rapper N.O.R.E. often notes his "half-Spanish" roots (he was born to an African American mother and Boricuan father). The overwhelming response to "Oye Mi Canto," which features Nina Sky, Daddy Yankee, and N.O.R.E., has made him an important component of the reggaetón movement in the States. The video for the song was the first to expose the music to MTV and BET television audiences. "This is the first time in my career and in my life where I feel like I am representing both sides of me," he says. "Even if I don't benefit from this 100 percent, per se, I am setting off a whole culture that I had nothing to do with creating, but I have something to do with helping promote."

The day after the MSG extravaganza, Tego finds himself in midtown Manhattan's Ameritania Hotel, where he's just back after shooting a scene for his forthcoming "Voltio" video. His dozy eyes are hidden behind his trademark dark shades (he wears them even at night). And a black-on-black Yankee cap barely crowns his massive Afro, which swells out from every side. When he speaks, he lisps in Spanglish. He's since grown to respect the power of what the genre has evolved into. And on the way to seizing the masses in his homeland of Puerto Rico, he says, "it caught on" in the States.

To say that reggaetón—an approximately 20-year-old fusion of dancehall, born in the poorest neighborhoods in Puerto Rico, with mostly Spanish-language rap and tropical rhythms—"caught on" is a modest assessment coming from Tego. "I didn't know I did anything for reggaetón until I came to New York City," he says with a laugh. "In Puerto Rico, they might like you but they won't give it up. Believe me, you do *not* get gassed up."

While Ivy Queen, Daddy Yankee, and Don Omar have the power of record sales, Tego Calderón remains perhaps the most respected—though even he didn't realize it until recently. His upper lip curls up on the left side to form a wry smile, revealing a rather engaging gap parting his front teeth. "The way I see it, calling me the king of reggaetón is almost like calling me the king of pop," says the Latin Grammy-nominated Hennessy pitchman. "In Puerto Rico there is a school of hip-hop, of purists that consider me a sellout because I'm commercial and I have success. But I used to be the same way, so I'm not trying to dis them. I used to hate reggaetón, too." But now, it's all love.

WAYNE MARSHALL

we use so many snares

when i "first" encountered reggaeton (i put *first* in quotes b/c it's likely i heard it before this moment), it wasn't called reggaeton at all. it was called spanish reggae, and a high school student at *CRLS*, where i was working as a substitute teacher, introduced me to it by showing me a caselogic binder containing hundreds of CDs by artists i had never heard of before—most of them, it seemed, from new jersey. i realized at that moment, back in 2002, that this stuff was already HUGE. since i had my laptop with me and was already demonstrating digital music techniques to the kids, i ripped a track, looped an intro section, and put a big smile on the student's face.

my next encounter with the stuff was in roxbury in the summer of 2003. while teaching some kids there how to make beats on computers, i asked a student who his favorite artist was, and he said "tego calderon." he raved about tego for a minute, piquing my curiosity, then ran home and grabbed a copy of *el abayarde* so i could hear it. i was floored, especially when i heard my ol' favorite, the mad mad riddim, appear on "bonsai"—an ode to marijuana that falls late in the album. (apparently, the song was responsible for a cancelled concert in the DR.) i began studying up on the music online, finding such interesting things as a poll where people we're voting on whether puerto rico or panama represented the origins of reggaeton. (puerto rico was winning, though panama was making a strong showing.)

the next meaningful meeting i had with reggaeton happened during yet another digital music workshop. it was the spring of 2004
and i was teaching sessions twice a week at UTEC up in lowell. for
those who don't know, lowell is an historic massachusetts mill-town,
and in the last couple of decades, its hispanic population has grown
considerably. as a result, most of the students wanted to make reggaeton beats. many of them were already doing so with their friends
at home, and several were already selling CDs out of their cars. a
couple kids, the producers of the crews, would come in with their
own CDs loaded with reggaeton samples. all kinds of things: kicks,
snares, cymbals, synths, basses, gunshots, spanish interjections, film
score snippets, you name it. but mostly snares. these kids used so
many snares. seriously, most of them had snare-drum banks that
numbered in the dozens and easily approached 100 discrete snare
samples. and most of them had acquired these sounds—in some
cases precisely the same sounds heard on all the big reggaeton favorites—by downloading them off the 'net or having a cousin
email/IM them from PR. no doubt: reggaeton is internet music.

i had noticed already in listening to the music that one of the
main ways reggaeton producers created form in a song was to
change the sound of the snare every 8 or 16 bars or so: keep it in
the same place, but change the sample that's being triggered. the
main change is therefore a timbral change—that is, a difference in
the "quality" of sound. there is thus an understanding here and a
focus on the sample as a fundamental building block in itself, and
an accompanying abstraction of sound—what is a snare after all,
once it is an array of sharp sounds, many of which weren't even created on an actual drum? reggaeton's approach to composition is
symptomatic of the age of the sample bank: why use one snare
when you can use several? one of the things that i like so much
about this approach is how electronic, how digital, it is. this kind of
a stylistic predilection is only really available (and plausible) in a
world of digital sampling technologies and easy-to-use sequencing
programs. (how many drummers you know carry around extra

snares?) reggaeton is digital music par excellence. it is, for better and for worse, fruityloops music—just listen to the unmistakable sound of the FL "pluck" instrument in countless reggaeton songs (yes, even those on the daddy yankee album).

such wide adoption of FL, and its concomitant effect on the sound and style of contemporary music, isn't so far-fetched, or shameful for that matter. i heard it through the grapevine that the mighty chrome riddim was built on FL. and i could have sworn the kinda-grimey bionic ras riddim was made with fruityloops, too. (the bass tone gives it away for me, not that the south rakkas crew haven't been advertising their use of FL with those silly robot-voice intros.) of course, a lot of grime producers and dubstep producers freely admit to FL being their primary tool, and the software is increasingly being used by producers across the board, even if some don't admit it. as techno producer jeff samuel puts it:

> A lot of people don't want to say that they use it because it has a stupid-ass name, and had gotten this reputation as a toy and not a serious program, but who cares? There are a lot of really established techno artists who are using it. I hear the kickdrum that's in the blank template when you open up the program all the time. (XLR8R, may 2005, p. 34)

and though the program, and its ease of use, can obviously make for some lazy, unimaginative music, its user friendliness and, yet, its flexibility and power mean that a great many more people are making music these days, and the world is no doubt richer for it, despite needing a few more filters (perhaps) to weed through it all. and that's what mp3 bloggers are for, no?

at any rate, getting back to questions of style, aside from using so many snares, reggaeton producers tend to stick to some tried-and-true formulas: bombastic synth textures, plucky melodies, 4/4 kicks (usually at a midtempo pace—say, 90–110bpm), and that good ol' dancehall-reggae 3 + 3 + 2 syncopation (played on snares, natch).

of course, the 3 + 3 + 2 subdivision is common to all kinds of caribbean styles. you can thread it through reggae and mento, soca and calypso, son and salsa, merengue and meringue. but when it comes down to it, especially when we're talking about kicks and snares playing the 3 + 3 + 2, reggae has come to claim this rhythmic pattern. moreover, with the recent resurgence of roots reggae in the dancehall, the pattern seems to be making a comeback in jamaica, as heard on such smashes as I wayne's "can't satisfy her."

the difference between soca and dancehall, between merengue and reggaeton is a mere issue of speed—at least in a basic musical sense; let's not forget, though, that the cultural contexts for these styles are often rather different. (of course, the arrangements—i.e., the rest of the voices/instruments in the texture—are often rather different, too.) similarly, at the same tempos, with shifted rhythmic patterns (away from the 3 + 3 + 2 and towards a more "four-square" beat), these kicks-and-snares would cohere into something more closely resembling hip-hop or techno.

dancehall's distinctive bomp-bomp, as put forward famously by the pepperseed riddim, boils the 3 + 3 + 2 down a kind of essence. before dave kelly cooked up that rhythmic rundown, though, the sound of dancehall reggae was the sound of the pattern above—the sound of 4/4 kicks and 3 + 3 + 2 snares. (think of the bam bam riddim as heard on "murder she wrote" or just about anything off super cat's don dada album.)

the sound of dancehall reggae from the late 80s and early 90s is the sound of reggaeton today. and that's no coincidence.

by the late 80s reggae had gained popularity around the world, and dancehall was increasingly popular in urban centers, especially caribbean urban centers. thus, spanish-speaking audiences in panama, puerto rico, and new york (which, yes, is a caribbean urban center) increasingly became not just consumers but producers and performers of reggae music. panama's longstanding relationship to jamaica, which had sent large numbers of migrant workers to help dig the canal, meant that panamanian artists like el general were among the first to record spanish-language reggae. early recordings, such as el general's "pu tun tun" (or "tu pun pun"), were essentially translations of contemporary reggae hits (in this case, little lenny's "punaany tegereg"), using the same riddims and often converting the lyrics of the original almost word-for-word. (see the album dancehall reggaespañol for a great introduction to these early recordings, including their sources of inspiration and featuring some rather informative liner notes.)

the popularity of these spanish reggae tracks in the tri-state area helped the approach to catch on among new york's puerto rican (not to mention dominican and cuban) communities, which in turn helped to fuel what was undoubtedly a burgeoning scene already in PR (which, lest we forget, is not very far from jamaica). ever the cultural crucible, new york nurtured a musical conversation among its post-colonial peoples. it is the crystallization of reggaeton style in san juan in the 1990s (in close conversation with nuyorican developments) that leads to PR's current, almost undisputed claim to reggaeton. interestingly, the riddim track that many people cite as being the "planet rock" (see, miami bass) or the "drag rap" (see, nawlins bounce) of reggaeton is the backing to shabba ranks's "dem bow"—a riddim produced by bobby "digital" dixon and a beat that remains a staple in reggaeton. (daddy yankee, for instance, talks about freestyling endlessly over the *dem bow* back when he was cutting his teeth.) while jamaican dancehall moved on to minimal and maximal permutations of that ol' bomp-bomp, reggaeton stuck with the ain't-broke boom-ch-boom-chick-boom-ch-boom-chick, recognizing that it overlayed rather nicely with salsa and merengue and claiming it as the new sound of (urban) latin america.

at this point, reggaeton has already gone global, riding on the coattails of hip-hop's and reggae's international appeal, not to mention the international sociocultural circuitry of the spanish-speaking world. although it is not surprising, it is significant that reggaeton has become the most popular youth music not just in the PR and DR and panama but in cuba, colombia, belize, and increasingly in mexico, chile, and non-caribbean latin america. of course, it's big in japan. and there appears to be a thriving scene these days in the UK, complete with a magazine/online-portal (if conflated there with spanish rap), a series of regular dances (alongside dancehall, of course), and some locally fueled coverage of the wider history and cultural significance of the music.

reggaeton has been mainstream in the US since nina sky and nore took it there last summer. daddy yankee took it to the bank this spring. and in yet another interesting development—and a weird flip-side to english-language reggae being adapted to *spanish*—i've recently heard some english-language reggaeton showing up on boston's "official #1" for blazin' hip-hop and R&B! this could be seen as a bit of a threat, as most of reggaeton's stars have yet to break into the american mainstream. (shit, we're still waiting for a true tego hit. maybe on the new album.) i don't think there is much to worry about though, as reggaeton's core audience isn't about to abandon don omar to whomever p.diddy trots out as the new face of urban music. (britney spears's attempt at the style, see "the hook-up" on in the zone [ignore the jamaican-sounding dude and listen to the beat], seems to have made nary a ripple.) what the appearance of english-language reggaeton *does* demonstrate is that reggaeton is not simply spanish-language hip-hop or reggae. it is a recognizable musical style in its own right, one that is evoked with kicks and snares and synthesizers. (and, no doubt, luny tunes are still the kings of the beats.)

the music has an amazing amount of momentum going for it right now, and reggaeton will undoubtedly change as it continues to find adherents in various local contexts around the globe. being such a diffuse scene to begin with (san juan's claim as capital notwithstanding), it would seem that reggaeton is poised to shift with its new circumstances. in spite of what some might perceive as rhythmic conservatism, it is reggaeton's steady caribbean polyrhythm, in all its modern, digital splendor, that gives the new style such compelling coherence, such distinctive force. and it

would seem only a matter of time before unremarkable synth textures and one-finger melodies are replaced by the vibrant strains of
salsa samples, indian flutes, and whatever else one wants to fit into
its solid template (making it an omnigenre on par with hip-hop and
dancehall, and one based, yet again, on the creative re-use of well-
worn materials). if in the meantime, however, you get bored listening to the latest confections on the radio, just focus on the snares.

posted by wayne&wax @ 12:19 AM

(For audio samples please visit: wayneandwax.blogspot.com/
2005/08/we-use-so-many-snares.html)

Selections from the 42 Comments

Joe Twist said . . .
Dope post! Your observation about the implications of multiple
snares is heavy . . . I remember realizing that I had become fully
absorbed into the digital world when I was listening to some old
Motown a few years ago and thought "Damn! These guys are using a different snare sound every time!"—then I remembered it
was a live drummer . . .
4:05 AM

jace said . . .
vaya sabidura! que fuerte, gracias por toda la informacion. the
most informative piece on reggaeton i've read anywhere.

you may have sparked a wave of snare-centric reggaeton listening, i know i'm gonna keep ears sharp for snare-switchups
midsong, i'd never noticed that b4.

i was DJing a latenite party in brussels & dropped some reggaeton & the crowd went wild, so i kept it up for 30 min or so,
mixing it then really struck me how that distinctive beat pattern is
a brilliant multipurpose anchor for all kinds of wildness on top,
"omnigenre" base like you suggest.
2:02 AM

Anonymous said . . .
and with the 3 + 3 + 2 . . . surely thats latin music takin back its
own thing?

I remember when punnany came out a lotta comments were

on the "clave fell/latin turn etc etc" I'll bet steely n clevie have
plenty to say about it
Pete M
3:13 PM

wayne&wax said . . .
though the clave (and latin caribbean music more generally) both
have a 3 + 3 + 2 component, i'd hesitate to grant latin music
"ownership" over that figure. influential as cuban music has been
worldwide, we find these 3 + 3 + 2 syncopations in simply too
many places to posit such a direct line of origins and so forth. definitely plenty of overlap there, though, which helps to make sense
of the embrace of dancehall's take on the 3 + 3 + 2 among latino/a
youth. when it comes down to it, though, "drop it like it's hot" is
closer to a clave than, say, the fiesta riddim or any typical reggaeton beat.
7:19 AM

DJ C said . . .
Great post wayne. All this snare drum talk is makin' me want to
lay down some beats . . .
I'm not so sure South Rakkas is using Fruity Loops. I had a look
around their photo gallery and the only computers I saw were
Macs. Sadddly, FL doesn't exist for said platform, which is probably the only "Reason" I don't use it myself.
8:20 AM

paul.meme said . . .
Wicked piece Wayne, as ever.
DJ C—fruity is well worth trying—different result than Reason,
which is better, but less immediate sometimes.
I suspect the robot voices are done the same way I do the ones on
my mixes—using the "Speech" control panel of OSX to speak
some text, and recording the result with Wiretap . . .
7:26 AM

Anonymous said . . .
For us musical novices, where does the term 3 + 3 + 2 come from,
and/or what are those numbers specifically referring to?
11:16 AM

wayne&wax said . . .

the term 3 + 3 + 2 is not widely used, except by me since i find it a useful way to differentiate this kind of polyrhythmic orientation from more "foursquare" or duple beats. i have seen some ethnomusicologists use this shorthand, though, to describe precisely what i am trying to describe: a breaking up of an even pulse with odd-and-even grouped accents—a practice that is quite common in, say, west african drumming traditions (which should not surprise students of caribbean music).

the numbers refer to the groupings of (micro/sub) pulses that create the dynamic polyrhythm that defines so many caribbean genres. whereas you might count through a bar from a hip-hop or techno song (though not ALL of them) like this—12341234— you would more likely feel/count a reggaeton beat according to this kind of grouping: 12312312. it's all about where the accents cut across the overriding pulse of the song.

since most popular music is in the time signature of 4/4 (i.e., four beats of a quarter-note length per measure), adding accents on the downbeat, the (sub)beat just before beat 2, and the "and" of 3 (or the off/upbeat before beat 3) gives you the distinctive rhythmic pattern that we hear in reggae, reggaeton, salsa, son, soca, calypso, merengue, meringue, konpa, etc.

of course, i suppose this still sounds like a lot of musical gibberish. if we were in the same room, i could easily demonstrate the difference using fruityloops. check my lessons on hip-hop and dancehall to walk yourself through (and hopefully hear) these stylistic differences: http://wayneandwax.org/lessons

i hope to address and clarify some of these things in a future post, too.
11:29 AM

2xmachina said . . .
i remember in the 90's there was this trend in europe (the netherlands) where dj's played their dancehall records on the wrong speed (speedy bubblin'); voices were all chipmunk sped up, but the crowds went wild for it at parties. with this bumped up bpm, they got to mix all the riddims with merengue/soca or even house music to cross genres without losing tempo or energy. it was perhaps the first time i noticed this similarity in syncopation you're talking about.
9:02 PM

Matthew said . . .
I love this article. Some very astute observations. The social ties
you made are wicked. Also, FL is a completely groovy tool. I have
been using it for years, loading my own sounds in. In music, and
in so many other forms of art, the tools you use are irrelevant.
Look at what some artists can do with a pencil, what blazing poets
do with words . . .
11:42 AM

Anonymous said . . .
Bubbling:
It began in The Hague (Holland) in Club VOLTAGE in 1988
with DJ Moortje, MC Pester and MC Pret. From 1990 it became
this kind of dancing, together with the music that was very popular in all the big clubs in Holland. The tabloids and newspapers
saw this, so called, Bubbling as a new sexy style of dancing. Some
say it first was an expression of hidden protest, born at the antillian youth culture.
   1.1 Bubbling in the media and at the clubs. When they talk in
the tabloids and newspapers about Bubbling, they mention always
the way of dancing. They say that Bubbling is a girldance. No
wonder that they call Bubbling dancing also "the art of the as-
turn" or "erotic dancing" "soft porn" or "dry sex". Bubbling
means also competition. Almost every weekend there is a contest
somewhere in the country for the best Bubbling dancer, the best
Bubbling DJ or the best Bubbling outfit. These contests are usually announced weeks in advance by flyers and posters, they tell
which DJ's are perform and which girlbands are coming and last
but not least, how much money you can win. Only the dancing is
rather new, because Raggamuffin, the music that comes with
Bubbling, is nothing else but to play a 33speed record at 45speed
together with digital Reggae-music mixed with Hip Hop. The
Bubbling rhythm sounds like Tambu, an old Antillian slavedance.
   1.2 The music style Raggamuffin is born in 1985 and has its
roots from Jamaica. The Bubbling in Holland is rather different
then the Bubbling in Jamaica and England, because in Holland
the Bubbling is played at a much higher speed then anywhere
else. This so called "Mickey Mouse" style comes from Holland.
The founder of this uptempo Bubbling is DJ Moortje from Cura-
cao. Since 1988 the most popular Bubbling DJ in Holland. He

played by accident in a club a reggae song at the wrong speed and the crowd went crazy, so a new style was born and became a big success.

1.3 But Bubbling is more than a popular dance and a music style, it is also an expression of protest, like Bubbling entertainers Rodrgo La Cruz and Reynaldo Chirino, alias MC Pester and MC Pret. They give a new meaning to this music style with their lyrics against the system in Holland and Curaçao, the Police and Justice, discrimination and other topics. Also in there own comunity the people do not like them because of these lyrics.

1.4 From 1990 Bubbling is played in all the big clubs in Holland with DJ's like DJ Memmie, DJ Son and of course DJ Moortje. But it began in The Hague at the Club Voltage in 1988 with DJ Moortje, MC Pester and MC Pret. From that moment this trio began to organize Bubbling parties. The people who came to the Bubbling parties where mostly mature Antillians from near The Hague. These Bubbling Partiess were also social events. During these events the people talked about the problems they are faced with. While DJ Moortje was playing the Bubbling records, MC Pester and MC Pret were doing their lyrics with the songs like "Balia Sanka" (shake your ASS), a song MC Pester made during his period as a street musician.

1.5 In the beginning the Bubbling parties were not a big success, so the owner of Club Voltage organised Balia-Sanka parties, and gave a price to the best hips and ass-swinging girl of the evening. After that, the parties became a bigger success, and the crowd became much younger.
9:26 AM

(Anon. English-language translation of "Bubbling: About Dance, Music Style and Antillean Youth Culture in the Netherlands" by Marion van San, in *Soundscapes*)

Anonymous said . . .
Hey . . . lol I feel stupid . . . but the sounds (kick, snare) showed on the picture doesn't sound the same in my fruity loops. How can I change the sounds of the snare to make it more "reggaeton"? LOL thx for the answer . . .
10:49 am

wayne&wax said . . .

no need to L too out L. that's a pretty good question. as you can see from the screenshot at the top of the post, reggaeton producers use a very specific—if large—pool of sounds, many of which are sampled from classic reggae riddims, such as "dem bow" or the "bangara."

if you want to make the pattern really sound like reggaeton, you'll need to insert the right sounds. you might be able to find sample packs on the web at this point, but i'd suggest finding some classic late80s/early90s reggae riddims and grabbing some kicks, snares, etc.

7:04 AM

john said . . .

yo bruh I dont know u but I bet I make a better reggaeton beat den you holla at me and lemme know wuss up ight 1

7:47 AM

wayne&wax said . . .

you could be right, john. i don't really make reggaeton beats that often, but I try to listen closely to how other people make them. but what would you like to bet?

why don't you have any of your beats on myspace page? if you put one of yours up, i can upload one to mine, and we can let the world decide. you see me? lemme know. peace.

8:02 AM

ANDREW HULTKRANS

Sweat and Lowdown

The Extra Action Marching Band is a thirty-five strong troupe of Bay Area drum-and-horn hellions who play an aggro blend of Balkan brass music, New Orleans second-line funk, and primeval Moroccan trance, preceded by a raunchy flag team that marches, bumps, and grinds in corsets, hot pants, and pasties. They have graced the prestigious Guca brass band festival in Serbia, sailed the playa at Burning Man in a self-built Spanish galleon, and rocked the Hollywood Bowl with fan and colleague David Byrne. They incite near-riots wherever they go, and may be some of the best public art available in our chastened century. So when the band came to Galapagos in Williamsburg to kick off the final run of their "Eastward Invasion" tour, I needed to be there.

After an opening set by the local Hungry March Band, which is more musical but less explosive, Extra Action snake into the room. The band members bring in da funk in more ways than one. After three weeks living and touring in an already pungent Green Tortoise bus, Extra Action smells, um, powerful. Their heady stench acts as a kind of aromatherapy time-machine, transporting the audience to an earlier, bawdier era—Elizabethan times, say—when public drunkenness was common, instruments were acoustic, and showers didn't exist. In the narrow, sold-out space, there is simply no escape from the all-sensory assault of these lascivious minstrels.

David Byrne cowers at the back of the room, unadvisedly wearing all white. I take a musty pom-pom to the face, the flag team's sweat permeates my clothing, and, straining to turn my head, I notice my female cousin receiving an unsolicited colonoscopic close-up from a thong-wearing male dancer named Roky.

After a riotous, deafening set that includes a version of "Back Dat Azz Up," a horn player opens the door to the adjoining empty room that used to be the venue's performance space. Both marching bands start playing and pour into the room, followed by the entire audience. Chaos ensues. Byrne, smiling, head-nods to the merged bands' spirited version of "Kalashnikov," a popular Balkan stomper. The lights are turned on and off, whether by the staff or the band I'm not sure. I look back through the open door to the now empty bar area, where the bouncer is reading the riot act to trombonist Ben Furstenberg. The music is so loud that I can't hear what they're saying, but I imagine Furstenberg explaining artistic license and Althusserian subjectivity as the enraged mook screams, "Shut your hole and get them the fuck OUTTA THERE!" Apparently sensing an impasse and abandoning further discourse, the bouncer re-enters the fray, trying in vain to get individual musicians to stop playing, a Sisyphean task that, in my view, only adds to the unhinged glee of the moment.

Meanwhile, the manager ascends to the soundboard deck and turns on a mic, pleading with the throng to vacate the room. Someone good-naturedly yells "Fuck off!" Clearly, the manager anticipated this gambit. Without missing a beat, he shouts, "That's right, you can fuck me in the ass, *but you still have to leave!*" The line is such a bold departure from standard managerial rhetoric that the crowd actually honors his request, politely filing back into the bar/stage room to continue the revelry.

This is not to say there isn't more trouble afoot. Returning from a cigarette break outside, I'm nearly bowled over by the now apoplectic bouncer forcibly ejecting Extra Action drummer Mutt Mule, just caught in flagrante delicto with two ardent fans in the bathroom. A petite woman in a green dress chases the fracas with a digital videocam. For a tour documentary, I wonder? For a lawsuit? Who cares? Least of all Mutt, who's back inside twenty minutes later to rejoin his bandmates.

The Defense Department's research into the "sleepless soldier" notwithstanding, the human body can deliver total mayhem for only so long. So it is with Extra Action, who can't possibly top the continuous climax of the past two hours with a grand finale. Instead, they wind down like battery-powered cyborgs. Eventually, the flag team collects their sweat-soaked pom-poms from the rafters; dancers slither their way from table-tops to the floor, where, exhausted, they nibble at random ankles; audience heads are removed from flag-team crotches. The band slows to a mournful dirge and peters out, leaving Galapagos in a state akin to the aftermath of a Dionysian neutron bomb—nothing damaged, but with obvious traces of a massive blast of energy radiating everywhere.

J. EDWARD KEYES

Where's the Party?

13 Hours with the Next Franz Ferdinand

12:00 AM

A six-foot black transvestite in a top hat is on stage, cradling a mic like a baby and screaming "Hello, Motherfuckers!" at what could pass for a thousand or so refugees from a Duran Duran video. This is Motherfucker, the 5-year-old New York City dance party that is one part *Caligula* and two parts *Candy Land*. It's the kind of event where people show up dressed as ducks and devils and dominatrixes and leave barely dressed at all. At a time when NYC clubs have gone either square or self-conscious, Motherfucker is the last of its kind, the rare party where decadence and flamboyance are celebrated rather than affected.

Tonight is significant because it marks the beginning of a brief stateside invasion for Bloc Party, a British band that has been hotly tipped to top charts and change lives, and every duck, devil and dominatrix inside The Roxy is acutely aware of that. The group's momentum has been building slowly since the Dim Mak label released a teaser EP last September, causing scores of ambitious MP3 bloggers to go gaga and igniting the kind of grassroots enthusiasm that record companies usually work hard to manufacture. The group's first full-length, *Silent Alarm*, will be out one month from tonight, a co-release between hipster haven Vice and mainstream behemoth Atlantic, but it's already been established by record execs and the press that Bloc Party is going to be huge.

And who can dispute them, when a *six-foot black transvestite in a top hat* is introducing 2,000 people to the band before their record is even out?

3:00 PM

Nine hours ago, The Roxy looked like it was about to host Olivia Newton-John's Sweet 16. Gaudy cardboard stars were strung from the exposed metal rafters, while disco balls the size of Jupiter's moons were spinning idly, unlit. I was sitting in a spherical chair that looks like it was snatched from the set of *THX–1138* talking to Ted, an affable, enthusiastic member of the Motherfucker stage crew. Ted is dressed from head-to-toe in black, wearing black boots and sporting a roughed-up midnight dye job—the dictionary etching for "rock guy." As it turns out, exactly the opposite is true. "Basically," he says, "I spent the last five years listening to techno. I'd kind of given up on guitar bands. But then one day I heard Franz Ferdinand and I was like 'Okay! I'm getting really into this whole Return of Rock thing.' We had the Bravery come out and play New Year's Eve, and those guys were just awesome." As we're talking, the members of Bloc Party enter the room from the back. If we weren't looking for them, they'd likely go unnoticed. Every member is absent of swelling-star attitude or flashy, body-hugging clothing. Drummer Matt Tong, for example, is wearing a gray sweatshirt with a picture of cartoon carrots on it.

There are two giveaways that they are a little more than lost NYU students. One: The minute they walk in, soundmen and crew lackeys begin quizzing them on potential setup times and amp locations. Two: They are followed into the room by seven people, one of whom is carrying a 6-foot, camera-mounted tripod. As it turns out, Bloc Party has been trailed for the better part of the week by this entourage, which includes two representatives from the group's British label, their American publicist and a representative from Vice. A buzz trails them like a cloud of hornets, yet the actual members of Bloc Party aren't saying anything. Guitarist Gordon Moakes has his Blackberry flipped open, and he's punching the keys in a fevered, steady rhythm. Kele Okereke, the band's frontman, is bundled in a deep blue pea coat and is wearing a pair of earmuffs the size of hockey pucks. After a few minutes, they deposit themselves on a sofa and immediately the man with the tripod sets up in front of them and starts click-click-clicking. The members of Bloc Party don't even seem to notice him; they're staring off, dazed and distracted, at some odd point in the distance behind him. Every so often, guitarist Russell Lissack leans over and whispers something in Okereke's ear, and the two of them start cackling wildly. What it is that he's whispering, though, is anybody's guess.

4:30 PM

Back when I was in Bible College, wheedling Youth Pastor–types would periodically distribute music comparison charts, telling you which Christian Rock bands you might like by comparing them to popular FM arena bands. So if you liked REO Speedwagon, for example, you'd look them up on the chart and then you'd go to the Christian Bookstore and buy a White Heart record instead. There seems to be a similar logic at work connecting Bloc Party to Franz Ferdinand. The Scottish quartet is mentioned in nearly every article about Bloc Party and undoubtedly in an equal number of conversations occurring across record counters and over tallboys. Some of this is unavoidable: Bloc Party got their start after Okereke mailed a demo tape to Franz's Alex Kapranos two years ago, prompting Kapranos to invite the young group to open for them at the

Domino Records 10th Anniversary party. But most of the time, the mentions are preceded by the word "next"—as in "Bloc Party is the next Franz Ferdinand." Just like with those comparison charts, the similarities are fleeting at best. Where Franz is foppish and flirty and gloriously effeminate, Bloc Party's songs are worried and guarded and terrified of intimacy. Their protagonists hear voices and eat glass and walk into furniture. Sooner or later in every Bloc Party song there's a crisis, and the consequence of that crisis, 10 times out of 14, is something awful.

At the end of the day, though, these contrasts go unnoticed. Case in point: later in the evening I will interview 10 different Mother-fuckers, and all but one of them will mention Franz Ferdinand in their response. For their part, the members of Bloc Party are beginning to get a bit aggravated by the comparison. When I ask guitarist Moakes about its persistence later in the day, he sighs heavily. "People are often incredibly unimaginative in what their angle is," he says. "If we're in a funny mood, we'll react strangely or goof around a bit or just tell outright lies. You get questions like 'What was it like signing a record deal?' or 'How does it feel to be hyped by all these people?' I mean, how do you think it feels? It feels good."

One of the people he's referring to is the MTV VJ Conor Bezane. MTV is one of around 50 interviews Bloc Party will be doing this week. Bezane looks young and nervous, seeming almost overly aware that he could, in fact, be in the presence of the Next Franz Ferdinand. Periodically, the group breaks out in more fits of raucous laughter, both the comedians and the audience for their own secret joke, and this makes him look very worried.

Midway through the interview, Thomas Onorato, a member of the Motherfucker staff, steals up the stairs and leans in close to speak to Jen, Bloc Party's publicist. They run through a litany of tiny details: what time the band should go on, the status of the guest list and the general backstage arrangements. When he's done with this, Thomas puts down his clipboard, leans in even closer and whispers,

"Now, I don't want to get your hopes up but there's a small, small, tiny chance that Hillary is going to show up. She and her boyfriend love-love-*love* the record, and they really want to come by and check out the show." Jen is buoyed by the news, which causes Thomas to quickly backpedal. "Now, seriously, it's a really small chance. Like maybe 10 percent. So don't put any money on it or anything."

As it turns out, though, bets should have been placed. Because at around two in the morning, Hillary Duff and her boyfriend Benji Madden from Good Charlotte will, in fact, show up at The Roxy to hang out with Bloc Party.

They don't know this now, though, as they sit on the couch running through the story of their origins: Domino's 10th Anniversary Party, how it took them three years to find a suitable drummer, how they were a pretty conventional rock band at first, but how all that changed when they wrote the hollow, haunting "She's Hearing Voices." They're probably explaining how Okereke's spur-of-the-moment decision not to play guitar on that song radically altered the Bloc Party aesthetic, demonstrating to them the power of blank space and the value of a thudding, propulsive backbeat. From there, they'll likely explain how their latest single, "Little Thoughts," has cracked the UK Top 40, how John Peel bestowed his blessing, how the NME proclaimed them the 907,000th band to "Save Rock & Roll!" and how they were snatched up by Vice and came to be considered the Next Franz Ferdinand.

I am guessing all of this because from where I am sitting, I can neither see the members of Bloc Party nor hear any of their responses. All I can see is the VJ, the enormous floor lamp, and the cold, blank eye of the camera.

7:00 PM

All 12 of us are outside now: the band, the publicists, the journalists and the guy with the 6-foot camera-mounted tripod, looking like someone unloaded the cast of a Fellini film in front of a New York rock venue on a lonely February evening. As they have done for most of the day, the members of Bloc Party separate quickly from the pack, scurrying down the street, whispering in each other's ears and engaging in playful shoving matches. We're on our way to a Thai restaurant in the meatpacking district, where Bloc Party will finally get to eat dinner and I will finally get my interview. It's started snowing, and the buzz from the crowd of handlers and hangers-on is echoing off the icy macadam while Bloc Party plays grab ass three blocks ahead of us. We come to a dead stop at the edge of the West Side Highway, where the gradual increase in both snowfall and hunger has convinced everyone that walking eight blocks to the restaurant is a sucker's game. In order to grab a cab, though, we need to cross the street—a tricky enough endeavor for two people in the sun, let alone a dozen in the snow. But this is New York and Motherfucker and the Next Franz Ferdinand, and so when the lights change the members of Bloc Party, their publicist, four label executives, two journalists and a photographer with a 6-foot tripod run across the West Side Highway in the snow, trying to flag down a taxi. This is a doomed venture from the start, largely because the West Side Highway doesn't have a shoulder, and so any cabbie brave enough to pick us up would literally have to come to a dead stop in the middle of the 6-lane freeway. The cameraman has planted his tripod on the sidewalk, and has started snapping pictures of the four members of Bloc Party, shivering, looking for a cab. We are about to turn around and go back the way we came when Okereke spots a cab creeping out of a nearby parking garage and he and Moakes and Tong and Lissack and Jen the American Publicist race after it. There's a few seconds of negotiating, but soon enough the five of them pile into the cab, leaving the buzzing journalists and the busy executives and the clicking photographer miles behind them.

7:45 PM

It becomes clear within 30 seconds of arriving at the restaurant that my interview isn't going to happen. For one thing, the restaurant is packed. We all have to stand in a waiting area that's roughly the size of a box of raisins while the waitstaff arranges a table big enough to accommodate the Next Franz Ferdinand and their entourage. The cameraman decides this is as good a time as any to snap off a few reels, and so he dramatically captures Bloc Party, arms folded, waiting to eat. The restaurant is playing aggressive booming techno, and playing it so loud that in order to be heard you have to yell, and no one particularly feels like yelling. After a few minutes we're all led back to an enormous butcher block table, situated directly beneath one of the techno-blaring speakers. Okereke immediately buries his head in his arms and the rest of the band open their menus. I attempt to ask my first question, but have to repeat it three times due to the noise and the confusion and the fact that Okereke has his head down. The repetition is pointless, though, as I can't hear their responses anyway; I can only read the curling, tightening and unfurling of lips. Of course, just as some headway is made with Moakes, the waiter arrives, and attention is quickly and enthusiastically diverted.

Sensing my desperation, Tong leans in close to me and says, "You know, we're pretty quiet people. As a rule, we're usually pretty reserved. All of this," he swings his hand across the table, "these backstage parties, all these people hanging around—we're pretty bemused by all this. We never saw this as a reflection of our personalities. This whole thing, being famous just because you're famous, it really sucks."

Another of the band's US publicists has arrived and is talking with Okereke and Moakes as the waiter is jotting down the drink orders for 13 people. "There isn't any reason why you can justify what you do," Tong continues, "you just do it. There isn't a massive guiding philosophy. There isn't any big principle there. When we come up with songs, the mind goes blank and we just play, and eventually Okereke will say, 'Yeah, that sounds cool.'" He pauses and I look down at the end of the table to see that we've been joined by a woman dressed as a magician and another who's dressed as a rabbit. After looking at them for a long time, I realize I'm not completely sure if they're members of our party or not. Tong regains his train of thought and continues. "I mean, look, Bono is up for a fucking Nobel Peace Prize or something, isn't he? That's *far and above* what it means to be in a band. I wonder if he ever thought, at their first practice, 'You know, I'd really like to be nominated for the Nobel Peace Prize.' I mean, don't get me wrong, just because you're in a band doesn't mean you should restrict yourself to certain pursuits, but as art forms go," he pauses to take a sip of water, "it's fairly basic, innit?"

10:45 PM

By the time we get back to The Roxy, the venue has filled up considerably, but something has tipped the atmosphere from merry to menacing. Without warning, a security guard yanks a scrawny boy off the dance floor by his shoulders and slams him into the wall, yelling "This is not a strip club!" over and over into his ear. He drops the boy suddenly and shoves him gruffly toward the exit and out the door. Two minutes later, a topless girl in red suspenders and black leather pants strolls lazily by.

A quick informal survey reveals that many of the people in the room have come specifically to see Bloc Party, but further investigation shows that the sentiment about the band's ballooning profile is profoundly mixed. "There's a fine line between exposure and overexposure," says one girl, named Rachel. "I would hate to see them get exposed on the level of, like, Franz Ferdinand." Her opinion is echoed almost directly by two other Motherfuckers, Les and Illyse.

"Look, I'd rather keep them under the radar," says Les. "I mean, why do we *want* Americans to be all over Bloc Party?"

"Yeah," Illyse agrees. "Franz Ferdinand were good for about a minute, but now they're played out. Same thing with Modest Mouse—I love their old work, but their new stuff's crap. Once you see it on MTV or Fuse, it's over." Their friend Lee summarizes it most succinctly. "As long as they stay under the radar, I'll keep listening to them," he says. "But if they become mainstream, I'm probably going to stop."

11:45 PM

I spot Moakes about 30 minutes before the band is scheduled to take the stage slumped over in a chair backstage. He looks exhausted. The rest of the band is milling around aimlessly, but he's staying stock-still, staring at nothing. I settle down next to him and ask how it feels to be at the center of such a maelstrom. "I think we're quite aware of what people expect," he concedes, "but I don't go to bed at night thinking, 'Oh, my God, tomorrow I have to live up to this role I have as the bass player in Bloc Party.'" He sits up a little, rubbing his eyes and swaying slightly from side to side. "I always close my eyes and think of Radiohead." He chuckles. "I know that sounds silly, but they're one of the biggest bands in the world and yet what do you *really* know about Colin Greenwood? He's not a public persona, and yet what he does is critical to what that band sounds like." He sparks up now, seeming suddenly struck by a small epiphany. "The first band I was ever into was Simple Minds. I had books about them, and I'd look at the pictures and just pore over it. I was almost obsessed. There was this desire to see somehow, within what they write or how they talk or how they look in a picture, what makes that band. What really is happening between those people. The *mystique* of it. What is it between a bunch of people that creates the music they make? Where does it come from? Who are they? What feeds it?" He smiles wryly. "I don't think you realize that when you're in a band, it's not really as romantic as that."

1:00 AM

If Bloc Party right now told every person in the room to grab a knife and stab the person next to them, there would be 1,000 dead Motherfuckers in the Roxy in New York City. Such is the strength of the hold the group has on the crowd midway through their set. And it's easy to see why: the group plays like they *mean* it, locking into a groove and letting all the song's parts click and whirr and spin like gears in a combine. They're in the middle of the song "Little Thoughts," the one that landed them in the UK Top 40 and on MTV2 and essentially set this whole insane evening in motion. If you had to imagine the song visually, you'd do well to think of it as a marathon, where all of the runners are keeping exact pace with each other in the opening mile. They jog together, side by side, bass, guitar, drum and vocal, a slow and steady stride with no aims on exertion. Then, in the last minute, the vocal finds its adrenaline, and it breaks away and sprints out from the pack, solitary and invigorated and alive. And that's the part they're hitting now, Okereke rocketing out from the crowd of crystalline chords, wailing out over and over again: "I figured it out! I figured it out! I figured it out!" And in this room, with so many adoring onlookers, it's easy to believe him. But what "it" is, and how "it" works is for him & the band to know and the rest of us—the Motherfuckers, the journalists, the executives and the guy with the camera—to try, usually in vain, to unravel or to invent.

MIKE McGUIRK

Iron Maiden,
Number of the Beast

The chorus of "Run to the Hills" is just about Bruce Dickinson's finest moment. The rest of this album is no less than great. From the toughness of "Invaders" to the satanic aesthetic of the title cut (a now-pervasive idea in metal), Maiden's ridiculously awesome twin guitar attack enjoys a sort of domination and artistic peak few bands ever reach. Maiden! Maiden! Maiden!

High On Fire

Part I: Ah, Windsor!
Bordertown (the Journey)

Ah, Windsor! Bordertown. Birthplace of my father. Referred to by acquaintances as "an armpit" and "profoundly uninteresting." Home of a casino and dense with strip clubs. Flooded every weekend by thousands of thirsty, horny Americans, spilling over the bridge and through the tunnel. My associates and I were playing a different game. We were going to Alvin's, in Detroit, to find our pleasure.

Saturday, February 19

We made the drive from Toronto to Windsor in two and a half hours. It's supposed to take four.

To make the trip, we (Sean, Jeremy, myself) had rented a car—a Champagne Ford Taurus with dark red stains on the driver's-side headrest.

There were three of us in the car, though only two of our names would appear on the guest list. The third's entry was unaccounted for, but then, he was the driver, so his place in the car was generally uncontested.

The ostensible reason for my joining the trip was to cover a concert by the metal band High On Fire. They have a new record out and it's called *Blessed Black Wings*. As the band's website describes it:

> HIGH ON FIRE are [sic] a supersonic exercise in conquest by volume. Equal parts molten metal and earthquake panic, HIGH ON FIRE's MOTORHEAD-meets-SLAYER roar is outrageously loud and absolutely punishing.

I listened to *Blessed Black Wings* from start to finish on the car ride, my attention split between the music and trying to entice truckers to blow their horns by sticking my arm out the window and pumping my fist like Tiger Woods at the Masters. Only four trucks obliged. The album, like the horns, sounded good—damn good.

Upon stating my plan to go to Detroit, I was told that to spend time in Detroit proper was to "take my life into my own hands." My mother asked me to "just be careful and don't do anything stupid." My father expressed his hope "that you have the sense to leave if it gets dangerous." These are the words movie mothers say to their beautiful young sons before sending them off to war. And afterwards, if they come back, they're not the same. Sister asks, "Mama, why doesn't Billy laugh anymore?"

The driver, Sean, didn't want to navigate the lonely streets of Detroit (where the band was playing), so he arranged lodging for us at a bed and breakfast in Windsor, just across the river.

When we hit Windsor, our last Canadian haven, we jumped ship, left the car behind, and boarded a bus to take us through the tunnel, across the border, and into Detroit.

Before you're allowed into Detroit, you have to get off the bus and go through customs. I waited my turn in line and then went up to the customs booth.

I was asked if I had ever been arrested. I hesitated (they wouldn't actually check, would they?), lied, and said no. The customs agent asked if I was sure about that. My stomach tightened. It took a moment, but I realized he was kidding. I laughed. It's that easy. We got back on the bus.

When we hit the end of the line, we hopped off the bus. Standing at an empty intersection, a man, short, maybe forty years old, approached us. "You guys know where you're going?"

What was his scam? He walked us to the cabstand. Told us that a bunch of young men walking around don't have nothing to worry about. The media's a bunch of bullshit—just selling bad news. There're no bullets whizzing. He assured us we had nothing to worry about because we were unknowns. He said people do bad things to people they know.

I was glad to hear that.

We walked into the club, and my name was on the guest list with a plus one. I laughed when the no-neck bouncer asked if I would be drinking. He gingerly applied the appropriate paper bracelet and the three of us entered the fray.

We needed alcohol. In a patriotic moment, we started with Labatt's.

In a matter of seconds it was time to order more beer. I asked the black-mascara'd waitress, heavy in a way that only made her more desirable, for three of whatever was popular. She didn't understand. It's the curse of the service industry: people told over and over what to do often struggle when asked to choose. If the customer's always right, what do you do when they don't know? I told her to give me whatever the kids are drinking. She handed us three bottles of Pabst Blue Ribbon.

Shots of whiskey and more beer.

No one had any drugs. This seemed unusual to someone hailing from Canada, where the drugs flow like water from the faucet—or so I said at the time. In a place like Alvin's, there are two ways people deny a request for drugs. The first method is the embarrassed apology. This is what you're getting when you're told, "Oh, just not here, man" or "Sorry, you should have caught me earlier." Those interested in saving face use this approach. These people are unlikely to share. They probably won't even point you in the right direction.

The second, more honest, approach is characterized by an economy of verbiage and palpable discomfort. It is the method of choice for underagers and prudes. They don't look you in the eye. They hope you'll just go away. I prefer the integrity of this rejection.

Part II: The Raccoon's Realisation (the Review)

Tuesday, March 1

The crowd was all hooded sweaters, faux-intimidating facial hair, and heavy boots. Uncomfortable-looking women salted here and there, standing by their men. I fit right in.

A terrible band was playing. A band so worried about their looks, they don't even realize that their hearts had stopped. Strictly for necrophiliacs.

Long, jet-black hair draped artfully across his sweaty forehead, the singer smacked his face in a bogus fit of cathartic hysteria, gathered himself in time to announce that the next song was about "fucking."

The preening singer was making my blood boil. Ten-year-olds on Halloween are more disturbing than this jerk. His music, his show, had nothing to do with real pleasure, pain, or anything else that makes heavy music heavy.

When the singer, shirt buttoned only to the navel, started grabbing the heads of people near the stage in mock holy-roller fashion, something had to be done. With his head down, and his focus on the cranium of a skinny young lady, he never saw me coming. I moved within arm's reach and made a fist out of my hand as my eyes locked on a prime patch of his thinning hair.

It had been a long time since I gave someone a noogie. But I've never forgotten the feeling of my knuckles burning into someone's scalp. It wasn't the best noogie I've ever given, but I can't remember a more satisfactory application of that schoolyard staple.

Out of the corner of my eye, I saw others laughing at the stage and nodding in my direction. I didn't do it for them. I did it for me. The band finished up soon after.

Another beer. Then High On Fire.

High On Fire are for real. It doesn't matter that it's impossible to discern what Matt Pike's singing about. It doesn't matter that the band offers almost nothing in the way of visual appeal. What matters is the music. The riffs are ceaseless and impossible to escape. The drums are furious, the bass pounding, the commitment unwavering. Boogie from the best bar band in Hell gives way to solos Slayer should die for. It's heaven.

I can't give you any details about songs played or the equipment used. What I can tell you is that I don't know how a metal band could be better. They are an Aristotelian ideal of heaviness. If you like metal, if you think you like metal, see them now. Two thousand years from now, children will wonder how the Devil got so good, and creaky old metal heads will wipe the slobber off their chins and whisper, "He sold his soul to High On Fire."

The previous band doesn't even have the guts to admit to their artifice; they just hope you'll see it as something else. High On Fire don't give you a choice. You might like it or you might hate it. But High On Fire are not liars. They are High On Fire. Rocking is what they do. End of discussion. But not the end of the story.

I tiptoed through a snipe of mic-stands and electrical cables and entered the backstage room. I saw Matt Pike. Minutes earlier he stood with one foot on the stage monitor, killing a yeti with nothing but his guitar, sounding like he just gargled with Satan's Scope. Now he was sitting silently on a ratty couch, looking small and tired.

I approached him and explained I was from *PopMatters* and asked if I could have a word with him. He agreed without hesitation. The bass player looked at me skeptically. I patted Pike's sweaty shoulder and told him I thought it had been a great show—even if "show" is a degrading word for what High On Fire does.

Then I explained to him that I would tell a story, and wanted to know what his music had to do with the story I was about to tell.

My story is:

Driving home late one night, I saw a raccoon that had been hit by a car struggling to crawl away. I pulled over to the side of the road, got out of my car, and walked over to the raccoon. We looked into each other's eyes. Its breathing was laboured and its eyes were glassy. Using only its front paws, it struggled to pull itself off the road.

A cop had stopped a speeder a few yards away. I told the cop there was a hurt raccoon in the middle of the street. He said he'd take care of it and that I should just go home. I got in my car and drove off. Less than a minute later, I turned around. When I came back, the raccoon was now in a heap on the side of the road. Again, I looked into its eyes. It was struggling harder to breathe; it looked away, then back at me again. Then it died.

I popped the trunk of my car and went to pick up the raccoon. I could feel its broken bones as I placed it on the floor of the trunk. I drove home, got a shovel, and then headed to a park. Shovel in one hand, raccoon in the other, moonlight on my back, I found a good spot and began digging. I placed the raccoon in the hole, didn't cover it, and went home. The next morning I went back to the grave. The raccoon was gone.

What does that have to do with your music, Matt Pike?
"Everything has to die," he answered. "Even little raccoons."

Sunday, February 20

Hunter S. Thompson died.

Monday, February 21

Back in the office, the inevitable Monday morning questions came. The kinds of questions where the answers are less important than the show of asking. This time was a little different though; the reactions were livelier than usual—surprise that I willingly went to Detroit and surprise that I liked the heavy metal I saw and heard there. Raised eyebrows, embarrassed smiles.

One of my co-workers tried to rationalize my trip by saying, "Heavy metal huh? I guess that can be a great escape from life sometimes." *Heavy metal is an escape from life?* The poor bastard. Heavy metal *is* life. Sitting in front of a computer for eight hours, engaging in phony banter, minimizing my web browser every time someone walks by, feeling guilty about stepping away from the desk too much, always knowing that finishing one boring task just means I have to move on to the next one—that's not life.

The little raccoon wasn't dying as it clawed its way across the street; it was living. It was doing all that it could to keep moving. It wasn't bogged down in maybes. What we call life is overflowing with alternatives—what we'd rather be doing, what we could be doing.

At a High On Fire show, when the music starts you can't do anything but scream and jump and go with it. It can be unbelievably hard to do what we have to do to make sure we're living and not dying. Sometimes we're not up to the task. We're told "that's the real world" and we put the bit in our mouth. Sometimes we can get away for a weekend, drive to Detroit, and see High On Fire. And sometimes, after decades of trying anything and everything to avoid choking on the bullshit, we wake up one morning in Aspen, decide we're too tired to keep living, and blow our heads off.

MIKE McGUIRK

Boredoms, *Super Ae*

The Boredoms offer those addicted to the mind-bending effects of nitrous oxide seven tracks of doom metal bash, hyper-speed astral travel and the healing power of New Age psychedelia. *Super Ae* marked a new era for this incredible band and needs to be experienced by anyone interested in music that goes too far.

MONICA KENDRICK

Bang the Head Slowly

*Uncomfortable, Unemotional,
Isolating Metal at a Snail's Pace*

(This is a review of an Earth show at the Empty Bottle in Chicago
on 9/24/05)

> *This is the light of the mind, cold and planetary*
> *The trees of the mind are black. The light is blue.*
> —Sylvia Plath, "The Moon and the Yew Tree"

When it comes to music, introverts get a bad rap. It's as though having an "I" in your Myers-Briggs profile means you love to get up in front of lots of people with nothing but an acoustic guitar, a sense of entitlement, and plenty of intimate melodramas to sing about—or worse yet, that you love to listen to that crap. But we introverts are fully capable of enjoying ourselves at raucous keggers or neotribal nekkid fests. We can orbit the same star as everybody else; we just do it out of the plane of the ecliptic. Sometimes the music is enough to occupy our minds completely, so we don't even feel guilty for not socializing, and other times we're half listening to that little voice in the back of our heads that's wondering if we'd be having more fun

alone on the couch with a glass of wine and a good collection of old
Mystery Science Theater 3000 episodes.

Sylvia Plath was right: very often the pleasure of solitude is cold
and planetary. And Earth—the Seattle-based band that basically
consists of guitarist Dylan Carlson and whoever he's working with
now—offers some of that same sort of pleasure. Ordinary lusty rock
'n' roll usually revs people up with speed—it takes the rhythms of
pulse and breath and throttles them up just the right amount. But
Carlson and company mercilessly refuse to play at a tempo that's
comfortable for the average human's body. They bring it way, way
down, past even Sabbathy 'lude rock, into an icy zone of dark-
matter density—you wonder if this deep, deep sludge is being
played by Ents or trolls or some other creature that has a longer life
span and a much slower metabolism than we have. They aren't setting the controls for the heart of the sun like so many psychedelic
rock bands—they're trying to tunnel to the center of the earth, and
they don't care how long it takes to get there. There's nothing com-
munal here, no reaching out to the audience—just riffing and every
so often drumming, slow and inexorable as water eroding stone.
There aren't lyrics or vocals or any other attempt to represent human emotion. The music aims for the transpersonal and ecstatic
through physical mortification and self-negation.

This was radical stuff in the early '90s, when Earth started—if it
sounds less so now, that's mostly because, à la the Velvet Underground, everybody who bought Earth's first record seems to have
started a band. (Joe Preston, who was on that first record, the 1991
Sub Pop EP *Extra-Capsular Extraction*, seems to have been in half of
them himself.) But Earth's first full-length, 1993's *Earth 2*, still
stands as a sort of limbo bar of heaviness—even now there aren't too
many people who can go lower.

That said, the current incarnation of Earth is sparser, leaner, and
cleaner than the early–'90s version: the band's new *Hex: Or Printing
in the Infernal Method* (Southern Lord) has the barren, melancholy
quality of a Nevada landscape, and could easily double as the sound

track to an even weirder version of Jim Jarmusch's *Dead Man* (maybe one that draws out a single grim moment for hours, like a Michael Snow film). Hell, if it weren't for the dark, clangy guitar tunings, you could convince yourself you were listening to an early Calexico album at the wrong speed—Carlson even plays banjo, swear to God. But I'm convinced that the relative calm of the album's first half hour is intended to lull the unsuspecting into dropping their guard before the elegant, incantatory, monstrous grind of "Raiford (The Felon Wind)"—which is, as it happens, also the track with the banjo. Carlson would scheme like that. He's already proved himself to have a kind of reptilian, Machiavellian patience in his music.

Drummer Adrienne Davies, currently the band's other core member, is de-emphasized in the album mix, but onstage at the Empty Bottle last weekend she was the spine of the beast, mesmerizing to watch as she bowed and swayed, just as involved in the beats she didn't play as the ones she did. Every eloquent thud seemed to come after a long anticipation—the aim of rhythm like this isn't to surprise but to crash down with all the inevitability of destiny. I'd never heard wind chimes sound so fucking *metal*.

The album makes effective and ominous use of near silence, but this can be hard to pull off live when your band's MO involves turning up to 11. The trio, rounded out by bassist John Schuller, didn't try terribly often—but when they did, they made it count. The lovely, menacing "Lens of Unrectified Night" is all about protracted tension, and Carlson landed on its climactic chords so viciously that I barely missed the ghostly pedal steel that shadows the main guitar riffs on the disc.

Earth wasn't a particularly warm or chatty band onstage, and that seemed appropriate. The audience was a picture of solipsistic bliss, like a bunch of long-haired, jeans-wearing slo-mo dervishes, all caught up in their own isolated pockets of mystic communion with the Force. You can't "party" to this stuff. You probably shouldn't have sex to it. You can't even really drive to it—unless you drive like a 90-year-old.

Myself, I was a little disappointed. This new, stripped-down Earth doesn't often land on your head like Judgment Day. The music's slinkier and subtler and at times even kind of boring—though Carlson and friends clearly aren't afraid of coming off that way. After all, they're not bored—they're going to their private happy places, and you're responsible for your own. That's why I wish the set had been longer: given that I was required to immerse myself in the music, rather than simply wait for it to draw me in, some more time would've been useful. As it was, I ended up admiring it from a distance, the way you might watch the moon inch across the sky.

Kraftwerk, *Man-Machine*

The Man-Machine is one of the most groundbreaking pop albums of all time. Forget about Bowie's ersatz space-robot shtick and practically all the synth pop that came in the wake of it; this is disco made by *real* robots. *German* robots. Kraftwerk basically encoded the language of New Wave here.

WILL HERMES
(AS ROBERT BARBARA)

Vegetarian militancy, sound magick, B&D, and the most astonishing live show of my life

"Bondage for Satomi Fuji"
—Merzbow

I just saw the most incredible show of my life.

Or maybe, to be more precise, I had the most incredible club experience of my life.

That's not it either, but hey—it's a lead. Let me explain.

My friend Ethan, who is a psychology student at Queens College, emailed me out of the blue to ask if I wanted to see Merzbow—a.k.a. Masami Akita, the Japanese "noise artist" and writer—at the Knitting Factory, the multi-stage avant-garde coddling music space in Lower Manhattan. Ethan is interested in extreme behavior, which is curious because he is a very mild-mannered, non-extreme sort of guy. I said sure. I've never really gotten into this sort of music—it all sounds, well, like noise—but I figured it would be interesting. So last night we went.

Opening was Jim O'Rourke, occasional Sonic Youth member, who performed a duet with some guy using a bunch of electronic boxes. It was a mostly undifferentiated mass of electronic shrieks and rumbles which heaved in some interesting ways. Next was Circle, a Finnish prog-rock group who were pretty great, with lots of anthemic crescendos and Arctic Circle howling and an excellent, krautrock-literate drummer who looked wicked in a black turtleneck and a black cat-burglar mask, like Batman's sidekick Robin if he was a skinhead philosophy grad student. Adding some visual amusement up front in the audience was a huge dude wearing a red headband, who was alternately taking pictures of the band and, during the really heavy parts, pumping both fists ecstatically towards the ceiling, presumably in a gesture of Finnish solidarity.

Merzbow came on precisely at midnight, and sat behind two PowerBooks, one 15″ and one 12″. (For some reason I'd thought he used a guitar, but whatever.) On one was a MEAT IS MURDER sticker, and the word FUR behind a red circle and slash.

Akita had long straight black hair that hung down to the small of his back, and wore small oval glasses. As a writer, he is known for his writing on bondage and S&M (http://www.bondageproject.com/public/history_e2.htm), so it might strike some as odd that he is also an animal rights activist.

I guess it's about consent.

The performance began with a stream, then a flood, of sputtering low frequencies, which increased in volume until it felt like a hundred subway trains were running beneath the venue (unlike Joe's Pub, in which you can usually hear only the #6 train during shows). Then higher frequencies came in: piercing laser-shots, screaming outbursts like buzzsaws against steel, lurching and grinding sine waves bending like girders collapsing under the weight of buildings, and around it all a cloud of static like a swarm of giant bees, or the magnesium-flare of a pyrotechnical display that just keeps sizzling. It felt like—here comes a rock critic cliché, but I'm at a loss for any more precise description—the soundtrack to the apocalypse, of buildings collapsing, calling to mind the World Trade Towers which fell only a few blocks away, and the German industrial group Einsturzende Neubauten, whose name in fact translates as "new buildings collapsing" and whom I was thinking about last week while stepping around mounds of dogshit and high-end babystrollers in the Kreuzberg district of Berlin, the group's old stomping ground. I closed my eyes, and I basically saw the money shots from old *Godzilla* films.

Yet there was also a stillness and an austere beauty to it all, as the chaos merged together into something almost ambient. The volume was admittedly terrifying: I had earplugs screwed in to the hilt, with a 25dB noise reduction rating, and that made it easier to parse the subtle, sculptural moves he was making within each group of frequencies. (Never have I been to a show where earplugs actually enhanced the music.) And there was the sheer physicality of it: the bass frequencies literally entering your body and massaging it from the inside, the high end grazing your skin like the tingle of ocean salt when it dries on your arm hair after a swim.

With your eyes closed—almost the entire crowd stood that way—you felt like you'd been physically taken over and manipulated by some *Alien*-like creature, although more symbiotic than parasitic. The act of bondage has never rated very high in my erotic top-ten. But I imagine that it might create a sort of sensory-deprivation dream-state much like the experience of this performance, where immobility and sensory deprivation make you acutely sensitive to your body while simultaneously freeing you of it, allowing you to step out of your flesh husk and watch yourself writhe.

It was pretty hot, actually.

But then things got weirder.

Whenever I opened my eyes, I'd see the crazy Finn with the headband up front, holding an SLR camera with a flash unit about four feet from Akita's face and firing off shot after shot—despite the fact that Mr. Merzbow didn't change his bookish expression or move, except to pivot his head a few inches between laptops, for the entire two-hour performance. When he wasn't taking pictures, the Finn was bellowing and pumping his fist.

It was after about an hour and a half that the guy let out another moronic stadium-rock yelp, and with his fist still up in the air, projectile vomited across the front of the stage. It was the most spectacular upchuck I've ever seen: it came out of both sides of his mouth in a wide spray that somehow missed Akita—who didn't so much as blink—and his equipment.

The music seemed to get even louder as the stench wafted back. People began moaning and moving towards the door, and soon half the room was empty. But Akita gave no indication that he'd even noticed, and there were still dozens of listeners who remained riveted to the floor, eyes closed, hands over their noses and mouths.

Then an even stranger thing happened.

Or maybe not strange at all. Other people began throwing up. A jockish dude near the left speaker cabinet puked violently into it. Two dreadlocked white guys, one following the other, hurled, side by side, against the side of the bar. And a beautiful Japanese girl, who I'd been watching bliss out whenever my eyes were open, put her hand on my shoulder and hurled onto my left foot before being led away by her girlfriend.

At this point, the lights suddenly went up, the volume seemed to arc up even higher, like the sound of Godzilla hitting high-voltage cables.

And then it stopped. Akita stood up and walked off stage, seemingly unaware anything unusual had happened.

Maybe this wasn't unusual.

Out on Leonard Street, the crisp night air returned my body to me, and relieved the nausea of being inside. People milled about, dazed, some hunched over, a few laughing and trying to find words for what had happened. I saw the Japanese girl get into a cab with her friends, which was a bit of a letdown as I wanted to try and console her. I looked down at my shoe, and there was a chunk of what looked like unchewed yellowtail sitting between the front laces and the toe. Disgusted, I kicked it off.

Then I had a fleeting thought: What if Merzbow's frequencies, coming as they did from an anti-meat activist, were designed to attack and sicken meat eaters?

"Interesting idea," said Ethan. "Good thing we had falafel. I'm going to Google that when I get home."

At the top of this post, an MP3 link to a 29-minute piece from Merzbow's out-of-print *Music for Bondage Performance 2*, to give you an idea of what I'm going on about. Do not listen to it after a meal at Peter Luger's.

But wait—I almost forgot the weirdest thing of all.

At one point during Merzbow's set, I left to pee, and went up to the balcony for a different perspective. I stood next to a tall, handsome girl in the first row of seats who was typing speedily into a 12″ Power-Book. She looked familiar, and when she looked up, she pointed in an accusatory way and smiled; a cute, snaggle-toothy smile. But given the volume, talking was out of the question. Since I couldn't recall her name or where I knew her from, I pointed back to her, nodded in that universal nightclub nice-to-see-you-but-I'm-not-going-to-talk-to-you-now code, and left to re-enter the maelstrom below.

After the show was over, it hit me: She was the waitress from Minneapolis—the one who brought the Bloody Marys during my interview with Conor Oberst at Hell's Kitchen, and who gave me a withering look when I chugged Conor's leftovers. Her hair was half blonde and half green then; now it was growing out brown with white tips, which is maybe why I couldn't place her at first. That and her out-of-context appearance in New York.

When I realized this outside the club, I went back in to find her. But she was gone.

I hope she didn't get sick. Judging from her build, she looked like a carnivore.

MIKE McGUIRK

Dream Theater, *Octavarium*

Dream Theater's 2005 release, their tenth full-length since the group formed in the mid-1980s, may boil down to synth-heavy, 12-sided-dice nerd metal, but that's not the worst thing in the world. There's always ritual murder, and you have to listen to *something* on the way to Laser Tag.

MOUSTAFA BAYOUMI

Disco Inferno

Yasir al-Qutaji is a 30-year-old lawyer from Mosul, Iraq. In March 2004, while exploring allegations that US troops were torturing Iraqis, Qutaji was arrested by American forces. News accounts describe how he was then subjected to the same kinds of punishment he was investigating. He was hooded, stripped naked and doused with cold water. He was beaten by American soldiers, who wore gloves so as not to leave permanent marks. And he was left in a room soldiers blithely called The Disco, a place where Western music rang out so loud that his interrogators were, in Qutaji's words, forced to "talk to me via a loudspeaker that was placed next to my ears."

Qutaji is hardly the only Iraqi to speak of loud music being blared at him, and the technique echoes far beyond Mosul. In Qaim, near the Syrian border, *Newsweek* found American soldiers blasting Metallica's "Enter Sandman" at detainees in a shipping crate while flashing lights in their eyes. Near Falluja, three Iraqi journalists working for Reuters were seized by the 82nd Airborne. They charged that "deafening music" was played directly into their ears while soldiers ordered them to dance. And back in Mosul, Haitham al-Mallah described being hooded, handcuffed and delivered to a location where soldiers boomed "extremely loud (and dirty) music" at him. Mallah said the site was "an unknown place which they call 'the disco.'"

Disco isn't dead. It has gone to war.

And it's everywhere: Afghanistan, Guantánamo Bay, Abu Ghraib, anywhere touched by the "war on terror." In Afghanistan, Zakim Shah, a 20-year-old Afghan farmer, was forced to stay awake while in American custody by soldiers blasting music and shouting at him. Shah told the *New York Times* that after enduring the pain of music, "he grew so exhausted . . . that he vomited." In Guantánamo Bay, Eminem, Britney Spears, Limp Bizkit, Rage Against the Machine, Metallica (again) and Bruce Springsteen ("Born in the USA") have been played at mind-numbing volumes, sometimes for stretches of up to fourteen hours, at detainees. And at Abu Ghraib, Saddam Salah al-Rawi, a 29-year-old Iraqi, told a similar story. For no reason, over a period of four months, he was hooded, beaten, stripped, urinated on and lashed to his cell door by his hands and feet. He also talked about music becoming a weapon. "There was a stereo inside the cell," he said, "with a sound so loud I couldn't sleep. I stayed like that for twenty-three hours."

Whatever the playlist—usually heavy metal or hip-hop but sometimes, bizarrely, Barney the Dinosaur's "I Love You" or selections from *Sesame Street*—the music is pumped at detainees with such brutality to unravel them without laying so much as a feather on their bodies. The mind is another story, and blasting loud music at captives has become part of what has now entered our lexicon as "torture lite." Torture lite is a calculated combination of psychological and physical means of coercion that stop short of causing death and pose little risk that telltale physical marks will be left behind, but that nonetheless can cause extreme psychological trauma. It's designed to deprive the victim of sleep and to cause massive sensory overstimulation, and it has been shown in different situations to be psychologically unbearable.

Clearly, torture music is an assault on human rights. But more broadly, what does it mean when music gets enrolled in schools of torture and culture is sent jackbooted into war? With torture music, our culture is no longer primarily a means of individual expression or an avenue to social criticism. Instead, it is an actual weapon, one that represents and projects American military might. Cultural differences are exploited, and multiculturalism becomes a strategy for domination. Torture music is the crudest kind of cultural imperialism, grimly ironic in a war that is putatively about spreading "universal" American values.

Yet the first reaction torture music inspired among Americans was not indignation but amusement. Finally, dangerous terrorists—like everyone else—will be tortured by Britney Spears's music! Most commentators saw it this way, particularly after *Time* reported that Christina Aguilera's music was droned at Mohammed al-Qahtani, the alleged twentieth 9/11 hijacker, at Guantánamo. The *Chicago Tribune*'s website compiled readers' favorite "interro-tunes" (the winner was Captain and Tennille's "Muskrat Love"). The *New York Sun* called it "mood music for jolting your jihadi," and a Missouri paper wrote cheekily that Defense Secretary Donald Rumsfeld had "approved four of seven stronger coercive tunes but said that forcing the prisoner to view photos of Aguilera's *Maxim* magazine photo shoot—in which she poses in a pool with only an inner-tube to cover her ferret-like figure—would fall outside Geneva Convention standards."

Thus, torture lite slides right into mainstream American acceptance. It's a frat-house prank taken one baby-step further—as essentially harmless, and American, as an apple pie in the face. It's seen as a justified means of exacting revenge on or extracting information from a terrorist—never mind that detainees in the "war on terror" are mostly Muslims who were in the wrong place at the wrong time.

"Without music, life would be an error," writes Nietzsche, but for Muslim detainees, it's the other way around. Mind-numbing American music is blasted at them with such ferocity that they will believe their lives are a mistake.

Torture music has a history. In 1997, while considering the regular Israeli use of the practice, the United Nations Committee Against Torture explicitly qualified it as torture and called for its ban. In 1978 the European Court of Human Rights confronted a similar technique employed by Britain in the early 1970s against Irish detainees, although in the British rendition, it was loud noise instead of music that was wielded against detainees. This was one of the so-called Five Techniques, scientifically developed interrogation practices that also included wall-standing, hooding, sleep deprivation and withholding of food and drink. While the Court stopped short of calling this torture, it did label it "inhumane and degrading" and found that the Five Techniques were breaches of the European Convention on Human Rights. Britain promised never to employ them again. (Questions have since been raised about British troops "hooding" prisoners in Iraq.)

In fact, the Five Techniques never disappeared. All five and a few more have materialized as an orchestra of effects in the prosecution of the "war on terror." Attorney Jonathan Pyle and his law partner, Susan Burke, have interviewed scores of Iraqis for a class-action suit against private contractors for their alleged roles in abusing Iraqis. They report that Iraqis repeatedly describe the same kinds of abuse—being hooded and handcuffed, sealed in containers, doused with cold water, subjected to strobe lights and blasted with brutally loud music. And according to the Fay report, one of the government's many investigations of the Abu Ghraib scandal, sleep adjustment was brought to Iraq with the 519 Military Intelligence Battalion from Afghanistan. Shafiq Rasul, a British citizen who was imprisoned for two and a half years, says he endured similar treatment in Guantánamo after October 2002. Citing a source familiar with conditions at Guantánamo, Physicians for Human Rights described how the "deprivation of sensory stimulation on the one hand and overstimulation on the other were causing spatial and temporal disorientation in detainees. The results were self-harm and suicide attempts."

With a little imagination, it's not hard to see exactly how. Of Britain's Five Techniques, noise was considered the hardest to suffer. In his book *Unspeakable Acts, Ordinary People*, John Conroy describes the "absolute" and "unceasing" noise that the Irishmen who were first subjected to the Five Techniques endured. While the other four techniques were clearly terrifying, the noise was "an assault of such ferocity that many of the men now recall it as the worst part of the ordeal."

A US military program confirms Conroy's observation. In July *The New Yorker* reported on the SERE program (Survival, Evasion, Resistance and Escape), a course that trains soldiers to withstand interrogations by subjecting them to the harsh treatment they could expect if captured. (The article suggests these counterinterrogation techniques have been twisted and turned into policy at Guantánamo.) Soldiers often believe the interrogation part of their program will be the most difficult, but according to the article, "the worst moment is when they are made to listen to taped loops of cacophonous sounds. One of the most stress-inducing tapes is a recording of babies crying inconsolably. Another is a Yoko Ono album."

Such distress noises (called "horror sounds" by one ex-detainee) have been reported in Afghanistan and Guantánamo. Erik Saar, a former Gitmo translator, describes in his book *Inside the Wire* how Qahtani "was subjected to strobe lights; a loud, insistent tape of cats meowing (from a cat food commercial) interspersed with babies crying; and deafening loud music—one song blasted at him constantly was Drowning Pool's thumping, nihilistic metal rant 'Bodies' ('Let the bodies hit the floor . . . ')."

Ex-interrogators at Guantánamo's Camp Delta described their methods to the *New York Times*. These included shackling detainees to the floor, cranking up the air-conditioning and forcing them to endure strobe lights with rock and rap music playing at mind-numbing volumes for unbearably long sessions. "It fried them," one said. Another admitted that detainees returned "very wobbly. They came back to their cells and were just completely out of it."

This is when the mind begins its rebellion against the body. After you end up "wobbly" or "fried," a severe post-traumatic stress disorder commonly results. Patrick Shivers, one of the Irish victims of the Five Techniques, developed a lasting and severe hypersensitivity to noise to the point where he was "disturbed by the sound of a comb placed on a shelf in his bathroom."

In Iraq we can hear about the beginnings of the same traumas. In a gripping *Vanity Fair* article, Donovan Webster searched for and found "the man in the hood" from the macabre Abu Ghraib photos. Haj Ali told Webster of being hooded, stripped, handcuffed to his cell and bombarded with a looped sample of David Gray's "Babylon." It was so loud, he said, "I thought my head would burst." Webster then cued up "Babylon" on his iPod and played it for Haj Ali to confirm the song. Ali ripped the earphones off his head, and started crying. "He didn't just well up with tears," Webster later told me. "He broke down sobbing."

Sounding brass in front of your enemy has always been a part of war, from Joshua's trumpets tumbling walls in the Bible to a mean fife and drum ringing out "Rule Britannia" across the Plains of Abraham. When American forces invaded Panama in 1989, Manuel Noriega fled to the papal nunciature, and American forces roared Twisted Sister's "We're Not Gonna Take It," and songs with the word "jungle" in the lyrics in front of His Holiness's house. During the siege of Falluja in April 2004, American soldiers cranked the volume on their AC/DC. Their preferred song? "Shoot to Thrill."

The calculated use of American music in interrogations is less about rallying the troops than destroying a detainee. The US innovation in the interrogation practice of blaring loud noises is the deliberate use of American culture as an offensive weapon. While culture has long been a rationalization for conquest (consider the "civilizing mission" of European colonialisms), and while much post-Holocaust European thought has viewed contemporary culture as coercive and potentially authoritarian, neither colonialism nor the Frankfurt School witnessed the transformation of culture into the very instrument of torture. For them, culture was more the end than the means of conquest.

But culture as warfare is Pentagon policy. Donald Rumsfeld and Lieut. Gen. Ricardo Sanchez approved its deployment in their lists of harsher interrogation techniques for detainees. Rumsfeld did so in April 2003 and Sanchez in September 2003, and their almost identical memos both specify, along with the use of auditory stimuli or music, that "interrogators be provided reasonable latitude to vary techniques depending on the detainee's culture." The Sanchez memo also allows the presence of military working dogs, which "exploits Arab fear of dogs."

Altering interrogations according to a detainee's culture is not necessarily damaging, but the Pentagon's multiculturalism doesn't run deep, just wild. With the dissemination of the Abu Ghraib photos, Seymour Hersh reported in *The New Yorker* that the "bible" among neoconservatives was *The Arab Mind*, a piece of trash scholarship more than a generation old that claims Arabs understand only force, shame and humiliation. When the book was reissued in 2002, Norvell De Atkine, director of Middle East studies at the JFK Special Warfare Center and School at Fort Bragg, wrote its foreword. This is "essential reading," writes the man who has "briefed hundreds of military teams being deployed to the Middle East." So essential, in fact, that *The Arab Mind* "forms the basis" of his "cultural" curriculum.

Despite (or maybe because of) the continued use of the book, military professionals' knowledge of other cultures is actually dangerously low. A recent article in the military journal *Joint Force Quarterly* reveals how little American forces understand Iraqi society, using an example of how the US military frequently misunderstands Iraqi hand gestures, leading to tragic consequences and preventable deaths. The article goes on to quote a Special Forces colonel assigned to the Under Secretary of Defense for Intelligence. "We literally don't know where to go for information on what makes other societies tick," admits the colonel, "so we use Google to make policy."

What the practice of sounding loud American music at Muslims reveals most is the power American forces associate with American culture. Any prolonged loud noise in the right circumstances stands a good chance of driving you mad. Yet narcissistically, American intelligence seems to believe American music will break you more quickly. "These people haven't heard heavy metal. They can't take it," a psy-ops sergeant told *Newsweek*. And in Guantánamo, they even have a name for it. The Pentagon's Schmidt investigation identifies it as "futility music"—that is to say, screamingly loud and deliberately Western music that will, per the Army field manual, "highlight the futility of the detainee's situation." (On the other hand, "cultural music," Schmidt reports, is "played as an incentive.") Twenty-four thousand interrogations later, "futility music," according to Schmidt, remains authorized.

Fifty years ago, the great Martinican poet Aimé Césaire wrote that the trouble with colonization was not just that it dehumanizes the colonized but that it also "decivilizes" the colonizer. Torture does the same. While transforming a human being into a thing of pain, it simultaneously strangles human society. Torture threatens to decivilize us today not only because its practices are being normalized within our national imagination but also because civil society is being enlisted to rationalize its demands. In most arenas, this process has elicited at least some vocal opposition. When it was revealed that medical professionals were assisting in abusive interrogations, debates among doctors and psychologists followed about torture, medical ethics and war. And while Administration lawyers have attempted to narrow the definition of torture and to authorize new methods of inflicting pain, other attorneys, including top military lawyers, have challenged interrogation policies on legal, moral and tactical grounds.

And so the B-side to the torture music issue flips to the music community's response to the practice. While many musicians may not even be aware of this instrumentalized use of their songs, Metallica's James Hetfield did comment on the phenomenon to Terry Gross on NPR's *Fresh Air*. Asked about a BBC report that described his band's music being blared during Iraqi interrogations, he responded with "pride" that his music is "culturally offensive" to Iraqis. Hetfield said that he considers his music "a freedom to express my insanity. . . . If they're not used to freedom," he said, "I'm glad to be a part of the exposure."

But Hetfield's voice must not be the only one. Where do other musicians stand? Will Eminem rage against the torture machine or will Bruce Springsteen speak out as his music is press-ganged into futility and pain? If American musicians oppose the use of their music in torture, it's time for them to make some noise.

Other Notable Essays of 2005

As Selected by Daphne Carr

Nitsuh Abebe, "Twee as fuck" (*Pitchfork Media*, October 24, 2005)

Judd Apatow, "Tuesday" (*Slate*, September 28, 2005)

Jake Austen, "A Kinder, Gentler Reality" (*Chicago Reader*, August 5, 2005)

Mark Baumgarten, "The warlord from Mars: Courtney Taylor-Taylor" (*Willamette Week*, December 7, 2005)

Janice Berman, "Ageless Charo keeps the cuchi, cuchi flame burning" (*San Francisco Chronicle*, August 6, 2005)

Andy Beta, "The World on a String" (*Stop Smiling*, October/November 2005)

Mark Binelli, "The Guru" (*Rolling Stone*, September 22, 2005)

Andrew Bonazzeli, "Extreme Metal Ballet" (*Decibel Magazine*, August 2005)

Gavin Borchert, Laura Cassidy, Liam Cole, Matthew Corwine, Lynn Jacobson, Heather Logue, Chris Lorraine, Michaelangelo Matos, Ann Powers, Rachel Shrimp, Kate Silver, Christina Twu and Rickey Wright, "A Day in the Life" (*Seattle Weekly*, November 9, 2005)

Hank Bordowitz, "Saving Ray Charles" (*Massachusetts Super Lawyer*, 2005)

John Bowe, "How Did House Bands Become a Filipino Export?" (*The New York Times Magazine*, May 29, 2005)

Hillary Brown, "Nature Versus Nurture" (*Flagpole*, November 30, 2005)

Sam Chennault, "The urban music community responds to Katrina and the aftermath" (*Miami New Times*, September 29, 2005)

Chris Dahlen, "The Chubawamba Factor" (*Pitchfork Media*, August 22, 2005)

Justin Davidson, "How we experience music" (*Newsday*, January 2, 2005)

Geeta Dayal, "noise" (*The Original Soundtrack*, August 8, 2005)

Andrea Duncan-Mao, "Big Boy Game" (*XXL*, September 2005)

Danny Eccleston, "Franz Ferdinand" (*MOJO Magazine*, November 2005)

Jenny Eliscu, "Motley Crue's Rock & Roll Circus" (*Rolling Stone*, May 19, 2005)

Dan Epsten, "Age of Quarrel" (*Revolver*, March 2005)

Sasha Frere-Jones, "Ring My Bell" (*The New Yorker*, March 7, 2005)

Jason Fry, "Rock's Oldest Joke" (*The Wall Street Journal*, March 17, 2005)

Chad Garrison, "Dirty Ernie" (*Riverfront Times*, October 5–11, 2005)

Zoë Gemelli, "Shrine of the Polymorph Madonna" (*Creative Loafing*, November 23, 2005)

Jeff Gordiner, "The Strange Art of the Male Soprano" (*Details*, September 2005)

Nick Green, "Board to Death" (*Decibel Magazine*, October 2005)

David Hadju, "The Royal Blues" (*The New York Review of Books*, June 23, 2005)

Keith Harris, "Kanye West gets an honorary degree in Afro-American Studies" (*City Pages*, September 7, 2005)

Dylan Hicks, "Ad Rock" (*City Pages*, June 13, 2005)

Hua Hsu, "Three Songs from the End of History" (*The Believer*, June/July 2005)

Edd Hurt, "Mod Lang" (*Nashville Scene*, September 1, 2005)

Rob Kenner, "Rude Awakening" (*Vibe*, September 2005)

Jason King, "So Amazing" (*Village Voice*, July 5, 2005)

Greg Kot, "Bono: 'We Need to Talk'" (*Chicago Tribune*, May 22, 2005)

Utrillo Kushner, "Comets On Fire tour diary" (*Magnet*, April/May 2005)

Jeff Leeds, "The Most Expensive Album Never Made" (*The New York Times*, March 6, 2005)

Jonathan Lethem, "The Beards" (*The New Yorker*, February 28, 2005)

Alan Light, "Long Road Home" (*Mother Jones*, July/August 2005)

Andria Lisle, "I Know a Place" (*Wax Poetics*, Winter 2005)

John Nova Lomax, "My Darlin' New Orleans" (*Houston Press*, September 8, 2005)

Jimmy Magahern, "Big Cheese" (*Pheonix New Times*, May 19–25, 2005)

Peter Margasak, "The Funk Archaeologist" (*Chicago Reader*, February 18, 2005)

Darrell M. McNeill, "Navigating the Metal Minefield" (*Creative Loafing*, August 31–September 6, 2005)

Bob Mehr, "The Godfather of King Drive" (*Chicago Reader*, April 22, 2005)

Gabe Meline, "Swallow That" (*North Bay Bohemian*, January 19–25, 2005)

Rick Moody, "How to Become a Christian Artist" (*The Believer*, June/July 2005)

Tom Moon, "Ryan Adams Gets His Feet Wet (Again)" (*Harp*, July/August 2005)

Paul Moreley, "Rock and Reel" (*The Observer*, August 21, 2005)

John Morthland, "Daddy What If" (*No Depression*, January/February 2005)

Mark Anthony Neal, "Rhythm and Bullshit?: The Slow Decline of R&B" (*PopMatters*, June 3, 2005)

Chris Norris, "The Revenge of Crazy Nate" (*Blender*, May 2005)

Jon Pareles, "The Case Against Coldplay" (*The New York Times*, June 5, 2005)

Brian Raftery, "Requiem for a Beam" (*Spin*, September 2005)

Dan Reines, "Still They Ride" (*SF Weekly*, February 9, 2005)

Simon Reynolds, "Seize the Time" (*Slate*, October 5, 2005)

Mark Richardson, "Green Eyes and the Other Guy" (*Pitchfork Media*, July 8, 2005)

Jody Rosen, "Billy Joel" (*Slate*, November 29, 2005)

Jay Ruttenberg, "Hill of beans" (*Time Out New York*, July 28–August 3, 2005)

Kelefa Sanneh, "The Strangest Sound in Hip-Hop Goes National" (*The New York Times*, April 17, 2005)

Jon Savage, "Third Eye for the Straight Guy" (*MOJO*, March 2005)

Philip Sherburne, "Epiphany" (*The Wire*, October 2005)

Julia Silverman, "Far from home, a gifted young musicians starts over after Katrina" (*Associated Press*, November 30, 2005)

Tom Sinclair, "School's Out" (*Spin*, September 2005)

John Soss, "An Elvis Kind of Christmas" (*Chicago Tribune Magazine*, December 18, 2005)

Keith Spera, "Katrina Blues" (*LA Weekly*, September 9, 2005)

Mark Stryker, "Reminiscing by ear" (*Detroit Free Press*, August 28, 2005)

Touré, "The Book of Jay" (*Rolling Stone*, December 15, 2005)

Lisa Tucker, "Helen Humes" (*Oxford American*, Summer 2005)

Gayle Wald, "'Have a little talk': Listening to the B-side of history" (*Popular Music*, Volume 24/3, 2005)

Matthew Weiner, "The Song Cycles of Jimmy Webb" (*Stylus*, February 28, 2005)

Eric Weisbard, "The Nine Billion Songs of Pop" (*Black Clock*, Fall 2005/Winter 2006)

Michael Patrick Welsh, "My House" (*OffBeat*, April 2005)

John Wirt, "New Orleanians carry city's musical spirit in their hearts" (*The Advocate*, September 16, 2005)

Geraldine Wyckoff, "Around the clock with Kermit Ruffins" (*OffBeat*, June 2005)

List of Contributors

Susan Alcorn is a musician, composer, and teacher who resides in Houston, Texas.

Moustafa Bayoumi is an associate professor of English at Brooklyn College, City University of New York (CUNY). He is the co-editor of *The Edward Said Reader* (Vintage) and has published widely, including articles in *Transition*, *The Yale Journal of Criticism*, *Souls*, *Arab Studies Quarterly*, *The Village Voice*, and *The London Review of Books*. He also serves on the editorial committee of *Middle East Report* and is a regular columnist for the Progressive Media Project.

Elizabeth Méndez Berry's writing has appeared in the *Washington Post*, the *Village Voice*, *Time*, and *Vibe*, among other publications. She is from Toronto.

John Biguenet is the author of *The Torturer's Apprentice: Stories* and *Oyster*, a novel, among other books. His play *The Vulgar Soul* won the 2004 Southern New Plays Festival. His fiction, poetry, and essays have appeared in journals such as *Esquire*, *Granta*, *Playboy*, *Story*, *Zoetrope*, and *Ploughshares* as well as in various anthologies. An O. Henry award winner and *New York Times* guest columnist, he is the Robert Hunter Distinguished Professor at Loyola University in New Orleans.

Geoff Boucher writes features about music, film, and pop culture for the *Los Angeles Times*. The native of South Florida has been in Southern California since 1993 writing for the *Times*, and in that stretch he covered crime and politics before moving to the paper's entertainment and culture pages. He is also author of the 1997 nonfiction book *Two Badges: The Lives of Mona Ruiz*, which tracks the life of a Santa Ana woman from her time as a street-gang member to becoming a celebrated police officer.

Jon Caramanica is a Senior Writer at *XXL*. His writing has appeared in the *New York Times*, *Rolling Stone*, *Vice*, *New York*, *Spin*, and the *Village Voice*. He is at work on a social history of rap music.

Raquel Cepeda edited *And It Don't Stop: The Best American Hip-Hop Journalism of the Last 25 Years*, which won a 2005 Pen Beyond Margins Award. Cepeda's written for many publications and television, and has edited as well. She's currently in production on her first film, a VH1 "Rock Doc" titled *Bling, A Planet Rock*, about hip-hop, diamonds, and the 11 year uncivil war in Sierra Leone, West Africa. She lives for her daughter Djali.

Robert Christgau began writing rock criticism for *Esquire* in 1967 and since 1974 has been a full-time employee of the *Village Voice*, where the masthead now lists him as "gray eminence." He has published three books based on his *Consumer Guide* columns and two other collections, *Any Old Way You Choose It* (1973) and *Grown Up All Wrong* (1998). "The First Lady of Song" was his first contribution to *The Nation*.

Kimberly Chun is a music columnist and the Music Editor/ Senior Editor, Arts & Entertainment, at the *San Francisco Bay Guardian.*

Amateur Brit crit **Tom Ewing** edits the pop culture webzine *Freaky Trigger* and founded sprawling music message board *I Love Music.* He has a day job in market research, and his current online project involves writing about every single to reach #1 in the UK. He is not looking forward to finding things to say about thirteen different Westlife records.

Bill Friskics-Warren lives in Nashville and is the author of *I'll Take You There: Pop Music and the Urge for Transcendence* (Continuum), which comes out in paperback this fall. His writing has appeared in the *New York Times*, the *Village Voice*, the *Washington Post*, *Rock & Rap Confidential*, and the *Oxford American*. His work was also included in the 2000 and 2004 volumes of *Da Capo Best Music Writing.*

Will Hermes writes for the *New York Times*, *Entertainment Weekly*, and many other publications; he also contributes to National Public Radio's "All Things Considered" and "All Songs Considered." He is co-editor, with Sia Michel, of *SPIN: 20 Years of Alternative Music* (Three Rivers Press), and author of the semi-fictional MP3 blog Loose Strife (http://loosestrife.blogspot.com).

Andrew Hultkrans is the author of *Forever Changes* (Continuum, 2003), one of the inaugural six volumes in the 33 1/3 series on celebrated rock albums. From 1998 through 2003, he was editor-in-chief of *Bookforum* magazine. Over the years, his journalism and criticism have appeared in *Artforum, Bookforum, Wired, Salon, 21C, Filmmaker, Tin House, Cabinet,* and the pioneering cyberculture magazine *Mondo 2000,* where he was managing editor and columnist for three years in the early '90s. He is at work on a book about surveillance in America.

Monica Kendrick is a staff writer for the *Chicago Reader*. She has contributed to several other magazines and ranted wildly on the Internet, secretly loves participating in panel discussions, and has been known to commit poetry and fiction on occasion.

J. Edward Keyes has been writing about music since 1997, and has contributed to *Entertainment Weekly*, *The Village Voice*, *The Chicago Reader*, *Philadelphia Weekly*, *MAGNET*, and various other publications. For two years he was a member of a one-man industrial band, about which the less said the better. He lives with his fiancée in Astoria, New York.

Frank Kogan walked a thousand miles while you were asleep, brags of his stained garments, and can be found online poking and winking at people any day of the week, though he nonetheless claims there's more to him than you've seen, and invites you to ask. Fragments of his journey are collected in *Real Punks Don't Wear Black* (University of Georgia Press).

After completing an undergraduate humanities degree at his hometown University of Toronto, **David Marchese** enrolled in NYU's graduate journalism program, where he studies cultural reporting and criticism. In addition to his work on *PopMatters*, his writing has appeared in the *Village Voice* and *Pitchfork*. He particularly enjoys guitar solos and catchy middle-eights. He resides in Brooklyn.

Greil Marcus is the author of *The Shape of Things to Come: Prophecy and the American Voice* (Farrar, Straus & Giroux, 2006). His other books include *Lipstick Traces*, *The Old, Weird America*,

The Dustbin of History, and *Mystery Train*. He writes a monthly column for *Interview*, and lives in Berkeley.

Wayne Marshall is an ethnomusicologist, DJ, producer, and blogger who studies and mixes the music of the Caribbean and the U.S. He has taught courses on music and society at Brown University, the Harvard Extension School, and the University of Wisconsin-Madison. He is presently co-editing a reggaetón anthology while working on an intertwined history of hip-hop and reggae. During the 2006–2007 academic year, he will be teaching at the University of Chicago as post-doctoral fellow.

Mike McGuirk is a freelance writer who cut his teeth discussing the merits of Led Zeppelin and listening to classic hits radio while he fried donuts for six years in his hometown of Maynard, Massachusetts. He has written for the *SF Bay Guardian*, the *Seattle Stranger*, *Index Magazine*, and *Chin Music Magazine*, among others. His primary job since October of 2000 has been writing blurbs for *Rhapsody*, an online music service.

Charles Michener, a former editor at *The New Yorker*, covers music for *The New York Observer*.

In 2001, **Anne Midgette** became the first woman to regularly review classical music for the *New York Times*. Her reviews and feature articles on music, theater, art, dance, and film have appeared in the *Wall Street Journal*, the *Los Angeles Times*, *Newsday*, *Opera News*, *ArtNews*, *Town and Country*, and many other publications; she has also written in German for *Die Welt* and *Opern Welt*. With Herbert Breslin, she co-authored *The King and I: The Uncensored Tale of Luciano Pavarotti's Rise to Fame*. She is currently working on a novel.

Geoffrey O'Brien's most recent book is *Sonata for Jukebox: An Autobiography of My Ears*. His other books include *Dream Time: Chapters from the Sixties*, *The Phantom Empire*, *The Browser's Ecstasy*, and *Castaways of the Image Planet*. He has also published five collections of poetry, most recently *Red Sky Café*. He is editor-in-chief of The Library of America.

Anne-Marie Payne (aka Miss AMP) lives in East London and writes stupid stuff for anyone who'll pay her. She's been writing for *Plan B* and its predecessor, *Careless Talk Costs Lives*, since 2001. Her work has also appeared in *The Guardian*, *Bizarre*, *Kerrang!*, *Marmalade*, and *The Face*. She currently sings in the band Shimura Curves, and is writing a book about the early 90s riot grrrl movement.

Ann Powers is the author of *Weird Like Us: My Bohemian America* and co-editor of *Rock She Wrote: Women Write About Rock, Pop, and Rap*. She has served in critic positions for the *New York Times* and *Blender Magazine* and has written for publications ranging from *Rolling Stone* and *Spin* to the *Nation* and *Slate*. She has also held the position of Senior Curator at Experience Music Project, an interactive museum in Seattle devoted to celebrating the creativity inherent in rock & roll. She is currently the Chief Pop Critic for the *Los Angeles Times* and lives in Los Angeles with her husband, the noted music journalist Eric Weisbard, and daughter, Rebecca Brooklyn Weisbard, and sees the Mekons whenever humanly possible.

Peter Relic. A postscript: Driving away from the hotel, after the stunning, check-left-unpaid conclusion to the Bushwick Bill interview, my cell phone rang. I picked up. "Hey, it's Bill. Listen, I want you to know, if they come after me, you're my co-defendant in this." I felt I'd just been bestowed with a strange, unexpected honor. At this time—and in that spirit—I'd

like to thank my faithful "co-defendants" at *XXL Magazine:*
Dave Bry, Vanessa Satten, and Elliot Wilson.

Alex Ross has been the music critic of *The New Yorker* since
1996. His first book, *The Rest Is Noise: Listening to the Twentieth
Century,* is forthcoming from Farrar, Straus & Giroux.

Katy St. Clair writes a diary-disguised-as-nightlife-column for
the *SF Weekly,* called "Bouncer." She is currently working on a
full-length book about the lives of her developmentally disabled clients (working title: *Let's Get Retarded in Here!).* She is
the former music editor of the *East Bay Express,* a job she managed to snag even though her favorite band is the Bee Gees.
No, really.

John Jeremiah Sullivan is an editor at *Harper's* and a former editor of *The Oxford American.* He is the author of *Blood Horses:
Notes of a Sportswriter's Son* (2004).

David Thorpe is a chain of 220 family-style restaurants located
throughout California and the Pacific Northwest. David Thorpe
offers buffet dining amid an atmosphere of nostalgic Americana,
and he contains modest gift shops in which diners can purchase
"shabby-chic" crockery, comfort food cookbooks, and large
wheels of cheese. Additionally, David Thorpe is a regular columnist for the venerable humor website *Something Awful* and for
Boston's indispensable *Weekly Dig* newspaper.

Dave Tompkins has written about hip hop since 1992. His first
book, *I Have No Vocoder and I Must Scream,* begins with a man
yelling at an air conditioner. Participants include: Ray Bradbury,
Rammellzzee, Can, a 16-foot hexagon called The OVC, a 96-
year-old WWII speech splitter named Ralph, Miami, Stanislaw
Lem, a Bavarian mental institution, Dr. Phibes, and weird little

kids and frogs. He lives in Brooklyn and writes for *The Wire* and *Wax Poetics*.

Marion van San works as a senior researcher at the Erasmus University Rotterdam. Her research interests include juvenile delinquency, youth culture, prostitution, and street crime.

Nick Weidenfeld was born in Washington, D.C. He worked with Linda Tripp and Monica Lewinsky at the Department of Defense before becoming co-owner and editor of *While You Were Sleeping* magazine. He is currently the head of Program Development for [adult swim] on the Cartoon Network and is working on his own series, "That Crook'd 'Sip" inspired by William Faulkner's *The Sound and the Fury* and David Banner's first record, *Mississippi: The Album*. He lives in Atlanta, Georgia.

Robert Wheaton has lived and studied in England, California, and the Netherlands. He studied American cultural and intellectual history, and has written on subjects ranging from the urban history of San Francisco to the contemporary resonance of William Faulkner. In music, his interests extend from hard cop to drum 'n' bass, from the Bristol Sound to Charley Patton. He lives in Toronto, where he works in the book trade.

Kevin Whitehead is a jazz critic for NPR's *Fresh Air*, and has contributed to *Down Beat, Chicago Sun-Times*, and many other publications. His book *New Dutch Swing* (1998) is a study of improvised music in Amsterdam; his essays have appeared in the *Cartoon Music Book* (2002), *Jazz: The First Century* (2000), and elsewhere. A member of the improvising band Starship Beer, he teaches at the University of Kansas.

Credits